The Best of Donna Magazine

The Best of Donna Magazine

Donna Kakonge

FIRST EDITION LULU INTERNATIONAL EDITION, September 2009

Copyright 2009 by Donna Kay Kakonge, M.A.

All rights researched under International and Pan-American Copyright Conventions. Published in the United States by Lulu.com.

Library and Archives of Canada Cataloguing in Publication Data

Kakonge, Donna Kay Cindy

The Best of Donna Magazine
ISBN: **978-1-926734-34-7**

Book Design by Lulu.com

Manufactured in the United States.

BOOKS AND CDS BY DONNA KAKONGE

What Happened to the Afro?
How to Write Creative Non-fiction
Spiderwoman
My Roxanne
Being Healthy: Selected Works from the Internet (edited)
Do Not Know
My Story of Transportation
Draft: eSpirituality Chats
"Nine" (CD)
Journalism Stories Collection
Digital Journals and Numerology
"Matoke" (Audio Download)
"Spiderwoman" (Audio Download)
The Education Generation
In My Pocket
Morning English Lessons
Where I Was
Radio and Television Announcing
Draft: Part Two
Ugandan Travelogue
School Works
Yes, School Works
School Works – Other Essays
Honest Psychic Chats
The Write Heart
Listening to Music
This is How the Egyptians Fell
Natural Beauty
Random Bibliography of Media Books and Internet Resources
My Mind Book
Stories in Red and Yellow: Digging up Work Done in Yesteryear
The Best of Donna Magazine

For my sister Lisa Kakonge-Clayton who was the co-creator of my first magazine *Miss Sassy*

The Master Weaver (originally published with Pride Newsmagazine)

In [Beauty](#), [Business](#), [Writing (all kinds)](#) on **December 16, 2007** at **20:26**

Rose Hibbert and Christos Cox creates magic with Donna Kakonge's hair

The Master Weaver

With her 1992 red and black Volkswagen Jetta, Hibbert drove me up to Hair & Wigs on the Danforth in Toronto to get the 150 per cent real human cuticle hair for the makeover. Her sister Ingrid Hart, who is an actor and had a long-running role on "Train 48," was seated in the back.

Once we got back to Urban Textures Salon, one of their locations in downtown Toronto, I asked Hibbert why it's important for people to change their hair sometimes for those people who have always been wearing the natural look, like I have for 13 years.

"I always say, there's nothing wrong with conforming if it benefits you," she says. "When people think carefully about that, use kids as an example. Kids will always be defiant. When you ask them to do the right thing and do this and do that, you're asking them to conform into something positive or into something that can help them in the long run. Same thing with hair – there's nothing wrong with getting extensions, especially if you know it's going to benefit you – whether or not it's short or long. It's going to emphasize your beauty, or exaggerate your beauty."

She tells a story about another sister of hers who started off working in the corporate company she presently works in with straightened hair. Now she wears locks and she's a supervisor.

"She's earned those locks," says Hibbert.

I came on a day to get my hair done where I had few other plans. Hibbert advises this because sometimes it can take time. The actually weaving of my hair only took her an hour and a half, but in the traveling time to get the extensions and do the moisturizing treatment I did before the process, this took up a number of hours.

"Look at this," said Hibbert pointing to my hair. "You feel the softness in your hair and how strong it looks already. Continue your treatments and you'll be set."

Hibbert can do all kinds of hair, but prefers doing the weave. She works freelance and has more challenges than just dealing with an invisible part to overcome.

Hibbert has a kidney problem in which she is currently undergoing dialysis. You'd never know it from her quick smile and easy laugh.

She has a cat and started weaving in her early years. Her entire family became her hair models to test out her skills. She's a specialist because she spends her spare time weaving. Although she does extensions, she also believes the importance of cutting hair.

"You have a house plant that's growing, and you have about five dead leaves on it – you're not just going to cut off half the leaves, half of each dead leaf," she says. "You have to cut off all the leaves, cut it all off – it doesn't matter if you have a little bit left. All you're doing is giving it more room to grow. Ever hear the saying one bad apple spoils the whole bunch. It's the same thing with your hair. No matter how you try to hold onto it, it's going to continue breaking and it's not going to grow. Cut it all off and you're going to notice how healthy your hair is."

My hair is doing great and now I have an easy to maintain look that makes me feel different in a good way. I have so many people telling me how natural my weave looks, and it's thanks to Hibbert. She is a master weaver.

Sometimes I miss the exposure of my natural hair, but I know it's underneath, growing – which is what I want it to do.

I can keep the cuticle hair for six to seven years and that will give a lot of time for my hair to grow. The style will last for three months because Hibbert is a "perfectionist."

If you're interested in Rose Hibbert doing your hair, contact her at Urban Textures Salon: 416-977-HAIR.

Options for homes (originally published with New Dreamhomes and Condominiums Magazine

In Business, Home Decor, Writing (all kinds) on **December 16, 2007** at **20:24**

Mike Labbé – President of Options

Options for Homes – Making Home Ownership a Reality – October 2005 – published in *New Dreamhomes and Condominiums Magazine*

Bring a community together from the ground up and give them what they need to own a home seems to sum up the Options for Homes belief system.

When President Mike Labbé, started the non-profit corporation he figured the best way to mobilize prospective buyers, would be by getting them to literally build their own condominiums.

"Really we're providing our expertise for the buyers to build their own homes," says Labbé. "They [the owners] hire the contractors, they hire the lawyers, and they hire all of the pieces they need to build a condominium for themselves. As a result they get it at cost. And we put in different things to protect against flipping and stuff – but that's the gist of what Options does. It pulls people together to build their own homes."

As Labbé said earlier, essentially people acquire the home at the cost price. The difference between the cost price, and the market value is then added in the guise of a second mortgage that will contribute to the individual's down payment, usually about half of the down payment goes to the Canadian Mortgage and Housing Corporation (CMHC) when people want to sell.

As long as they stay in the home they don't have to give that money back to Options. It's an incentive for owners to stay there as long as possible.

"So there are a very small number of investors that come along," says Labbé.

Labbé says Options does not prevent resale because then there's no advantage to purchasing. You can buy and sell any time you want. But when you sell, you pay back that differential.

Weston Village was the first project. Options for Homes had three condominium sites under construction. One at the Distillery District, one at 650 Lawrence Ave, two in Pickering and one in Scarborough, near Eglinton and Markham. The one at Markham and Eglinton was completed by the spring of 2006. Another project near Markham Road was scheduled to begin in the fall of 2005. Options goal would be to construct three to four projects a year, and this model is one that has spread to Montreal and Waterloo.

Where Options manages to keep costs down, is in not offering any facilities or amenities. Most of their condos might have a meeting room with a kitchen that could hypothetically allow owners to meet and mingle, but that's about it.

"We don't put pool and sauna rooms in normally," says Labbé. "The only exception to that was in Pickering where the amenities were already built, they were already there. Normally we don't do this because it reduces the caring maintenance costs and reduces the capital costs."

Just because Options lack amenities doesn't mean there are no condominium fees, fees do exist, but are usually five cents less, a square foot than the general market. Labbé says the condos are about $300 to $500 less a square foot than a regular condominium.

"We can reach people that have $10,000 to $15,000 less in income than the regular condo owner. You still need to have a good income. You still need good credit. You still need to qualify for a mortgage in all cases. By starting a lot lower, we can get a reasonable two-bedroom into people's hands for $1,100 a month – which is about what it costs to rent. And that's where we've done really well, getting homes to people who otherwise couldn't have owned homes at all," says Labbé.

Sometimes Options can help people with $40,000 of their down payment says Labbé. That allows a lower income group to get a mortgage.

"We have people much more varied in income," Labbé said.

The way they do their marketing, usually 40 to 50 people come out to an information meeting. After that they put down a non-refundable $100 deposit.

"Special thing is that dreams people have to get rich enough to buy a piece of land to build their own home they can help make reality. Create a community participatory community, energy conservation, creation own home," says Labbé.

Options for Homes marketing plans are low-key. I once saw a poster on the subway, and they have a website at www.optionsforhomes.ca, but outside of that, if you've heard about them before someone you know may have told you.

"A lot of their marketing is word of mouth," says Dee Gibney, narrator of promotional video.

One Options for Homes owner expresses how she feels about home ownership in the promotional video.

"I feel very wealthy" Nona Segal, an Options for Homes Owner.

Options have support from the Ontario government.

"This is a win-win-win for the government housing options of this province," said Minister of Public Infrastructure Renewal, David Caplan.

Canada Mortgage & Housing Corporation's Manager of the GTA, Mark Salerno says Options for Homes was given a Housing award in 2002 that is granted every two years.

The promotional video also shows how Options has support from writers like June Callwood.

"I think this concept is one that's going [to] sweep the country," says Callwood.

You can find out more about Options for Homes from their website, www.optionsforhomes.ca.

How to make your mall experience a free one (originally published with The Shoestring.com)

In Business, Entertainment, Events, Writing (all kinds) on **December 16, 2007** at **20:24**

How to Make Your Mall Experience a Free One

Being in a shopping mall can be an overwhelming experience – especially when you don't have cash to spend. But, there are ways to have a good time without spending a cent.

Before you go shopping, you want to make sure you look good. Visit a makeup counter and get a free makeover and look gorgeous while you walk through the mall. It's also a great form of exercise.

First and foremost – know about samples. Rather than buying anything you need, you can always ask for samples of things and stock them for supplies. This goes for just about anything. For example, I had heard that there was this great hair product called Phyto and went to the mall to get samples every time I needed some. You can do this for face creams, body lotions, and many other toiletries.

Trying on new clothes for the fun of it could give you some great ideas to find cheaper versions of what you love at discount places or to get hand-me-downs from friends.

Once you're done with looking your best, catch some entertainment by going into an electronics store and watching some of the stuff they have on their screens. Some really nice stores have chairs set up and might even have a new DVD on. You could always ask them to put on something interesting so you can see the quality of the latest flat screen monitor, without having the money to buy it.

What is this world without music? Even the smallest of malls will have one music store and the bigger ones will have more for you to choose from. The best way to find out what's hot and what's not is to look at the racks and see how the different CDs are ranked. You can even mellow out by checking out the listening stations in places like HMV and enjoy the tunes.

Speaking of how things are ranked – check out the bookstores for the bestsellers. Books from Dr. Phil or the upcoming biography on Bob Denver you can read for free at Indigo or Chapters. Take your time; some bookstores have places to sit so you can be there for awhile. Or squat on the floor.

If you have a child, spend that special time in the children's department of a bookstore reading to your little one. Toy stores are great ways to keep the kids occupied. Perhaps if they can play with that doll or toy truck in the store, they'll tire of it and won't hound you to buy it.

Get decorating ideas that you can do on the cheap from places like the Pottery Barn.

After all this excitement, go to the furniture department and take a nap on one of the luxurious couches of any of the big stores like Sears.

Now after you've experienced a fulfilling free time, look for loose change in pay phones and on the ground (it can pay to walk with your head down) go to the mall's bank and make a small donation to Hurricane Katrina relief (every penny counts as you know).

If you do have a little cash to spend – The Dollar Store is always a great place. For example, I bought a pair of sunglasses for a dollar with black frames from there and took them to a one-hour optical place and paid way more for the prescription lenses than the frames. People are telling me all the time they look like $300 glasses – but I didn't spend any thing near to that.

When you get hungry, try checking out places like Baskin Robbins and many others for samples to get a quick fix. If you go to enough fast food joints for samples, you might even end up feeling full.

All this will make your shopping experience pain-free for your wallet and enjoyable. Have a good time and remember to throw a penny in the waterfall if your major mall has one!

Dim sum for the Murmur Project aired on CBC Radio 3

In [Entertainment](), [Health](), [Music](), [Radio Podcasts](), [Restaurant Reviews](), [Writing (all kinds)]() on **December 16, 2007** at **20:20**

Dim Sum & Friends

"Every time I see you falling, I get down on my knees and pray."

The techno-rhythms and words of New Order blared in Sharon's car as six teenagers were squeezed inside. We were going down to Kensington Market as part of our late 80's ritual, coming from "Asiancourt."

Finding parking and walking through alleys to get to Pearl Saigon was all part of the adventure. The whole way, in the car, while parking and through the alleyways, me and my friends chatted about our week at school and our part-time jobs so we could have the extra cash to shop at all the second-hand stores in the market.

The owner of the Saigon knew us by now. Every Sunday brown-faced me and my Asian girlfriends would enter the restaurant and fight the crowds for a table to fit us all. That day I had news for them.

"Did you see what so-so was wearing on Thursday?" Sharon asked us.

"Of course!" said Catherine. "Fuchsia is not a colour to be worn, or a colour to be missed."

That was all I heard of the conversation. My mind was drifting on finding the right words to tell my girlfriends my news.

"Donna!" Yoko snapped her thin fingers in front of my eyes. "Come back to earth."

"Oh, sorry." Okay, now was my moment. "Ladies, this is the last time we're having Dim Sum together."

I almost let the tears fall. Meeting with my friends over Dim Sum was like the therapy I'm lucky enough to have OHIP cover now. It was a good, old-fashioned, positive moaning session.

"Oh ma God. You don't like the food or something, Dee?" asked Sharon.

"No, that's not it. I'm going to school in Ottawa. I got my letter on Friday."

There was silence. Out of those six girls who were my chums, the silence continues to this day.

I never knew then that it would take more than a decade to eat Dim Sum again and have my moaning sessions. This time I had one companion, my friend David. He would pick me up from downtown and we would drive to the market. The first time we went, I marvelled at the fact he took me to the same place. We even parked in the same lot and started our moaning (I guess his groaning and my bitching) in the alleyway on our way to the Saigon.

I still do shopping in the market with whatever job I have at the moment. Now my tastes have changed. I shop for Shea Butter at 426, drums from Uganda at the African shop on St. Andrew, and incense and candles at the store next door.

What hasn't changed is my love for Dim Sum and friends.

Jully Black

In Beauty, Entertainment, Music, Writing (all kinds) on **December 16, 2007** at **20:16**

Jully Black – Home-grown Talent

The first time I met Jully Black was while she was working with the Princess of Wales show "Da Kink in my Hair." I was walking out of a swanky store in the Eaton Centre of Toronto and she was walking in. With a huge smile on her face, she greeted me and said "hello."

"Why not say hi. You cut us all, we bleed red. Why are we surprised? It's great that we connected on a human level."

It's this type of down-to-earth nature that Black has. I interviewed her the day after she performed live at the Toronto Street Festival and rocked the crowd. The first thing I asked her was about her segments on CTV's "ETalk Daily."

"I love doing those segments for "ETalk Daily." They let me be me and I love them. It's fun"

She was at the Juno Awards and her feet were hurting her, her heels were burning her and they had a room called the Pantene Room that she was sitting in and she wasn't supposed to be there – but she was resting. Someone from "ETalk Daily" came over to her and said "Aren't you Jully Black? What are you doing sitting by yourself? Why don't you come over and join us?"

She went into the room where the "ETalk" crew was and she was causing trouble, bothering Ben Mulroney and Tanya Kim.

"I was telling Tanya that my dress is better than her dress. Meanwhile, her dress is 20 grand and my dress is like 500 bucks."

It was just a whole bunch of fun, Black said. "ETalk Daily" ended up running Black's footage more than anyone else who had won. Then, they invited her to do weekly diaries for the entertainment show where nothing was scripted.

She was able to bring her Mom on the show, too.

"My Mom is the love of my life," Jully says. "She raised all 9 of all us all by herself. She migrated from Jamaica in 1972. She had me in Jamaica and I was a twin. I had a brother, but he didn't live. She didn't even know that she was having twins until she delivered us. She's just been my pillar of strength, my inspiration. As much as I can I bring her out. She's older, she's 69, and she had me in her 40s."

Black also notes that the fact that her mother is alive and well to see her live out her dream is worth more than a platinum album to her.

"My career is still in its infancy. I'm so proud of the accomplishments. I was signed to a label in America that folded and Universal Music Canada still kept me and that's practically unheard of because usually when the Americans go away, so does everyone else."

Black lost her sister in 1990 and left children behind.

"I've definitely been through a lot in my young years – I'm only in my 20's. But, that's definitely helped me become the woman I am – just not taking anything for granted."

Black talks about how a lot of the arts magazines have helped her rise to success like *NOW*, *Eye* and community magazines like *Pride*.

For the future, Black has "television, television and television" on her agenda.

"I definitely want to record many, many albums. I'd definitely like to have my own company and sign many artists. But, I'd ultimately love to have a television show that caters to all walks of life that is definitely a music show. It would kind of be like Oprah meets Ellen and bridge the gap. Where the youth can come home from school and watch the show with their parents and it's still cool."

Black says she just wants to follow her spirit. "I'm everybody. This album is entitled 'This is me.' I'd like everybody to give it a chance and see this album like another Olympic Gold medal. I use this analogy because it unifies us. I'd love to be added to the bunch of Canadian icons that are recognized for their talent and still not compromise."

A sprint to a clothing line (originally published for
Pride Newsmagazine)

In Beauty, Business, Entertainment, Writing (all kinds) on **December 16, 2007** at **20:15**

A Sprint to a Clothing Line

Published in *Pride Magazine* – June 29, 2005

Ben Johnson, the fastest man in the world according to a 1988 World Record time of 9.79 seconds, is now in the clothing business.

"I just like good clothing, good fabric, good taste and I think that this type of business is the right thing for me to get involved in," Johnson says. "I've done this many years ago. I've done this for 30 years and this isn't the first time I've had my own clothing line. In 1987 I had my own clothing line in Italy and it didn't really take off because of the public. So I decided to come back 18 years later and do my own stuff."

The official launch of Ben Johnson's new line was held at Metro in Toronto at 296 Richmond St. W. on Thursday, June 23rd. Lucid Options, a multi-service advertising agency helped to organize the event.

"I've been flying by the seat of my pants for the last four weeks," Christeena Mitchell, Business Director with Lucid Options said. "It seems like everyone is having a really good time so far. I think what's really important is to show Ben's clothing in the most positive light."

About two hundred people came out for the event, including media and wholesalers looking to market Johnson's line.

Although Johnson made an attempt in the clothing business in the past and it didn't work out he thinks now is a good time. "If you can't start, you can't finish. So this is the time to do it."

"My target market is kids between [the] age[s] [of] 8 to 35 years old, but the clothes are widespread. Anybody can wear it," Johnson says.

Johnson describes his clothing as the design being nice and the colours being different.

"It's good quality stuff," Johnson says. "It's not anything cheap. But the price is not high-end stuff, the price is right in between the other apparel clothes, but it's very good quality."

Johnson does most of the designing because it's something that he's been involved in for 30 years.

"I've worn a lot of clothes over the years, I feel the fabric, I feel the quality, and I make the adjustments. I say I don't want this, I want this. Everything is fresh. It feels very soft, the material is very beautiful."

Johnson also has running shoes.

"The running shoes are different because they have more support on the heel, on the arch, because most people have a low arch. And the heel is not very thick to get the compact of running – you can have problems in your hip or in your back. So I've made sure there's an extra cushion for everything."

Di-anne Hudson has a background in law and also helps with the designing of the clothing with Ben Johnson. She mentions that Johnson's family has been in the clothing business for years. His mom and sister both sew and make clothing and he grew up with that around him.

Where Johnson is responsible for the athletic wear, Hudson is responsible for the casual wear.

All the materials for the clothing are made in Canada, which is something everyone involved with the Ben Johnson Collection, is proud.

To visit Ben Johnson's Collection online, go to: www.benjohnsoncollection.com.

Restaurant makeover (originally published for Pride Newsmagazine)

In [Entertainment](), [Health](), [Restaurant Reviews](), [Writing (all kinds)]() on **December 16, 2007** at **20:14**

The show "Restaurant Makeover" helps restaurant owners to makeover their businesses. All you need to do is to send in a letter or a call and they decide whether they're going to take the project on. The show, which airs on the Food Network Tuesday, Wednesday, Saturday and Sunday, matches the money that owners put into the renovations dollar-for-dollar.

Alison Ruthland is owner of First Class Delites at 1156 Weston Rd. She wrote a letter to "Restaurant Makeover" highlighting her situation.

"We were away from the business for a little while because I had twins in November," Ruthland says. "One of the twins was born and she immediately went into heart failure. We spent a few months at Sick Kids and my husband was back and forth. So that took up a lot of our time. She was our priority at that moment."

Ruthland says that because the business got neglected, she took a look at "Restaurant Makeover" and found that it was a great show to fulfill her needs.

"I figured why don't I give them a call and see what they can do. We wrote in and they responded right away. It's been a very fast process."

The show that "Restaurant Makeover" is featuring First Class Delites heavily focuses on Ruthland's daughter. The Ruthlands have decided to open up another restaurant in name of their daughter called Sydney's Island Restaurant.

Shaam Makan is the producer of Tricon Films who does "Restaurant Makeover" for the Food Network.

"She [Ruthland] emailed me the story. I went down to visit and as soon as I met the family I knew this is a story I'm going to do," Makan said.

Ruthland worked with the designer, saying that they wanted a "totally fresh, new look."

"Apparently, one of the top designers in the city worked on the restaurant," Ruthland says. "I'm not sure what she's going to do. Apparently it's tables, chairs, ceilings, floors; it's going to be the whole place. Because when we came in the whole place was demolished. The ceiling was going, the floor was ripped up, the counter, everything. It was a bit of a shock to see the place look like that, but we're really excited because we know the place is going to look completely different."

They're shooting right now for season two and First Class Delites will be featured in November. Makan advises you check out "Restaurant Makeover" at www.foodtv.ca to find out when First Class Delites will be on. The show has had one season.

You'll have to go down to First Class Delites to see the new and improved restaurant. Also, check out Sydney's Island Restaurant at 5120 Dixie Rd. in Mississauga that opened recently.

In terms of the recent response to the renovations made at First Class Delites:

"So far we're getting a great response," Ruthland says. "We're getting a lot of new f aces. We haven't changed the menu, but we've added in some new things on the busier days. Our fish cakes are popular every day."

The Ruthlands have four children, the twins are seven months old and Sydney is doing much better when doctors had thought she wouldn't make it home.

Power pics

In [Culture](), [Writing (all kinds)](), [cars](), [travel]() on **December 16, 2007** at **20:11**

He's 29…he wears T-shirts about trucking companies and jackets about old diners called Dickie's. He's also an artist and an IT guru exhibiting at the Guerrilla Gallery on College Street.

David Larraguibel is a Chilean born Jew whose varied work of skinny bodies scarred by stitching and nostalgic photos of the way the Lakeshore used to look like before the condo developments is only a portion of this man's abilities. With his super tiny black bike, reminding those who remember the BMX style, we met at a Starbucks on the northwest side of Bathurst and College in Toronto, then continued our conversation at the TeaShop down the street.

"I feel one half almost joy…a cathartic feeling getting images out sometimes," says Larraguibel. "When I see an image in its production, sometimes I see it and it hits something – I guess it's like with most people. I'm starting to begin to communicate what I didn't even think I could communicate. It's almost like at same moment I wonder if it's a meaningless pursuit, almost because it takes so much for me to see what I think I see, that I wonder if there's even a miniscule chance that I will not see what I think I see."

Larraguibel says everyone his age and younger is doing this really "poppy" and socially meaningful and confrontational work. They're trying to say something really important about the world.

"I don't know enough about the world – not really – to feel like I have something valid to say that it hasn't been distilled down to me by all these other artists or other politicians. I can get angry like anybody else gets angry about the smog and the people on the streets that don't have homes. I don't feel like I have enough right to talk about it, like I've studied it or had to experience it in my own life – I haven't. All I have to talk about is me and my own work and what my work means to me and why it happens more often than not to revolve around issues of the body and how it breaks down and wondering what I would look like if I didn't have a leg or injured beyond repair – all these things. All I have is me."

Although Larraguibel is 29, he doesn't look it. His extremely youthful appearance makes him get carded every time he goes to the liquor store. At the same time he can feel his body creak as he gets older.

"Things that were so easy five years ago or two years ago are not quite as easy as they used to be," he says. "It's this inward and outward process of watching this so-called…decay. I see it happen in everybody else, everybody I love, and everybody I hate. It's happening to all of us. There's nothing we can do to change it."

His work concentrates on living and dying in the body we were born in. There's a second aspect to his art which involves urban landscapes with Larraguibel, his bicycle, his camera, his tripod and his music at 3 a.m. or 4 a.m.

"It's not just that the environment is different at night. It's like the buildings are singing – they're communicating to each other. The way they play off one another is this dance – it's a beautiful symphony. It's such a surrounded feeling when I'm out in the city alone at night…even walking, sometimes driving – though I rarely drive."

Larraguibel was driving down the Gardiner, it was a foggy night. He was coming down the Gardiner and smiling the whole way down. He was having this conversation inside his head: "it's so beautiful, you're so beautiful."

"The lights coming down on to where the 427 meets the Gardiner, passing by those twin towers close to Kipling, slicing through the air, it's black above and there's this beautiful swirling yellow light and it just dots along into the distance. I lit up a smoke and drove really, really slowly up York Street, across Queen Street and everything was resonating that night. In some way or another – everyone seems to be feeling it.

The streets were packed that night. Maybe they're not feeling what I'm feeling – but, they're feeling something."

For Larraguibel it's about being on that bike and roaming through places where he has a history and sometimes no history at all. It's just about being there.

His third style of art he does is influenced by German artist Max Ernst born in 1891 and died in 1976. It involves wood carvings and etchings. He has one piece called "Baby with Machine Gun Wings." He was inspired by an illustration of a baby grinning playing with a bar of soap. When he was in high school with his ex-girlfriend, she wrote on the cigarette packages that were coming out with the health warnings. The one she focused on was "Smoking Can Harm Your Baby." David's ex-girlfriend took a black marker and turned the message into "Arm Your Baby."

David found this to be a powerful message for his art.

"I feel like we're becoming armed to become prepared for a war – a war of any kind. Society is always trying to build some kind of conflicts into your child. It's already too late for us – we're forced with having to stand on a difficult side of any subject. I thought it's catchy."

It was his first piece and it's still one of his favourites. He cut the head off the baby picture and put a piece of machinery from *Popular Mechanics* of 1919 or 1920. He put a spiky bar instead of the bar of soap.

"It's now called 'Mother and Child,' which I thought was kind of lame," says Larraguibel. "It used to be called the 'The Return to the Arms of the Wicked.' With that style of work I just am trying to do something that sings to me…some sense of truth. Maybe the landmine looks more right in the baby's hand than the bar of soap does. I have no idea what the truth is. My friends seem genuinely excited to see it, so I'm hoping I'm on the right track with that one."

Spain (originally published with Rozaneh Magazine)

In Culture, Writing (all kinds), travel on **February 16, 2008** at **01:08**

This is the Spain where it is easy to play Red Rover on the beach, but hard not to shop. This is the country of siesta, cheap shoes and sangria that flows like a river. You must order your water like this: "aqua sin gaz," which means still water. But this country is not still. Everything moves, and it moves to the rhythm of a Spanish guitar as you dance the night away meeting Spaniards and Brits who have had too much beer.

Almost anyone could recognize Spain, because Spain is that kind of country where all your expectations are fulfilled. Even Barcelona is the city where Olympic dreams come true.

The south of Spain is where I spent most of my time close to the water. I saw places like Costa del Sol, with my souvenir pen for proof. It doesn't work anymore. I saw Torremolinos and the famous Rock of Gilbrator. I had to resist the urge to climb the rock in newly bought heels.

In the south of Spain it is also easy to see the tip of Africa, Morocco. A dingy of a boat can take a small group over for a nominal fee. The day I was supposed to see Morocco the water was choppy and the captain of the ship decided that we shouldn't go, but this did not ruin my traveling experience.

Spain is a place where you can relax and enjoy the ever-present sunshine. It did not rain one day when I was there. Getting up early in the morning to shop and see the castles of old, the whole country shuts in the early afternoon for siesta. Usually this takes place after the noon meal. Being a tourist, I preferred to do my sleeping on a beach towel on top of the sand, rather than in my 5-star suite.

Shopping

Shopping is fantastic in Spain. This is the land that created the fashion outlet Zara and the clothes are feminine and form-fitting for the ladies, stylish and sleek for the men. In Barcelona, a good part of the Eixample is where you can find numerous select fashion shops and jewellery stores. On the Passeig de Gracia and in other parts of the Eixample, shopping arcades abound.

More shopping after siesta, then it's off to the hotel to get ready for the nightlife. Spain has a vibrant life at night and one of the clubs I went to was called the Coliseum and had the colonial-style white columns to match.

You never have to be alone in Spain, not if you don't want to. There are museums, art centres and monuments, exhibition centres, art galleries and antique shops, cultural activities and events, parks and gardens and plenty of food and drink.

Art

In Madrid there is a street known as the "Avenue of Art." Those with an eye for luxury can enjoy the Prado, Thyssen-Bornemisza and Centro de Arte Reina sofia Museums. With these three places of art, you will be exposed to the best in the world.

The Prado Museum has the finest collection of Spanish paintings. There are masterpieces by El Greco, Valazquez and Goya. You may already be one of the select few who have some these magnificent pieces gracing your walls at home or in your office.

What you will not find in The Prado, you will find in The Thyssen-Bornemisza Museum. Unlike the Prado, with its single masterpiece of the period, Fra Angelico's Annunciation, the Thyssen-Bornemisza showcases Italian Primitives. There are also superb examples of German Renaissance and Dutch 17th century paintings (of which the Prado only has a few). There are also 19th century American works of art, virtually non-existent anywhere else in Spain. From the first stirrings of modern art, as Impressionism, up through the harsher years of German Expressionism and Russian Constructivism, to experiments with Geometric Abstraction and the tongue-in-cheek irreverence of Pop Art…all are represented in this wide-ranging retrospective that is the Thyssen Collection.

Leaving the other two galleries behind, your last call will bring you to one of the most famous and in its time controversial masterpieces of this century, Picasso's Guernica, now hanging in the Centro de Arte Reina Sofia. The permanent collection here is primarily made up of Spanish painting and sculpture: Picasso, Gris, Miro, Dali, Chillida and Tapies, along with newer contemporaries.

On the "Avenue of Art" you will be dazzled by all the beauty great minds like yours have had to offer.

After the shopping, the gallery-hopping, the times at the beach and the nightlife, you will need to replenish and refresh the body with Spanish Catalan cuisine.

Food & Drink

Catalan cuisine defies summarizing with a few typical dishes. Dishes with deep-rooted country origins from the humble escudella to the rich and varied seafood cuisine, from grilled fish to excellent suquet de peix can be sampled in Barcelona. There are also many different ways to prepare codfish, an ample repertoire of fowl and game, including rabbit with snails, Catalan-style partridge or boar, and numerous specialities from Ampurdan region, such as duck with pears, chick with shrimp or lobster, etc. Finally, I must not forget dishes using duck and goose as their main ingredient, as well as snails and mushrooms.

Desserts are also varied and are not limited to the most typical ones, such as crema catalana (custard with a caramel topping and mel I matao (cottage cheese and honey).

Catalunya is a land of good wines, particularly the wines from Penedes, Costers del Sergre, Alella and Peralada. Penedes is the region par excellence of the sparkling wine called cava. This all makes for decadent and delightful meals.

There is so much to do that you will find that seven days is not enough and 10 days is just about right. If you would like to fit in Portugal in your trip, which is a short jump away, plan to stay longer.

I left Spain with the feeling that if there was anywhere in the world I would like to live other than where I'm living now, I would chose Spain. You probably will fall in love with it, too.

Hair – by Donna Kakonge (published December 1999/January 2000 – Panache Magazine)

In Beauty, Media Writing, Opinion, Technology, Writing (all kinds) on **November 2, 2008** at **14:27**

Back in the mid-80s, watching Oprah Winfrey's bouncing and behaving hair was like a dream come true. I never knew that black hair could do that. I rushed to a salon, telling them to duplicate the Oprah 'do on my head, and they did. The bad part is that just like what once happened to Oprah, my hair fell out. I was left with no hair on my head to duplicate any 'do.

Nina Simone sings "Black is the Color of My True Love's Hair" and actually I once thought my true soulmate was a bald man. But the inside love (that's me) does have black hair. Learning to love myself and my hair is a never-ending project, so much so I've decided to make it my concentration of study at the graduate level.

I was sitting with some friends of mine at a Montreal university pub, talking about what I often do – hair. One of them said to me, "why don't you do research on hair." I thought she was crazy, and that I would never find information on the topic, but I was wrong on both counts. I had been thinking and talking about hair for so long that I was sure my first thought as a baby was a kinky one. It was a natural choice for me to do research on hair.

I found out that everybody is talking about black hair these days. It's like when Dr. Ruth came out talking about sex and everyone was discussing it. I don't know who started the black hair talk, maybe Jesus himself, but black hair is top pick of writing topics, music, documentaries, and Internet sites.

With the growing sophistication of technology, and the millennium on its way, I decided to catch up with the times and do my master's project as an Internet site.

Finding a metaphor for the site was easy. I had spent a lifetime searching for the perfect salon. A salon with hairdressers that paid more attention to your head than the telephone. A salon that encouraged you to feel beautiful naturally. A salon with top-rate service, but low-rate prices. With the dream world one can create on the net I built a virtual one called Salon Utopia.

There's a receptionist, Betsy, who greets you as you enter. Hairdresser Mariame fashions the inside of your head as well as the outside. Music plays in the salon that makes you want to let your hair down.

There's a resource room with a head full of information about black hair. And a hairnet café links you up with a selection of other sites about hair. Most importantly, just like any good hair salon, there is a freedom to chat and an opportunity to participate in an on-line discussion about hair politics.

The on-line community, linked through Excite Communities, is the vital part to the research coming out of this site. The most active elements of the site are the calendar and the discussion threads. Both aspects have been up and running since November 18, 1998. The calendar acts as a bulletin board for everyone who is part of the community, and visitors as well. The community is like a clubhouse, where members and visitors are free to check out at all times of day and night what is going on. Member «nubchewy» includes information about her magazine, and most important is the discussion section.

The profile of the community and the members involved in the on-line discussion is quite diverse, and a bit 'sketchy' to explain, because on the internet, you can be whoever you want. I believe the make up is like this: out of 17 members, which makes `The Politics of Black Hair` one of the top communities under political issues in Excite Communities, there is one Asian male, three Asian females, all of these people coming from Canada, two black men, one from Canada, one from the United States, five black women (including myself) from Canada, but Rootswoman I`m not too sure of her race or location, two mixed race women, one from Canada, one from the States, a white woman from Canada, two more black women from the United States, one with a great name like SafFroNfox, and a mar2sad that I don`t know anything about. I hope that adds up. Mainly I found the members of the community through word of mouth, flyers at events about hair, and through search engines. I also sent hundreds of invites to everyone on my email mailing list. The people tend to be mainly of the same class as myself, the educated, middle to upper class. Unfortunately, these are the people who mainly have access to the internet. And although I`d hoped for a more international spread of members than just in North America, some people have told me that certain characters in my website address make it difficult to access in Africa, for example.

Speaking of Africa, Tojane, one of the members of the group, has an interesting anecdote about hair there. She says: «Here is a little tidbit of politics that takes us beyond the side of the Atlantic. Back home, in

Nigeria, locks have very definite meaning. The only people who wore them were either crazy, a part of a certain caste (outcaste) of society, or a "rastafarian." I went back a couple years ago, and had a lengthy discussion with my aunt about them. She just couldn't understand why anyone wouldn't want their hair free. Of course, she had a long, flowing weave in her own hair.» Tojane talks further about wanting to put locks in her own hair, and Alice Walker promoting taking the «dread» out of the word «dreadlocks.» It seems like she was utilizing the community to sort out her own hair issues, and get sharing and feedback on such a visible topic as hair.

This is the kind of discussion that has been going on for many months in the on-line community. «Ask the Administrator,» and «Locks.» have been the most popular discussion threads. Through the research in the on-line community I have managed to do what so many researchers dream of, debunk some of the myths of their subject. Some of the myths of natural black hair is that it's difficult to deal with, Alice Walker herself even says this in a kind of loving way. But Tojane gives a different perspective. She wears her hair natural and actually sees it as «fun» rather than «hard.»

Other myths about natural black hair include black men. There are many black women who believe that they must have long flowing hair like Tyra Banks, Naomi Campbell, or any of those other (I will admit) beautiful women on the runways. But a black man from the United States gives voice to men that don`t desire black Barbie dolls, or fake breasts and fake hair: «Speaking from my current state of consciousness, I love black hair. By black hair, I refer to hair belonging to people of color – of African descent. I prefer it in its natural glory, with all its "kinkiness," curls, "naps," bends and loops. I must admit however, I haven't always felt this way about black hair. At one time I was swayed and influenced by all those straight hair, blond blue eyed, pale-skinned commercials. I wanted my hair to move when the wind blew just like my t.v. favorites. Black entertainers also upheld the image of whiteness by frying, and dying, and relaxing hair that was meant to stand firm, stand tall…God has given each one of us a certain uniqueness. And there's nothing wrong with experimenting with fashions and styles, but to alter ones looks to appear more acceptable to another culture is a form of self-hatred.` Say it again, Sam as they say.

Another myth I managed to debunk with this web community is that white people do not care about black hair politics, and that they do not have their own hair issues. The white female member of the group pointed out an interesting article appearing around March in *The New Yorker* about hair colouring, history and white women. That article also lead her to relate to some of the issues in my website.

The contribution of the white woman in the community lead me to think, is black hair and its politics just one those `black things,` or is it part of a larger cultural issue (can`t do question marks on this keyboard). The answers, like they often do, came from the website and the members. Tojane looked to the media and positive images of black women in the mainstream popular culture to explain black women representation. She says it best: «Until we start seeing positive images of BLACK women in mainstream popular culture, we will continue to aspire/pain ourselves to that white ideal that has been affecting us for centuries. Now-a-days, its in to be not too black, to have "good" hair, and figures that fit within this societies ideal of who we are. Black women have yet to appear in positive ways on TV, in our magazines and on the fashion runways (if they exist at all). When they do show up, their skin tone and hair texture are used as props in themselves to push the exotic image that we tend to fall into sometimes–hypersexualized and hard. Either that, or we are chocolate images of our white counterparts. Aside from this there is a virtual absence of positive Black female images. This could be said of all women of color. We tend to remain silent or remain sex objects for male spectators.»

In many ways nubchewy through the community has a chance to agree and share with Tojane when she talks about locks. `I know that a lot of sisters who have

perms say "I would wear my hair natural if I could get long locs right away" but they are still dealing with that 'having hair hanging down' issue.» What nubchewy says echoes in many ways Tojane`s sentiments that many black women are buying into and being sold the white woman as beauty ideal myth. This is more than just a `black thing,` it has social, political, and economic ramifications that affect our lives as viable members of our non-virtual communities.

Economics is a big issue, work and black hair was an important topic in the community which generated two interesting stories I will note.

One woman who lives in Toronto said: «My own father warned me that I would be "unemployable" since braids do not fit the corporate image. As a black man, he has always expressed a deep distaste for black women who wear natural hair. Women who maintain a short afro are called "mannish» or "lesbians" and women with braids or dreads are "radicals" This view is strongly held outside the black community as well. My white friends express a fascination with the process of braiding, but clearly do not consider it to be an ideal hairstyle. It is exotic or strange. I wear my hair in ways that it is comfortable to me, but I am aware that working in a corporate environment in which the very few black women who are there sport conservative, relaxed styles. Will I pay a penalty for having natural, braided hair all year round? I think, sadly that the answer is yes. Secretly, I admire black women who wear short afros, but I don't think I would be brave enough to face the criticism and derision that comes with such a choice.»

The woman from Toronto raises some realistic points in a virtual way. Another story from nubchewy displays the drastic lengths some people will go to to avoid having employees with natural hair. «I work part time is a computer trainer for professional adults. When I went to the first job interview and the callback, I wore my natural hair in neat cornrows with a bun. I was offered the job but told that I must complete a 2-week unpaid trial run to ensure that I had the right stuff for the job. In desperation, I had a sistahfriend of mine braid my hair for me so that it could last 2 weeks. At the end of two weeks, the boss (a white, Jewish woman) told me first thing in the morning that I had done excellent work and that the company

wanted to "reward me" for working so hard without pay. The reward was a

so-called day of pampering and the company would foot the bill. She said, and I quote, that it was time I "stopped looking like a University student and started looking like a professional woman." I would be sent out that very same day with the receptionist (the only other black person in the office) to get a new suit, new shoes, makeup, a manicure and get

my hair done.` Nubchewy had to negotiate with the receptionist, who wore a blonded Jherri curl herself, what to do with her hair. The boss really wanted her to perm her hair, but nubchewy refused and compromised with braids, which she ripped out a few weeks later. Nubchewy proudly wears a wild `buckwheat` afro as she puts it, and still has her job, because in the end, her excellent job performance outcurled even her hair.

These things that have happened to the black women of the community are awful. But don`t be fooled that the politics of black hair is a `black people`s thing.` There are other races that have black hair too, just not quite, never quite, like black people. A female Asian member of the community makes comments on Asians (and blacks) and their hair politics. She `wonders why Asian women get perms to look like poodles, and black women straighten their hair to have something that looks like an oddly shaped bob – she also mentions that women of colour strive for a Caucasian aesthetic and when will it end a denial of ones spiritual essence. Some would even say that it is a form of self-hatred.»

While I've been putting together Salon Utopia, I've gone through braids, to a natural look, to twists, to neo-dreads, to blow-dried straight, to cornrows, to braids again, and my latest style is an afro with a band. I have learned a lot through hair, great stories, great hairstyles, how to do a website, read many good books, and seen interesting movies. Last but not least, I've met many interesting people – through the net, at conferences, and at hair documentaries. But the most important thing I've learned is that on this journey of ever-increasing self-love, hair, and education, like the thousands of strands of hair on my head – I'm not alone.

Forging a Career in Aboriginal Film and Video (originally published in Heartbeat of the North.com)

In Culture, Media Writing, Movie Reviews, Writing (all kinds) on **December 2, 2008** at **11:53**

Marie-Helene Cousineau is a video and filmmaker who I first met by being her teacher's assistant at Concordia University in Montreal back in 1997. Her career path has lead her to many opportunities to work with Aboriginal people in Nunavut. She is founder of a women's video collective called Isuma.

"Just the fact that I moved to Igloolik, this was not something I planned ahead," says Cousineau talking about how she came to form Isuma. "I was working with women's groups and individual women before moving to Igloolik, so I was working for people that were there."

Cousineau preferred to work on films rather than on papers for school.

"Everybody's interested in film and video and I was interested in art and I started to make images and I started to make images as a student in school making slideshows, and it was kind of normal to go towards the moving images."

Among many of Cousineau's accomplishments is her involvement with Atarnajuat (The Fast Runner). This is the first feature film in Inuktitut that has had world-wide appeal.

"My name is in the credits as the still photographer," says Cousineau. "I was involved in the technical team, I did some public relations, and I worked on the set. I was there for the whole process. It was a very intense experience. It was hard to produce the film to find the money to do it and convince people in the film system in Canada that it was a good idea. To convince people in the film system that a feature film in Inuktitut would have a mass appeal. Mostly the actors were from Igloolik, everyone had to learn as they were going."

Cousineau says the reason why the film worked against the odds is because despite the fact it was the first time for everybody to do a feature film, people had already some experience.

"I think it worked because people were really convinced that it was a great story and great script. The people who were doing it weren't giving up and didn't make any concessions. They really pushed it all the way to the end [with] their convictions. They didn't take no for an answer."

Marie-Helene Cousineau says the problem in Nunavut is that the territory has existed for about six years now and the structures are not in place to support a film and television industry. What was in place in the North West Territories, when it changed to Nunavut, were lost.

"People who are now there are not acting really fast on that dossier, I don't know if they really believe in that dossier," says Cousineau. "You don't feel like there's a real political will to make this an issue. If you work in any other province in Canada, there is support there."

Cousineau does mention that there is a Nunavut Film Commission now and they've hired a film commissioner about five months ago, but it's not really functional, so you can't rely on it.

"You have to do things in all sorts of weird ways to find money to make a film. I can't even imagine what they [the commission] can do. That's one big problem."

There are other problems, like distance, says Cousineau. Traveling to the North is more expensive than traveling to Australia. Food is expensive, hotel rooms are expensive, you need to train people as you're doing things, and then you need to find money to train them.

"If you train them, you need to get them a job after. If you train them you need to have a support system to offer jobs to people and you need to have support from the government and it doesn't exist. At the same time there are big needs for jobs in the North, and the jobs in that area need to be transferable to other jobs, not just driving a truck for a mining company. Most of what the government is supporting is mining in the North West Territories and northern Quebec and Ontario. We're back to selling Canada to big corporations."

In Cousineau's personal life, she has two sons, one named Sam and the other Alex. Alex is an Aboriginal five year old and was adopted.

"Adoption is kind of a usual thing in Igloolik or Inuit communities, maybe anthropologists would call it circulation," says Cousineau. "In every family there are kids that are given in adoption, there were spiritual reasons and practical reasons. The Elders would control the welfare of the community like that. This tradition is still going on right now."

One day a woman that Cousineau knew for 10 years was pregnant and asked her if she wanted to adopt and she knew Cousineau was open to adopting an Inuit child.

"This woman is kind of a sister and I was kind of part of her family and [knew] her boyfriend. I already had a child, so when she gave birth, she gave me the baby, he's going to turn five next week, we love him very much. We just finished a film about adoption called Unakuluk, Dear Little One, that's the name of the movie that finished three months ago. It's a 46-minute documentary and my son's name is Alex. In the story I visit with his grandmother and one of his great-grandfathers and they tell the story about how it happens and why for adoption."

Right now Cousineau is preparing a feature film based on a Danish novel that's taking place in Greenland.

"I wrote a script based on the book The Day before Tomorrow. It's a fiction feature, for me it's going to be like a first experience."

Cousineau is on her way to Legosier, Guadeloupe where they will be buying videos that the video collective Isuma makes.

Citizen and Refugee (Originally Published for Orato.com)

In Culture, Opinion, Writing (all kinds), travel on **December 3, 2008** at **12:18**

African beauty displayed in this statue

As the end of the year draws near and the death of former President of Uganda, Milton Obote passes, it brings back memories. Memories of a life I was meant to live in my Dad's home country and all the loved ones lost in the wars which have ravaged Uganda.

I was born August 12, 1972 in Kitchener, Waterloo, Canada. My Dad was doing his PhD in biology and zoology on a Commonwealth scholarship at the University of Waterloo, and my Mom, who is originally from St.Vincent and the Grenadines, had moved from Toronto. The plan was after my father's graduation my family would move to Kampala, Uganda where Dr. Sam Kakonge would teach at Makerere University. I would grow up and receive the same kind of education a solid middle class African girl would and most likely only return to Canada to study abroad.

My Dad became a PhD, his wife Yvette became my Mom, and all three of us left Canada to make Uganda our home in September, 1972. Now, at the age of 33, I still have the scar from the booster shot I received in Uganda on my upper left arm.

That turned out to be the first of the scars left. My Uncle John was head of the youth party for the Uganda People's Congress, Obote's party. As former President Idi Amin overthrew Obote in a coup d'état, Uncle John went missing.

My Dad has told me with passion many times over the years how much he loved his brother John. He quickly was involved in searching for his brother.

My Mom tells me that one of my Dad's sisters came to the house we were living in. This was a time when the former British colonialists influence was still on Uganda and milk was brought to your door. My Dad's sister did not bring milk, but instead a message that the police were looking for my Dad and if we didn't get out of the country fast, he may go "missing" as well.

This is where I became a refugee to a country where I was a citizen. My Mom left behind many precious things like her wedding dress in Uganda, but with me tucked in her arms we returned to Canada after five months of being gone. My Dad followed later on as he needed to tend to his work situation.

Like so many Ugandans, Uncle John was never found. Over the years my Dad has also lost family members from more than just Amin, but from AIDS.

I returned to Uganda in September, 1996 almost 25 years after my first visit. President Yoweri Museveni is presently in power and the weekend radio shows call the names of those dead, mostly from AIDS.

My family grew; I have a younger brother and sister in that order. They were both born in Toronto, did their education mainly in Toronto and work in Toronto. My parents divorced when I was 15, 1987, but they remain good friends as my Dad often reminds me how other divorced couples bicker. If only the once unified continent of Africa could get along so well.

War is what plagues Uganda. When I was there from 1996 to 1997, I stayed and worked mostly in Kampala which is a bustling city, but many of the buildings at the time show signs of wear. In my trip there, I found the potholes in the road to one of the most dangerous daily encounters.

My Dad, once he returned to Canada worked mainly for the government. Now he delivers The Toronto Star and owns six houses in downtown Toronto which he renovates. He has not been back to Uganda, but returning is part of his retirement plan, where he would like to restore his old family home in Hoima, Uganda in a village near Rwanda. I saw that home when I was in Uganda in 1997 – he has a lot of work to do.

Would I go back to Africa? With the beat of my heart I would, however my heart also beats for Canada and all it has to offer. My Mom, my Dad, my Aunt and my country kept me safe from Dictator Idi Amin. As another year passes, and old Ugandan leaders die, the best I hope to do is have a peaceful and productive life in my native land.

Get radical (originally published on Canoe.ca)

In Beauty, Writing (all kinds) on **December 7, 2008** at **17:23**

Trends in hair fashions are keeping tempo with music and other media. Looks change from the rock and roll and out of bed, straight with no frizz and shiny as a mirror like classical or jazz, or alternative radical styles with no half measures and no compromises.

The desired look with StudioFX

Many young people are adopting these trendy looks and in every way letting their hair hang loose.

"[I have a] curly look," says Elle Spencer-Lewis, a part-time editor. "Usually I'll put on some kind of glossy hold product when it's wet, and then put on a spritzer when it's dry, and blow dry it slowly."

Spencer-Lewis is fairly familiar with this season's hair trends. She's glad she does not have to straighten her hair anymore.

Possibly a good product for Spencer-Lewis might be the "radical" brand of products of L'Oréal Paris's new Special FX line, which is supposed to be great for pasting, shaping and setting.

"Extreme hold is guaranteed," says manager of public relations for L'Oréal Paris, Caroline Badger. "Radical gel's original 'glue' texture is enriched with fibres to create extreme effects almost hair by hair – with a hold that just won't quit!"

Caroline Künzle, 27, and a part-time theatre usher, isn't looking for a radical look with her wavy to straight, relatively short hair. She wants less structure.

"My hair maintenance is quite low," says Künzle. "I'm growing it out, and decided to go for a longer look. It's kind of in that awkward in-between stage. I'm kind of trying to go for that palm tree look. The look I want is the out of bed, and as unkempt as possible."

GET RADICAL

Künzle likes the unwashed look.

The new Special FX line "out of bed" product, aimed at the under 30 age group, promises to tousle and unsettle.

"A bonus benefit, the formula is extremely pliable and allows one to change the direction of the style during the day – to create a unique 'remix' as the day goes on," says Badger. "Whatever movement is fashioned, hair remains shiny and supple…and stays that way!" Angela Li, a 29-year-old financial analyst with naturally straight hair, sometimes tries to make it even straighter.

"I wash, condition and blow dry my hair," says Li. "I don't do much to get it straight. Sometimes when I want it really straight and shiny, I'll use a flat iron."

L'Oréal Paris's Special FX line "straight" promises to add sleekness and smoothness to anyone who desires a straight look.

"The perfect partner to blow-drying, 'straight' can straighten to the max! Non-greasy and with no 'weighing down,' 'straight's texture smoothes the hair and provides a sleek, smooth look – all day long," says Badger.

The Special FX line of products will be available October 2001 in large retailers and pharmacies. The suggested retail price of each product is $7.99.

Creating a Canvas (originally published for Pride Newsmagazine)

In Beauty, Business, Entertainment, Writing (all kinds) on **December 11, 2008** at **03:22**

Guess what? That beautiful mane on the head of Miss Universe, Natalie Glebova – it is a weave.

Christos Cox and his team at Urban Textures Salons created the winning look for Miss Universe like any artist creates their canvas.

"I didn't even know at that time sitting in the salon that she had won Miss Canada," says Cox.

He got an emergency call from the President of Miss Canada. "He came by that day to let me see her hair. We recommended darker, longer hair," says Cox. "She wanted a Chinese perm. The type of straightening that she wanted would have been very detrimental to her hair. They insisted on having her hair retexturized. We did it. We were thinking about the fact she would be in Thailand and dealing with intense humidity. We chose to use a relaxer system that is used for super curly hair textures, but the mildest form of that. It's somewhat exclusive to us in Canada."

Cox wouldn't mention what the product is – a trade secret.

"We retexurized her canvas," Cox said. He sees hair the way artists see canvas – it's a foundation from which to create something beautiful. "We extended her hair 10 inches. We try to come up with the concept and design first. That's where Rose comes in, to put structure where there was no structure."

Rose Hibbert, the weave specialist who did the work on Miss Universe, used 150 per cent real human cuticle hair.

Hibbert says in the packaged hair, there's only 10 per cent human hair, even though it says it's 100 per cent human hair, it's not. She got the hair from Hair & Wigs on Yonge Street.

"A lot of the product [used in weaves and extensions] us as black salon owners are using, coming from Thailand and Japan and different parts of India are toxic, cancer causing," said Cox. "They're working with different types of chemicals that they use masks in the factories. We need to be really careful of what we're putting in their heads."

Both Cox and Hibbert emphasized that the synthetic hair is material and not good or healthy to use.

"Cuticle hair is used by people like Beyoncé and Janet, people like that use the hair for six or seven years," said Hibbert. "A lot of people tend not to make the braids neat enough, like French braids."

Hibbert advises that if you would like your hair weaved, you should come prepared – don't make any plans. "The trick to maintaining the hair is to get good quality. Always get quality things, that saying you get what you pay for is so true."

"We're not the cheapest game in town, but not [really] expensive," says Christos Cox.

Hibbert says the term tangle-free does not exist unless it's cuticle hair.

"Urban Textures is the only place that has this quality in Canada. We do weaves that are naturally yours. It's a natural extension to your hair."

Other tips Hibbert has for maintaining the weave: "Vive Serum from L'Oréal is a genious product. And Spray Stopper along the edges of the weave keeps it from fraying."

"Weave will never be out of style. Take care of it. The days of it looking tangled in the back should be over. You'll love it once you start. Weave is addictive." Hibbert lives by it.

Christos Cox mentioned Oprah has been staying away from weave for years because every weave she saw was a ghetto weave that looked like weave. Then when she found out that you can spend $500 on a weave to get someone else's real human hair – she did it.

"We don't do the dancehall weaves here," said Cox.

"We usually tell people during a consultation, bring a picture from a style you like and that's what we'll do," Hibbert says.

Hibbert advises not to leave a weave in longer than three months on super curly hair because the hair will tend to tangle underneath.

Christos Cox met Natalie Glebova at his long-time mentor Robin Barker's salon on Yonge Street.

"I did Natalie's hair during the Miss Canada's pageant of 2003. Frizz was her issue that year. I put in some really long weave and blended it into her hair and flat-ironed it. She came in 2nd place. I did her hair again for another show that they did. She won Miss Canada last year."

"The runner-up [of Miss Universe] had frizzy hair on her pony-tail and whatever Christos told her [Miss Universe] to do work well," said Rose Hibbert.

Also, Thao Nguyen did the colour for Miss Universe. The colour chosen was chocolate.

"We pulled a team together to deliver all the different services we required," said Cox.

Some tips on colouring hair include if you have highlights, get them done every 6-8 weeks. If you have full colour – go every 4-6 weeks to get the grey out.

"It's not easy to cut a weave and blend it in to look natural."

It's something Urban Textures does. You have to go to them to get it done. Urban Textures Salons has two locations – one downtown at 44 Gerrard St. W. (at Bay St.) and the other in Scarborough at 45 Milner Ave. (at McCowan Rd.).

Girl power in hockey (Originally Published in Amöi Magazine)

In Culture, Entertainment, Writing (all kinds) on **December 19, 2008** at **23:22**

Fran Rider, Executive Director of the Ontario Women's Hockey Association says Canadians are born with an interest in hockey. She came from a sports-minded family and started playing around 1967.

"It has powerful opportunities, many of the girls are teachers, professors, they're highly educated," she says. "There are many police officers. The young girls have role models in life, not just in sport."

When Rider was younger, she says there weren't many opportunities for women to play hockey. They could watch the sport, but playing was a different story.

"I saw an ad in the Toronto Telegram, I used to go to the Leafs' games and played in the backyard and always desperately wanted to play and when the opportunity arose I got involved."

Currently, there is no professional women's hockey like in basketball, football or hockey for men. The AA league is for recreation. The AAA team is national women's hockey where the women travel and are in the Olympic Games.

The Ontario Women's Hockey Association was formed in 1975. When the association first started out they received support from Shoppers Drug Mart and Mississauga Mayor, Hazel McCallion. The International Ice Hockey Federation moved towards a full world championship in 1990 making it possible for Canadians to play in the Olympics.

"The goals of the OWHA have been to grow the interest of the game throughout Ontario, Canada and the world," says Rider. "It's a universal game, the bigger objective of hockey is to win the game, but the bigger objective is to get more support for women's hockey and the sport."

Rider also says diverse women playing hockey creates role models.

"Angela [James] was one of the superstars by far and way ahead of her time," Rider says.

Angela James played for the Olympic women's hockey team. She grew up in Flemingdon Park in Toronto.

"It's funny because I'm retired from hockey now," says James. "When I was younger, I played in my neighbourhood with my friends, played in the outdoor arena. It's pretty much what everybody did in my area."

James is a Senior Sports Coordinator at Seneca College on York University's campus.

"I'm biracial," James says. "My father's from rural Mississippi and my mother's from Ontario. My father who probably has never put on a pair of skates in his life – most of his kids play hockey and are [good] at it. I don't know if it goes back to the faster muscle twitch."

James, who lives with her partner, has three children. Chatting with her on a traditional hockey night in Canada, she reflected on the highlights of her hockey career.

"The first world championship…the second world championship was another. The provincial championship was always a great highlight. There were so many it's hard to say which one. The action on the ice, the way the game is played, the skating. It's a winter sport, I enjoy that. Also friendship, it's a team sport off the ice.

"I was playing up until last year," says James. "I officiate; I'm involved in coaching my son's team. It's pretty much still a hockey house here."

James hasn't decided yet whether she will be returning to hockey this year.

"I'd play out of York University; they do have a league there. I'd probably play the AA, I could play the AAA, but it's just too much of a time commitment."

For all of James's success with hockey, she has recently been inducted in the Black Ice Hockey and Sports Hall of Fame based in Nova Scotia.

Diverse women of the North (originally published in Amöi Magazine)

In Culture, Living, Writing (all kinds), travel on **December 22, 2008** at **00:32**

Yellowknife is a well-kept Canadian secret.

Kate Wilson who is the Director of Family Housing for the YWCA in Yellowknife is from Ghana. She is a teacher by profession, trained in Ghana. Wilson did adult education at Aurora College in Yellowknife, as well as taking career development and life skills coaching through the YWCA. She's been living in the city for 12 years with her husband, who is an electrical engineer, and their four children. Wilson currently finds housing for people who are temporarily homeless. "It's a very enjoyable job and very rewarding," she says. "You're working with people and with families so I have the opportunity to be with children and their parents and to be in their lives. I have a wonderful staff and we all work with the clients that come here and you see their lives going from A to B to C. It's good to see the humankind going in a very positive way. There's a joy in giving, it's a selfish reason too. When you give, it comes back to you. I really enjoy the work I do here. Working with people from all walks of life. Not many people get the opportunity to do that. It's a beautiful thing." Wilson calls Yellowknife the United Nations of Canada. "You find everybody from everywhere," she says. "It used to be that there weren't too many black people, now you find people from all over."

Wilson describes Yellowknife as a small town with a small-town way of living.

"The air is so clean, we don't get smog and all those things," she says. "It's actually nice to breathe up here. There's work here, with all the economic boom. We find quite a few black people coming here. If you want work, you'll get work. For a black person living here, colour is not really a barrier. When I first came here I worked for the Native Women's Association. Colour is not a barrier, not as far as my life has been in Yellowknife. From my view, I'm very well accepted." Yellowknife is such a close-knit community that when the Ambassador to Ghana came to the city, Wilson was able to entertain the Ambassador in her home.

"I brought her to my home," she says. "Could you do that in a big city? We all gathered together in my home. That's the beauty of Yellowknife, it's easy access. Theresa Handley with the Status of Women and her husband is the Premier of the North West Territories. Joe had lived in Ghana before…we've had a beautiful relationship since then – it's easy access. When you go to Toronto and you see all those people hovering around with degrees and they don't have jobs. They should come up north. Canadians haven't really taken the time to know Canada's north. If you want a relaxing, restful life – Yellowknife is where to live."

Sandy Lee agrees with Wilson. Lee was elected to the 14th Legislative Assembly of the Northwest Territories in 1999. She was re-elected to the 15th Legislative Assembly in 2003. For both elections, she was one of two women elected and she is the highest-ranking Korean-Canadian elected official in Canada and the world.

"It's a surprise to me because I never would have imagined I would be in politics growing up in Korea," says Lee. "I was 14 years old when I left Korea. We came to Yellowknife. Nobody ever talked about politics, but when I got here, I thought of Canada as a land of opportunity, somewhere where I could go to as much schooling as possible. It's very expensive to go to schooling in Korea. All I wanted to do here is get schooling; I didn't care about the degree."

Lee started a business degree in Calgary, but eventually gradated in political science from Carleton University in Ottawa with the encouragement of a friend.

"I absolutely fell in love with politics," she says. "It was the best thing that ever happened to me. I came from such an underprivileged background, especially studying politics I felt so empowered. I was practicing law away from politics and someone asked me to run a campaign."

It was right after Nunavut and there were positions coming up. Lee figured if she didn't get in, she would get back into law. It turned out she beat out four guys.

"When I went door-to-door, I realized all these people were people I grew up with," Lee says. "Every second door I knew them, or they knew someone I knew, or my family. I didn't have a political profile, but I had a good reputation."

Lee gives talks to the Korean community and other ethnic minorities in Canada.

"Everyone looks for economic power first," she says. "People know how to do that. But I think we need to know that we need to be involved in the political process. More minorities getting elected and the composition of our political institutions should reflect our diverse backgrounds."

Lee notes that there are 160 countries represented in Yellowknife.

"I went to the citizenship swearing-in ceremony last winter and there were 200 people sworn in, and they were from every country you can imagine living in the north," Lee says. "The diamond industry has brought a lot of new people. We have six or seven families from Mauritius. We have people from Nigeria, Somalia, Uganda, and Thailand. When I was growing up 30 years ago, we had Chinese business people here. We have a huge Filipino population here compared to other places. The colour of our city has changed over the years. A lot of diamond producers here are from Australia, South Africa. Hardly any Koreans here. I'm just a Yellowknife girl."

The Biracial Generation: Embracing Cultural Diversity (originally published in Amöi Magazine)

In Culture, Living, Writing (all kinds) on **December 22, 2008** at **23:37**

There are more than 70,000 biracial people living in Canada according to Statistics Canada in 2001. They may have any combination of heritage including Aboriginal, black, white, South Asian, Chinese, Korean, Japanese, Southeast Asian, people from the Philippines, Arab/West Asian and Latin American. Christine Chin who is a salesperson with Conservus, a concierge company, calls herself Jamaican-Canadian and Canadian ultimately.

She was born in Liverpool, England and came to Canada at the age of 10 ½.

"My parents migrated to Canada in Christmas of 1972," Chin says. "My father is from a little village in China and my grandmother had 13 children and my father is in the middle. All the children were born in Jamaica."

Chin's great grandmother on her Mom's side is Scottish with some Cuban heritage.

"My mom looks more Spanish, European or Portuguese," says Chin. "I have two brothers and a sister. They all look different. The brother born after me had red hair when he was born."

Chin's natural hair colour is jet black. It would look blue in the sun like the body of flies. Now with her brown highlights, she could pass for people for the Philippines, Spanish or Puerto Rican.

People think she looks like her father who has a Vietnamese and Chinese background. People speak in Spanish and Chinese to her.

"Canadians say I'm not Canadian because I look ethnic. Jamaicans say you're not Jamaican because I'm not a 'yardy.' The culture at home is definitely Jamaican. With Jamaicans too I'm not fully black. Chinese don't think I look Chinese. Some say I do, some say I don't. I don't fully participate in the culture. I do have Chinese culture – it's west Chinese, but it is culture."

Chin says people try to put her in a box she doesn't fit in. She says people can't peg her.

However, there are positive things to being biracial.

"It's opened the door for conversation with lots of people," Chin says. "Men will think I'm intimidating because of my looks. I'm not intimidating."

Her former husband is Chinese-born and was raised in Jamaica. She has two boys who look Asian, but you can see the influences of other cultures in their faces.

Christine Chin's beauty has led to interesting experiences.

"I've been approached to do modeling. A man approached me at the Four Seasons in Yorkville. He did a painting of me."

The handsome Kim Barry Brunhuber whose father is from Cameroon and mother is white South African has also had dynamic career options being biracial. His step-father is Puerto-Rican and his mother had a daughter with the step-father who is his half-sister. Brunhuber grew up around different cultural influences that have inspired his career.

"I've had many various professional experiences: writer, broadcaster, even (to a small extent) actor," says Brunhuber.

Brunhuber was born in Montreal and grew up in Ottawa. He doesn't know how being biracial has affected him professionally.

"I think on balance it has been neither a blessing nor a curse," Brunhuber says. "Certainly in television it is a double-edge sword… a station could want to hire you simply because you're a non-threatening visible minority."

Brunhuber is the author of a book called Kameleon Man.

"I wanted to foster a discussion about race and identity in Canada, and specifically what happens when you invest all of your identity in the way you look. It's a world of disappointment, disillusionment and failure, and what better setting than the world of modeling."

In terms of identity, Brunhuber sees himself as a Canadian with African heritage. He does respond to "black" or a "person of mixed race."

His parents met at Cornell University in the United States at the African Students' Club.

"My mother, though white, felt utterly alienated by North American culture and identified more closely with African students, who were happy for the most part to accept her."

Brunhuber says he can move easily between different cultures. He has a love for languages and a keen interest in other cultures which accounts for his love of travel. He speaks English, French, Spanish and some German – enough to order a beer, not enough to buy one for someone else.

He's currently working on a novel set in Africa. He's working in Sierra Leone for a year with Journalists for Human Rights. He reflects on the way he's perceived internationally.

"It is an odd experience, as I am usually perceived as white," Brunhuber says. "In Uganda I'm a muzungu, in Ghana I'm an obruni, in Senegal I'm a toubab… all names for 'white man.' I have had many debates with Africans trying to convince them that I'm 'black.' It's strange, because I could represent my African heritage in Canada by wearing African dress to a function and no one would question it. But I would never be able to represent my German heritage by wearing lederhosen. Only in Cape Town and Cuba where there are large populations of brown-skinned people can I pass as a local."

Brunhuber doesn't see a shared future for biracial people in Canada. He says recent Canadian statistics state that 75 per cent of Canadians would not marry outside of their race.

"I believe the numbers to be higher. Any large-scale change will happen at the pace of human evolution – at glacial pace. Never underestimate the power of nationalism, ethnocentrism, racism and xenophobia."

Jamaican-Canadian Christine Chin says that in the 1970's when she first came to Canada, it wasn't' the best time to be non-white. However, she says things have changed.

"The barriers aren't here these days," says Chin. "Toronto is different.
Some cultures are prejudiced. My parents felt, marry for love."

Hushing People to Try on Clothes (originally published in Pride Newsmagazine)

In [Beauty](), [Business](), [Writing (all kinds)]() on **December 24, 2008** at **02:49**

Owner of Hush Boutique, Stephen Phillips stands by his creations

He was one of those people who answer his phone, but you get put on hold a lot because he has so many calls coming in. After three tries, I was finally able to set-up an interview with African-Canadian Stephen Phillips.

Who's he? You may ask that now, but just watch this young man and you may not be asking that much longer.

He's the owner of Hush Boutique & Yoga on 785 Queen St. W. near Bathurst St. and while I was waiting for him to do the interview, I saw a black cat on a hot tin roof.

That's how Phillips has been feeling these days, like a cat on a hot tin roof. His phone rings constantly as he plans a shopping trip to Hong Kong. He recently came back from Montreal where he is looking at property for his boutique. He's also looking to relocate to a different spot on Queen Street because the rent he's paying is too high.

It's not easy designing your own clothes and owning your own boutique. But, Phillips is doing it and looking to expand.

He started working in fashion with Giorgio Armani. When he left to own his own boutique, he knew there was only one place in Toronto where he could set up shop.

"I wanted to have my store on Queen Street because this is the place for fashion. All the great stores are here," says Phillips.

Hush Boutique & Yoga opened in 2003. His store is a unique blend of fitted street wear and yoga wear. One of the pieces he has hanging in the window is a shirt that says "pending" with the bottoms saying "approval." It's fun tongue-in-cheek fashion like this that captures the essence of Phillips' line.

He calls the store "Hush" because he wants to encourage the kind of atmosphere that when people come in, he quiets their questions about the clothes and just encourages them to try something on. He knows that when they do – they will find an outfit they like.

He has clothes for men and women. All of it is the kind of fashion that has a distinct look that goes beyond the clothes you would find in a mall. This is the type of clothing for making a statement. Along with clothes, he also sells accessories like bags, jewellery and belts.

Right now, he mainly has petite sizes, but for the fall collection and onwards he's going to start catering to guys who are 6 feet 6 inches and women with voluptuous figures.

"They'll be something for everyone," says Phillips.

He went to school at George Brown and Ryerson Colleges before he worked with Giorgio Armani. He also studied in Germany, but is originally from Ghana. He's spent most of his time in Canada.

"Most of my education came from working at Giorgio – doing fashion shows."

You can definitely see the influences of Giorgio Armani in the colours he uses. Browns, army greens, white, black and more traditional fashion colours accent his street wear. The yoga wear is a bit different with splurges on colour like intense pinks and blues.

His store has everything from jackets to tops to pants to handbags to jewellery and Phillips love all of it. His passion for fashion came at a young age.

"Why I love fashion is that I love clothes. When I was young and all the boys [his siblings] would get the same jacket and pants to wear – I would put different buttons on and do things to make mine unique."

He also mentions that because he exercises a lot the idea of combining street fashion with yoga wear came from one of his mentors he worked with at Giorgio. Phillips learned a lot about making clothes distinctive.

He uses a fabric called modal and is experimenting with bamboo fabric for his clothes. He uses nylon, tactile and spandex on the yoga wear pants because it makes them more comfortable. But, Phillips has more than just making clothes in his future plans. He wants to give something back to others.

For his future plans, his planning to work on something where a portion of the sales of his clothing will go towards HIV/AIDS, breast cancer or feeding the hungry in Africa. Although he is an African-Canadian, Phillips wants his clothing to appeal to everyone.

"I'm trying to cater to all the masses," says Phillips. "My fall line will include from short men to tall men. It will include from voluptuous women to skinny women. I want them all to wear Hush clothes."

To make sure you can visit Hush Boutique and find the exact location, please feel free to give Stephen Phillips the owner a call at (416) 361-3361.

Let it Go or Organize it (originally published in New Dreamhomes and Condominiums Magazine)

In [Home Decor](), [Writing (all kinds)]() on **December 25, 2008** at **00:38**

Getting a new dream home or condo is a great thing to come into your life. It's getting and keeping it organized that is the key.

Feng shui the Sharon Hay way includes less clutter so the energy flow is better in the home and condo. That is not an event but a lifestyle.

"The more you de-clutter the more comes in and opportunities and other things fall into place," Hay says.

Hay says there are nine stations of life and different elements enhance aspects of life. Each element has a colour and a shape.

"I get their [clients'] year of birth which gives me which directions are best for success," Hay says. "I find out how many bedrooms, how long they've been living there how old the building is…what's been going on in their life, if they just got married, if they just changed careers? We go forward to remove any blockages and enhance with the elements."

Landscaping inside and outside the home is important in organizing the feng shui way. Artificial trees, pictures and plants help to avoid the negative environmental influences. Even with a condo you would need more pictures of flowers and vibrant colours of plants and trees.

"Too much red is too stimulating, too much fire energy," says Hay. "If someone has a lot of kids they have to keep it fairly grounded. Oranges, beiges, taupes, yellows and things in square patterns. You can have square pillows on the couch. It gives a lot more of a feeling of security. [The parents] have to try and keep the toys under control and if things are out in the hallway and picking the rubber ducky off your kitchen counter – things become chaotic, hard to think, hard to focus, the relationship gets stressed."

Hay says a lot about organizing is going with your gut feelings. Holding onto things you do not need can make you lose money or lose out on opportunities.

"The more you let go, the more new fresh vibrant energy comes in. It's been handed down through generations – give it away." As Nada Thomson, professional organizer with Artful Organizers was preparing to set her parking time on her cellphone over breakfast she added her experience to organizing a new dream home or condo.

"It was a beautiful home in Oakville…a beautiful new community there and the home was just sprawling and lovely and architecturally interesting and there was a lot of storage available in the kitchen," Thomson said. "They put a lot of thought into how they were going to organize the kitchen – what cabinets they were going to order. So I helped them with the unpacking of their move. I wasn't around for the packing – they were coming from another city. They brought me in to help them unpack all of their stuff."

Thomson was at work with her clients to help them to use the space. She had to ask them many questions. "Are they bakers, do they love to cook, what age group are the guests, do they have sleep-over guests, do they need a home office? All of these things I needed to know about in order to plan the storage use for them."

Thomson mentions there are two ends of the scale when it comes to storage space that is so important in organizing your new home. There are some places that do not have enough storage and others that have more than enough. The home she worked with in Oakville had more than enough.

"I've seen in other homes that have had an excess amount of storage space that there's really very little thought that goes into unpacking things. So there'll be baking material all over the kitchen, they'll be food all over the kitchen and in every cupboard. There's no flow. It takes time to find things and then things get cluttered up because people don't know where to put things back and then the next person can't find what they're looking for, and the process goes on."

Thomson found baskets at Canadian Tire that come in three different sizes to use for storage space.

"They were about three inches deep and they come in three sizes and they're actually perfect for deeper shelves," Thomson said. "We could put all the snacks into one and all of the dog treats into another one and canned goods so it becomes this drawer that they could pull out so they have the freedom of using the drawers without having to have custom drawers made on each shelf."

Rose Cerullo is a professional home organizer with Inspiring Spaces.

"That's the key thing about organizing," says Cerullo. "By making organizing a process so you develop a system. That makes it fun. Organizing is constant change. For example just putting 15 minutes a day over a month is hours which is a movement towards your project which makes you feel good. People think it's going to take so long but taking a baby step [you can] have enough energy to do other things. Do a little bit more, do a little more, like creating a memory that organizing is ok." Cerullo encourages her clients to organize things in 10 to 15 minute spurts. This way it becomes a regular practice that is like a journey similar to Sharon Hay's approach that does it through feng shui.

"I've been doing this for four years and when I started, I started helping clients who were pack rats," says Cerullo. "They were collectors and didn't necessarily tune into the energy of how it doesn't feel good having all that stuff in their place. People who are organized, who are busy and are sensitive to how their environment feels there's a common denominator with all of them they want a better system. They have other things that are a priority who ask for your services. 'I'm spending too much time doing this over and over and over again, how can I make it more efficient.'"

Cerullo describes a client of hers that was magazine perfect when it came to her décor but needed help with a dozen work projects she was doing from home. Her file folders were flowing. "I asked her do you use it [documents] regularly, occasionally rarely, or never. Then I asked her to get post-it's in front of the drawers that she never uses. I had her sit at her computer and identify all the broad categories of her project for the next 12 months. And all the broad categories I had her type them in caps – creating an index. Then the sub-categories were determined in small letters."

Cerullo left her client with 15 minutes of homework and organizing an appointment with herself. Going to one of those drawers that she rarely uses and get a banker's box and put the files in the box the order she had them in her drawer. Then they were to be labeled on the outside and relocate it to another area in her room like her furnace room because that is where she has the extra space. The client would e-mail Cerullo and this establishes the habit.

"The key is to schedule time and to follow through with the organizing. Then you feel energy to do something else. You can apply it to any area of your life. In bite-size chunks and feel energetic after you do it – that's the key thing you want to feel good about it."

Cerullo says she is attracting more people who see the value of being organized. They don't feel overwhelmed anymore. If you're looking for someone who could help you organize your dream home or condo, please look up the Professional Organizers in Canada for contact information to find someone right for you.

TTC Time Travel (originally published in the Toronto Star)

In Education, Opinion, Writing (all kinds), cars on **December 25, 2008** at **23:48**

I took the hour commute by TTC to Seneca College on York University's campus to teach. On my way a woman spoke in what sounded like Polish on a cell during the moment of light on the northbound University-Spadina line. I caught all my buses and subways. I even made sure I was the third person off the bus to Dupont Station through the turnstiles and I think this helped me with my luck at getting the subway right away.

The class went well. I teach media writing on Thursdays, but it takes near daily work in-between.

As I was heading home I smoked almost two full cigarettes before getting onto the bus and this is after listening to the Smoker's Helpline to delay at least 10 minutes to have another one. I paced. That's how long I waited. Finally, the 196A Rocket bus came to go to Downsview station. This bus passes by C.W. Jeffreys Collegiate.

I was the second person on the bus and it was packed with kids. I did what I always do – I looked for a seat. I struggled to keep my balance as the bus rounded a corner. As I was heading to the back and the bus moved, I didn't have enough time to grab a bar. I heard gasps before I fully realized what happened. I oh so clumsily fell at the feet of some seated children. I propped myself on my palms to get up and the teacher escorting the children extended her hand. I was uttering apologies to the teacher and the kids as I struggled to get up.

When I was a child, the TTC was 25 cents. I was mean, if I were with my friends I may have laughed to see someone fall. When I fell, no one laughed – not even the kids. This is amazing. How does Toronto find such good people? Even as I moved to the back for a seat, a middle-aged white man gave a fairly young black woman like me his seat saying: "I'm going to get off anyway."

Rosa Parks – you would be proud how things have changed.

As the bus got to York University the crush of people moved, laughed and stepped off. A few new TTC commuters came on. The ride to the subway station was peaceful.

A small eatery inside Downsview run by South Asian women handed me a chicken patty for $1.35 upon my request. As I took the stairs down to the subway to head home I chose to sit at the front of the train. I had a book in my bag and eyed the newspapers lying around. Since I already had the Star waiting at home I looked through the front of the train and felt like a child, excited by the rush of dark and light as the train headed to Dupont Station.

Maybe it's the dirty red seats I love…maybe it's the savings to my bank account. Maybe it's watching the mice at Yonge station…maybe it's having the pleasure to say "hello" to a kind bus driver. Maybe it's the crowded smelly bodies I love…maybe it's the visual circus of people-watching while being driven. Whatever the reason, I'm grateful for the

TTC and public transportation. It sure is better than being in Africa and trying to hitch a ride in a minivan ("taxi") and getting your favourite dress ripped because the taxi was moving with the doors open.

I have no bruises after my fall on the 196A Rocket – and no one laughed – not even the kids. There was even change on the floor and a pen – no one dashed to pick it up. It was still there when I got off the bus.

It was a beautiful and bumpy ride on the TTC.

Hot home Office for Resale

In [Business](), [Home Decor](), [Living](), [Writing (all kinds)]() on **December 26, 2008** at **06:37**

The second floor office had books everywhere floor to ceiling and a little laptop. It was part of a house going on the market for re-sale.

Nada Thomson with Artful Organizers went through the books and boxed the ones that weren't really attractive.

"We staged the bookshelves with about a quarter of the books, rather than it being like a library, it was more of a decorative bookshelf arrangement – more than a functional library," Thomson says.

The lowest shelf had books from side-to-side; the other shelf had some books to the left, then some ornaments. The shelf above had a picture with some books, so they would be loosely stacked. Thomson also removed some book spaces as well, to make it a more comfortable space.

"I don't remember how quickly it sold, but I know they had more than asking," said Thomson.

Thomson had to clean up this office – this is her job and it took a number of sessions to complete. She is Founder and Chief Consultant of Artful Organizers. Among the many tasks she does, she helps people who want to sell their homes organize places like their offices.

"People buy up, they don't want to buy parallel they don't want to buy down," Thomson says.

This is why it's important to help potential buyers imagine living there.

"If you invite people into your home you would have them in the most welcoming fashion," Thomson says. "Because you have special guests coming over, you pack those things away. It's not that much different when you have buyers coming into your home."

If your office is polluted with paper and the bookshelves are crammed full, it's exhausting to be around.

The number one rule for Thomson is zoning. Everything of one kind must be stored together for ease of use. Thomson also needs to know a bit about who she is working with; specifically, are they right-brained or left-brained or somewhere in the middle.

"With right-brained people, I endeavour to keep their zoned categories in highly visible places and with left-brained people; I endeavour to tuck their zoned categories well out of sight," she says. "You see, the 'righties' need to see it for it to 'exist,' so, I will do things like put side-labeled tickle file boxes, only about four inches deep so they can separate categories without taking up copious amounts of space, on bookshelves – taxes; bills; medical; hobby – and the like."

This way, Thomson says there are no drawers to open to fully grasp what you must deal with.

"'Lefties' have the visual filing system in their brains, so it is OK to put their stuff into drawers; they actually prefer things to be completely out of sight.

"Then there are people like me who fall into the middle – I like some things to be visible and some things to be tucked out of sight; any way it is set up, I can find it."

These things will help in figuring out how to organize your home office for re-sale.

Thomson advises that small spaces shouldn't have clunky computers. The office space area should show the computer, the chair, the printer and the basic things you need. You need to be realistic in making the teeny, tiny little room show organization. Sometimes it's just a table that tucks in.

She says black plastic cabinet boxes for organizing are recommended. When planning a move, box as much stuff as possible ahead of time. Try to gain space – pack up and store. For things you need to have on hand it needs to be containerized in an attractive way.

When it comes to larger spaces there is the luxury of more space. You may use a bedroom for an office. People coming in will wonder if it's big enough for a bed. When advertising a place and showing a place, you should show the number of listed bedrooms.

"If there's any question on size, we need to relocate that office to a transition area like a basement if that's a possibility or transition the idea as a guest bedroom/office. Pack up one of the angles on the desk. It's not going to be ideal to live like that, but you would have to live like that."

Most people can use any room as an office. Louise Edwards is a Sales Associate with Re/Max and helps people to move up. She says so many people work from home and questions the advantages in one for resale when it comes to taxes.

"Is it advantageous in resale?" Edwards asks. "When it's time to resale on a home office you must pay taxes on it upon the profits from the income."

She also says many people will still work from home – simply without claiming the income and the space on their taxes. Then it doesn't become an issue for being a hot property.

The future of home building (originally published in New Dreamhomes and Condominiums Magazine)

In Beauty, Business, Environment, Home Decor, Writing (all kinds) on **December 30, 2008** at **01:27**

While driving a rented car on his way to get his two boys their first movie ever, Antonio Gomez-Palacio, the chair of the Toronto Society for Architects, discussed his work and vision for the future of home building in the Greater Toronto Area.

"My experience is much more around urban planning and a broader city-building perspective," said Gomez-Palacio. "I'm immersed in the debate of residential as it pertains to the broad city vision."

His work involves such things as growth management strategies and heritage preservation. One of the projects he is currently working on is looking at Mississauga and how it should grow in the next 100 years.

"I think the more important question to ask is what does the city look like and what should it look like into the future? There are two futures for residential. One based on the trend, the other on the imperative. The trend is a form of residential that is based on sprawl and single land use. That only includes residential, a very uniform type. Single-family detached over vast areas."

Gomez-Palacio said that when you look at the city it is a recent phenomenon – widely established over the last 30 to 20 years.

"We started to see some of the social consequences of developing in this sort of way. Taking Mississauga as an example. A lot of the current growth pattern of residential was presented by the opportunities of the automobile. They are designed for people to drive everywhere. There is a trend that the mast majority gets built under a very similar format. The pendulum is coming back. The number of condos downtown outnumbered the number of single-family detached units."

Gomez-Palacio says this trend started on the west coast that is a complete community. People could meet all the needs of their everyday life within walking distance. The shift is towards relying on walking rather than driving.

"You can start to see it's going to transform the vast majority of neighbourhoods over the next couple of decades," Gomez-Palacio says. "Some small detached houses. Apartment buildings. Everything that happens in a complete city all within walking distance rather than driving distance. There is a huge push over the past decade to get kids to walk to school. There is a huge problem that people don't walk to buy a gallon of milk."

He says the notion of mixed use and mixed type of residential homes is also a critical notion.

"If you have the ability to work from home and if you have a coffee shop your ease of staying home is much easier. I have two little kids and I walk them to daycare everyday no matter the weather. We live in a part of the city that allows us to do that. We can design a city that allows you to do that. What's more important is that we need to design a city in that way. We can no longer afford the type of lifestyle and the type of sprawling cities that consumes such vast amounts of land and depends on cars in that sort of way.

"When you ask people what are their favourite cities in the world, they talk about compact cities. They can't imagine building it for themselves."

This includes residential building that promotes a sustainable and healthy lifestyle. An environment that is more compact is healthier for us and healthier for the environment.

"I think generally the majority of the Greater Toronto area is pretty much built out and there isn't a lot of green-fill left," says Bindya Lad, a master's student of architecture at the University of Toronto. "I see a lot of developers taking sites that can accommodate greater densities that are maybe underdeveloped."

Lad also works for the Toronto Society of Architects. She has a previous background in urban planning and lives in Mississauga.

"So I know some things about development. I'm in my third-year at the university. By the end 2008 I would have graduated. I'm hoping to get onto licensing and acquire more experience and knowledge in the field. What I'm really interested in is multi-family housing."

What Lad is talking about is similar to the kind of "Who's the Boss?" type of living, if you remember the former television program.

"With a lot of immigrants coming in they can't afford any houses and they share the house with their relatives," Lad says. "Then you have elderly families living with their sons and daughters. People who cannot afford a house and they live in many houses. In my point of view it's kind of a better way of living it promotes greater living in single-family homes. It's better utilization of space. Multi-families can form support for one another."

Lad plans to do her master's research on this topic.

The Toronto Society of Architects has 1,000 members. They include historians, environmentalists and anyone who is generally interested in architecture and urban planning.

As the chair of the society, Gomez-Palacio also does work in Halifax, Regina and Moncton. As he was driving his rented car, his sons were looking for a documentary on squirrels. At the ages of 2 and 4, Gomez-Palacio said they do not even know what a documentary is. With a future in home building that is more sustainable as both Lad and Gomez-Palacio suggest, the boys will have the chance to watch real-life squirrels as they are walking from their homes to buy milk when they are older.

Life Long Learning

In [Education](), [Writing (all kinds)]() on **December 30, 2008** at **06:27**

Phil Schalm heads up the Chang Ryerson School

The G. Raymond Chang School of Continuing Education is a name that has been around for about two years. The continuing education program has been around since the early 1980s. It's been around a long time.

Phil Schalm is the Program Director of Community Services for The Chang School and has been with them since 1989. He has worked with other universities many years before he joined Ryerson.

"What is special about how it is structured here is that continuing education is tightly linked with the faculties," says Schalm. "So that in a given year, we have around 40,000 people who come through continuing education and take individual semestered courses. It's a relatively large population. It's by far the largest university delivery system. At least 80 per cent of those are credit courses that can be put towards certificate programs. They can be delivered as degree programs."

Schalm mentions that there are many new initiatives at The Chang School.

"Part of what we're trying to do here is to create an environment where [students] can learn about what the expectations are – to create a portal. To have access to that kind of information on the web or in person and to provide that kind of array of support services for them, ranging from ESL, to prior learning assessment and learning about what are the gaps in previous methods and what do I need to fill and learn here. Hook them up with mentors and give them some workplace experience."

They're in the process of developing a program around integrated developing technology professionals, engineers, IT specialists, technology-based scientists, and the medical sciences.

"I'm very excited," says Schalm.

For example, if someone wants to learn marketing, they can come to the program and get into the certificate program and receive specialized knowledge and later carry the credits into a degree.

"It's designed to give someone a degree in a specific area on a part-time basis," says Schalm.

They're also offering courses over the Internet all over the world. The students are invited into Toronto for a week. In nursing and in non-profit sector studies, there are hybrid courses which are a combination of Internet and face-to-face studies.

"You might come together for two or three days and do the rest of the studies on the Internet," says Schalm. "You would do the rest of the studies on your own. This is making it more accessible."

In terms of making it more financially accessible, about seven or eight years ago, OSAP fully funded the part-time program. Currently, you need to be taking five courses, which is about a full-time course load to be OSAP eligible.

"No part-time student can take a full-time load and still be working," says Schalm. "OSAP has become almost inaccessible. We're really aggressively building a bursary program."

This bursary program is for the part-time students. There is also one for the full-time students. There is $20,000 available in funds. This is non-repayable funding support. It helps with tuition and books.

"So many of the people that I've talked to are having to hold down two or even three full-time jobs, and on top of that needing to get into their professions – and how do you do that? We need to have some funding support to help them focus on getting their professional access."

Ryerson has 1,200 courses where many of them lead to degrees. They are professionally-minded programs. Whether it's magazine publishing, occupational health & public safety, nursing or radio and television arts – they can all lead to degrees or certificates. They profile their students and out of the 40,000 students at Ryerson, over half of them have been in Canada under five years. They already have degrees. They need courses like the Chang School offers, the mentoring and the work placement. Because of low incomes, there is a need for bursaries and The Chang School and Student Council is working on increasing the funds.

Charming the home inside and out (Originally Published in New Dreamhomes and Condominiums Magazine)

In Home Decor, Writing (all kinds) on **March 8, 2009** at **03:51**

Lorissa Leslie, an interior decorating student at George Brown College, believes in charming the home inside by getting back to basics.

"Back to basics, back to nature and calming…serenity and staying away from the chaos from the GTA," says Leslie.

These are her tips for how to create a beautiful home on the inside. She is strengthening the foundation of these tips through study and developed the foundation of these tips from where she grew up.

Leslie came from the east coast because there are not many colleges east of Montreal where she had an opportunity to study interior decorating.

"I thought I would have to do it online in New Brunswick but I had the opportunity to come here so I just came."

Leslie does not know what drew her to interior decorating – to travel across Canada with the aim of studying the art.

"I don't know I just get excited over accessories and sourcing and finding those pieces that match and fit perfectly together."

Leslie works at a furniture store and finds there are certain trends she sees in interior design.

"Grey is really popular right now," Leslie says. "Chocolate brown is still going strong of course, as in chocolate brown leather. We have a white lacquer item that is popular."

The trends follow with Leslie's recommendations of what she feels make for a wonderful sanctuary in any dream home or condominium. She suggests a look that is contemporary but comfortable. Something with clean lines yet casual – sophisticated but still casual makes a strong impression and feels great.

"[These are] part of the principles and elements of design," says Leslie. "Horizontal lines make us think of lying down. They are more calming. Vertical lines are more formal. On a pillow this has an impact. Natural elements and earth tones, different browns, different shades of browns – which wasn't so revered in some years before but still is in the last couple of years."

For the past 35 years Peter Carelli has been a painter. He does have a true talent of making things beautiful. Sitting down with a young man named Cyrus in his neighbourhood he was teaching him how to draw. When it is cold and it's hard for him to get work to make homes beautiful with painting them inside and out. Times are difficult however he sticks with it.

"I like art, like painting."

He has been married for more than 30 years and has three older children. He makes his living painting houses when the weather is good – making them beautiful on the outside.

He does know how to read English well, however he can speak it quite well and is fluent in Italian.

"It depends on when I got the job, if I don't make money, I don't get the job."

He did not go to school for art. "It's a personal talent – born artist."

His favourite paintings are of European villages. "Because it's a little bit more difficult to paint – it's more talent."

He has not ever had a gallery opening and cannot afford to pay a gallery to show his work. So he paints houses and sometimes works at pizza shops to make money.

He lives downtown and owns his own house. His wife takes in sewing.

"If I haven't made nothing 'till now…I'm not going to make nothing. I've lost hope. That's my mind – it makes me believe when I do it – when I don't."

At one of the most hopeful times of her life as a student, Lorissa Leslie does not own her own home however she has been told by people who visit her place that it is "cozy."

"I'm still in a rental so I haven't done everything that I'd like to. I do get compliments though that it's very cozy. I haven't gone crazy with the colours yet. I haven't painted yet. I'm working on improving the patio. There are more natural elements with the sea glass colours in the bathroom. The kind of glass you find in the ocean…I love that. The greens and blues you find in the ocean – the magical little pieces – the sparkling little gems that I get when I'm walking on the beach."

These are just some of the people in the Greater Toronto Area that work to make a living and make a home charming inside and out.

Making Your Move Stress-Free (Originally Published in New Dreamhomes and Condominiums Magazine

In Home Decor, Living, Writing (all kinds) on **March 8, 2009** at **23:55**

Moving all your precious things and making a new home is stressful, yet, people do it all the time. On October 20th, the Guilfoyle family, with their eight-month-old baby, packed up their belongings from a two-bedroom apartment and moved into their three-bedroom detached dream home within 10 kilometres in Toronto.

"We were renting before and we purchased a house, this is the main reason why we moved," says Cheryl Guilfoyle. "We were married for the last couple of years and we had a child and we were looking for a house and one sort of came up and then we moved."

The house is 65 years old and they had to redo all the wiring so the electrical work needed to be done. In the basement they're doing some work on one of the rooms to make it fully finished and have it carpeted. The renovations delayed their moving date, but the Guilfoyle family had a stress-free move.

"It was great, it was seamless," says Guilfoyle. "We did all the packing ourselves, they had four guys that came and from their perspective they looked around and walked through every room first and it took about 10 minutes to assess all that, and they just got to it. From start to finish from the old house to the new [they] started just before 9 a.m. and they were done by 11:15 a.m. or 11:30 a.m."

Guilfoyle says that it was a whirlwind for a couple of weeks looking back; they had to push their moving date back by a couple of weeks and had grandparents coming in to help with the baby.

Guilfoyle has some advice on how to make your move as easy as hers.

"Start early on the packing and always allow that extra buffer time [because] unknowns and the unforeseen can pop up. We took possession in the middle of September and we moved in about five weeks later so allow for that extra buffer zone."

The company the Guilfoyle family went with for their move was Consolidated Movers.

Jackie Cowan who is the owner of Consolidated and The Box Spot has more suggestions on how to make your move stress-free.

"Start packing as soon as possible," says Cowan. "Book your move well in advance. Basically go through the house and purge. You don't want to be packing things you don't need for your new house. You can have a garage sale and make a few dollars there. You can go out and have a nice dinner once the move is done when you're about ready to collapse. Try to pack a little earlier than last minute so to speak. Choose a good mover. Most people they'll check references, they'll have referrals from friends, there's good and bad in every industry. A lot of our work is referral, it's repetitive. We've done three generations of some families."

Melanie Bradley who works in sales for The Box Spot says, "a lot of people will come in and they have their questions normally. We'll try to suit them up the best possible, get them a good start with the standard boxes and some paper. Some bubble wrap for their fragile items. Usually it depends on the person. The person will give us an idea and we try to suit it to the best of their needs the best we can."

Bradley and Cowan have both seen when it comes to the end of the month and people haven't started packing yet, they see a lot of stressed out people coming into their store. They have rental boxes, dollies, furniture pads and "everything and anything" needed for renovating and shipping. Some people even come into their store to ship Christmas gifts.

"There's a guy that we've been moving on and off for 10, 15 years," says Bradley. "He constantly comes in here to get his materials to move him, his office moving, his girlfriend's moving in, everything like that. You get those kinds of people who have been with us for a long time."

"Our estimates are firm and that's makes people happy," says Cowan. "We don't take deposits, we trust the people who are booking. Most people who have moved with us are going to come back. I'm very happy when they've had a bad experience because they come to us."

Although Consolidated has had many happy customers like the Guilfoyle family, they have heard of horror stories which make business better for them.

"There was one lady who called maybe three months ago and she was waiting for her movers and the other people turned up with their furniture ready to move in," says Consolidated owner Jackie Cowan. "They took some of her stuff out and put it in the driveway and it was starting to rain. The woman was crying on the phone, and it was so sad and we didn't know what to do [because] we have six crews and we don't overbook."

Melanie Bradley says a big reason why people get into trouble with movers is because people will get numbers off a telephone pole or in a grocery store.

"You feel bad because they're in a dire situation and people are right there ready to move in and they're not ready to move out."

"You want to make sure with a mover that you ask a lot of questions and they have an address so that if you run into trouble, there's someone you can go and talk to," says Cowan. "That's the problem if you go with a number off a [pole], because a lot of times it's just a cell phone number and something like that is questionable. Are you going to trust you're possessions with someone like that, that's not probably even insured, just because it's a cheaper hourly rate? And most of them it's cash, there's no receipt, you're not able to deduct your expenses because they have home offices or something. If you don't have a receipt and your television is damaged, who are you going to come after?"

Cowan and Bradley both note that there are a lot of movers now that are hiring people to do telephone calls. Boris is always on the phone from Best Price Movers. There was one person they know that took him 10 hours to move a one-bedroom apartment because all he had was a little truck to do it.

"They get you one way or the other," says Bradley.

Consolidated Movers offers $70,000 worth of insurance to protect your belongings. There's a discount on The Box Spot when you go with their movers. Every Thursday there's free delivery of packing supplies.

Cheryl and her husband Andrew Guilfoyle, with their baby, have been living in their new house for only a short time. They have lots of boxes around mainly because the basement still has to be finished.

"Every day we try to unpack a box and get things back on the walls," says Cheryl Guilfoyle. But she says that it already feels like home.

Everything has a place (Originally Published in New Dreamhomes and Condominiums Magazine)

In Home Decor, Writing (all kinds) on **March 9, 2009** at **13:16**

Rose Cerullo, Professional Home Organizer with Inspiring Spaces That's the key thing about organizing. By making organizing a process so you develop a system. That makes it fun. Organizing is constant change. For example just putting 15 minutes a day over a month is hours which is a movement towards your project which makes you feel good. People think it's going to take so long but taking a baby step and having enough energy to do other things. Do a little bit more, do a little more, like creating a memory that organizing is OK.

It's likely you'll devote the 10 minutes and stop cause you know it's a process it's not an end.

Sometimes they don't know how to get the ball going. They don't know where to begin. So that requires someone else helping them whether it's a professional, friend, colleague. But that's a learning thing.

I've been doing this four years and when I started I started helping clients who were pack rats were collectors and didn't necessarily tune into the energy of how it doesn't feel good of having all that stuff in their place. People who are organized who are busy and are sensitive to how their environment feels there's a common demoniator with all of them they want a better system they have other things that are a priority who ask for your services. I'm spending too much time doing this over and over and over again, how can I make it more efficient.

I had a client that was magazine perfect, the décor, everything has a place and she walked into the office and I asked her how can I help you. She has about a dozen new projects and thefile folders are filed in her drawers and she doesn't have enough space.

I asked her do you use it regularly , occasionally rarely, or never. Then I asked her to get post its in front of the drawers that she never uses. I had her sit at her computer and identify all the broad categories for her project for the next 12 months. And all the broad categories I had her type them in caps. Creating an index. Then the sub-categories were determined in small letters.

I left her with a 15 minute homework and organizing an appointment with herself. Going to one of those drawers that she rarely uses and get a banker's box and put the files in a banker's box in the order she had them in her drawer. Then lable on the outside and relocate it to another area in her room like her furnace room because that's where she has the extra space. Tehn she would e-mail Rose and this establishes the habit. The key is to schedule time with herself and to follow through with the organizing. Then you feel energy to do something else.

You can apply it to any area of your life. In bite size chunks and feel energetic after you do it – that's the key thing you want to feel good about it.

I'm attracting more people who see the value of being organized. They don't feel overwhelmed anymore. Sharon Hay – 647-222-8151 e-mail: info@fengshuihay.ca Feng Shui way by Hay – The less clutter the energy flow is going to be a lot better in the home and condo and that's not an event it's a lifestyle. The more you declutter the more comes in and opportunities and other things fall into place. There are the nine stations of life so different elements will enhance different elements of your life. Each element has a colour and a shape. I get their year of birth which gives me which directions are best for success and fullness rest. I find out how many bedrooms, how long they've been living there how old the building is. What's been going on in their life, if they just got married if they just changed careers. We got forward to remove any blockages and enhance with the elements.

Usually there's not much landscaping outside and because we're only four seasons there's only certain things to enhance that. Even artificial trees, pictures, plants help to – missing the negative environmental influences. Even with a condo, they would need more pictures of flowers and vibrant colours of plants and trees.

For stability, interlocking brick is nice, you can have so many trees that you can't find the house. It's about balance. Too much red is too stimulating, too much fire energy. If someone has a lot of kids they have to keep it fairly grounded. Oranges, beiges, taupes, yellows and things in square patterns. You can have square pillows on the couch – a lot more a feeling of security.

They have to try and keep the toys under control and if things are out in the hallway and picking the rubber ducky off your kitchen counter

– things become chaotic, hard to think, hard to focus, the relationship gets stressed.

Muted colours in rooms with kids – in a room where they're going to spending a lot of time – pastels are better. Too many hard lines and also have the vibrant colours the parents would be feeling I would just like to get in and get out. The clouds and softer shaped things and especially the ones that are new to feel more relaxed.

Nada Thomson with Artful Organizers is a professional organizer for home and office.

Family Fit and Your Home (Originally Published in New Dreamhomes and Condominiums Magazine)

In Home Decor, Living, Writing (all kinds) on **March 10, 2009** at **03:39**

An expanding family is a one of the many great reasons to look for a bigger home. Andrea Grace and her husband Ted have a 13-year-old girl and a 10-year-old boy and changed from being renters to homeowners.

"We started off renting an apartment," says Andrea Grace. "We had our daughter while we were living in that apartment. I had to have a backyard for our daughter as she was becoming mobile."

After the Grace family moved out of their apartment they started renting a house. They needed the extra space and it was also becoming difficult moving basic things like groceries into the apartment while having a young one at your feet.

Now Andrea, Ted and the Grace children have gone from renting a home to owning one in Richmond Hill.

"We bought a re-sale home, at the time we were renting our house we couldn't afford a new home," says Andrea Grace. "We bought an older home and did a lot renovations."

They gutted the house because it was in bad shape. The original house had wallpaper and they had to rip down a wall as well as the carpet.

"We didn't have to do anything to the basement. Every single room needed attention," says Andrea.

The renovations cost the Grace family about $20,000 right off the bat and they are still ongoing.

Andrea is happy that her family has moved into the new home. Her husband Ted was always against buying a house.

"Now we own this home and it's great. It's such a great feeling to do whatever we want to do to this house. In a few years I'd like to move to a bigger and newer home."

When Andrea is not taking care of her boy and girl or renovating her new home she is the owner of Mommy and Baby Fitness.com. The company does post-natal fitness, mom and baby yoga, aqua classes, and workouts.

They use colourful parachutes and bubbles to increase brain and motor skill stimulation in babies.

"It's a good way to meet other moms. The babies learn early social skills and songs and rhymes. It's better health for babies," says Andrea.

Christopher Dolson works for Aluma Systems in sales that does forming and shoring in the concrete industry. He has two girls, five and two with his wife Michele and also bought a bigger home because of an expanding family.

He bought his new home about three years ago. The Dolson family wanted something a little bigger when their second child was coming.

"We were having our second kid," says Dolson. "It's a two-storey and it's called a link home."

The family paid around $300,000 for their three-bedroom home in Markham.

"When we were looking we gave a price range that we were interested in and our agent kept showing us houses that were at the top end of what we looking in," says Dolson. "We realize that with these bigger homes you still have to sink money into them. We'd have to do things like carpets and things like that. We kind of had to sit down with our agent and find something at the lower end of the price range and sink more money in. Once we started looking for homes like that…once they came down in scale like that. It was our second home that we looked at and that's the one we went with."

Chris Dolson and his family now have a little bit more room than the townhouse they were living in before. The new home has a two-car garage and bigger backyard.

"We're on a cul-de-sac so it's a quiet street."

Everyone needs their space including children. With the boom in the housing market and many new homes available all over the GTA there are many options available for families who are looking for a home with the right fit for their needs.

Choosing the Colours Right for You (Originally Published in New Dreamhomes and Condominiums Magazine)

In Home Decor, Writing (all kinds) on **March 12, 2009** at **00:38**

Many people have their favourite colours, just like they have their favourite lottery numbers. The number 1 is associated with the colour red. The number 3 is associated with the number yellow and the number 8 is associated with the colour rose pink. These theories come from an ancient science that you may or may not believe in known as numerology. Some of these methods can help you personalize your living space and when in doubt, you can always go to a colour consultant.

Tara Ford, owner and colour consultant for West Toronto Paint gets to know her clients well to help them choose the colours that are right for them. She also takes a close look at the design of the home and the structure of the home in determining just the right colour scheme for her clients.

"The first thing is that you have to look at the major pieces in the home…what has to stay," says Ford. "Your colour has to match with your flooring. You look at the major pieces, you look at the fridge and the floor and the back splashes and all the major pieces that go with that."

Some of Ford's tips for how you can brighten your home with colour include the lighting of your home.

"The next thing that would come into play would be lighting," Ford says. "The best time to look at your room is during the day. If you are often in that room during the day, then you would turn the lights on. If you have a lot of light coming in you can go with a darker colour. If you do not have a lot of light coming in I would not recommend going too dark."

Ford has some of her personal favourite design options that she likes to recommend to her clients.

"It's always good to work with contrast," says Ford. "If you have a lot of dark furniture, dark things in the room, say if it is all in a black tone…it may look really sharp to go with something lighter like a muslin – the lightest you would go would be if you have a lot of black. Raspberry truffles is really nice, if you have some black and white artwork."

Having a feature wall or something that can really grab the eye of your guests and loved ones that come to visit can really make a difference in how you use colour in a home.

"A lot of times people want to do a feature wall," says Ford. "Either that wall has really amazing architecture, a beautiful hutch or your bed is on that wall. Your eyes are automatically going to go there so you have to have something really beautiful there because your eyes are automatically going to go there. So you can do a nice red touch or a lighter tone."

Ford also says that a lot of people are using colour on their ceilings.

"Another option too is if you have really high ceilings and your paintings are flat, people are painting their ceilings now and it adds interest. If it is dark, it brings the ceilings down. You do a colour on the ceiling and it is for interest sake…then you want to have a really fabulous chandelier."

Colour trends are moving away from taupe that has been extremely popular for years now.

"Gray is turning into the new taupe, even in décor," says Ford. "We have a lot of mirrored pieces in our décor, I have been doing a lot of colour consults and gray is the new taupe and it is really popular right now.

"Taupe has been around for so long, even if you look into fashion, fashion translates into home décor. When I go into a consultation I ask people what they like to wear, what they like in colour. It is a new era into fashion design and it is all translating into home design too. There is a lot of art deco, a lot of modern design. You will see a really beautiful old style chair that has been painted creme and reupholstered in a funky fabric."

Whether you look further into the fascinating science of numerology, or hire a colour consultant, consider adding more vibrancy to your home.

Pets and Homes (Originally Published in New Dreamhomes and Condominiums Magazine)

In [Home Decor](), [Living](), [Pets](), [Writing (all kinds)]() on **March 13, 2009** at **00:03**

Your beloved pet could be what motivates you to buy a home, or what could be causing you problems. Imran Javaid, a realtor with HomeLife Miracle shares his stories of dealing with clients who have had pets.

"Recently I was working with a client, not into buying, but helping them to lease the property and they had a very lovely dog," says Javaid. "The way this couple's daughter would talk about him or her in their absence, it told me how much they were attached to their pet. Getting a property to lease with a pet was very difficult, they actually started looking to buy. Giving up their pet was a decision they did not want to take."

Javaid has been in real estate for more than two years. His approach to real estate is that it is a long term relationship and unless he is very honest with his customers and his clients – his business would not take him anywhere. He strives to be very honest to answer customers' and clients' questions. He says he tries his best to make one of the most important decisions of his clients' lives very easy.

"During our showings, say if I am working with a buyer, we do get the messages of do not let the cat out or do not let the dog out. In a busy schedule of six or seven appointments I can look at the lock box number of the pager and every realtor should really look at the number of the pager and let the realtor know there is a cat and dog in there. And every realtor should know to not scare the pets."

Javaid tells a story about a daughter of one of his clients who is about four, and she said "look there are turtles there" when the family went to visit a house. She just stood there while she was on the main floor.

"When I was going upstairs, she did not want to go upstairs because she was so involved with them," Javaid says. "If the daughter of the client was so involved with their pets – imagine how the owners of the home was."

Javaid says he thinks landowners out there should not say "no" to pets. It could be a tiny little well-kept dog. He gets lots of e-mails and calls from people begging him to find a place where they can just have their pet.

"When you are negotiating, that pet can be part of that," says Javaid. "Many of those pets, do not really harm the properties. They do have restrictions on some condominiums when it comes to pets."

For a person Javaid helped to buy a house in Haliburton just recently, she lives in Bracebridge right now and they were living in a basement and when Javaid met her first time, it was a referral through his cousin. She is in her late 40s and she wanted her own place and her boyfriend was moving with her as well and they just wanted a very nice home for themselves. Affordable, they wanted to stay under $200,000. They have a pet. She is doing two different jobs with automotive and also nursing home care. The man works with a resort. Their mortgage was rejected and she was very disappointed, but Javaid helped her find one in Toronto.

She has a big backyard and they actually have a long leash around the backyard – it is like a long island rope and then there is a leash hanging down. The dog can still go 300, 200 feet there. When they saw it in their backyard they were very happy their dog could be walking around. There is a deer park around there. They are moving in soon.

There are many realtors like Javaid who help their clients with pets make their experiences with finding a home much easier. Make sure that if you are looking for a home, starting with looking for a realtor, you make sure that are pet-friendly if this is something that is important to you.

Move that air around (Originally Published in New Dreamhomes and Condominiums Magazine)

In <u>Home Decor</u>, <u>Writing (all kinds)</u> on **March 13, 2009** at **11:10**

Air quality in a home is important for feeling comfortable. If you cannot breathe – the multiple thousands, if not millions you have spent on your dream home or condominium will seem like a huge waste of money. No one would want that and many people would not wish that on their worst enemies.

The solution – fans.

Fans have been around for thousands of years. Not only have been useful through the ages for moving air around, they are also seen as a status symbol.

Michael Gladstone the general manager of Royal Lighting says that the usefulness of fans in your dream home or condominium is something you may not talk about or even think about – yet it does have meaning.

"One place where fans are great are rooms that do not have enough air circulation," says Gladstone. "A lot of older people, 50 plus, are buying fans to help them sleep in the summer and the winter. The cooler air helps them calm down and sleep more. Even with air conditioners this works too – summer and winter."

Royal Lighting has a huge selection and a wide variety of floor and ceiling fans that can make living in your home more comfortable. So does Wilcorp Ceiling Fans.

"We have different colours, different sizes for types of ceilings," says John Maraj, the sales manager at Wilcorp. "There are fans that when you put them up they really, really work very efficient. You can get any colour you want to suit your décor."

Maraj says people send him pictures and they make great mention about the look of the fan and how gorgeous it is. Wilcorp sends out questionnaires to former clients to see if they are enjoying their purchase. Maraj says that some people say they have had their fan for 30 years and it is still working like day one.

Maraj gives other reasons to Gladstone why people buy fans.

"Circulation of course, to bring the hot air down. In the summertime, when you have your air conditioning on the cool air falls and your feet are all frozen. The cool air from the fan lifts the air up so your feet are not frozen."

At Wilcorp, there are different fans for different room sizes.

"You have fans that are noiseless. Fans that are wobble-free and the motors are lifetime. Most of the fans now that are manufacturing are star-rating, meaning very, very less hydro to operate the fan. You can leave the fan 24 hours a day and all you spend is a penny and you save dollars while they are working."

At Wilcorps, the fans start from $69.00 and go up to the thousands. It all depends on the material and the size of the motor.

"All ceiling fans have bearings," says Maraj. "But some bearings are better than others. All bearings have grease. Like lithium grease, is better. They need different capacitors that really make the fan so quiet. You cannot see the space in the router. The components create the magnetic field. The height of ceiling gives you different lengths of rods to go with the ceilings. [A cheaper] $69.00 fan would give you the little air movement."

Wilcorps has been around since 1965. They used to manufacture the fans themselves.

"We service throughout Canada," says Maraj. "Barbados – Sandy Lane Hotel and most of the fans in the Bahamas. Definitely homes as well. We do a lot of circulation of fans. We have thousands, and thousands of satisfied customers."

Michael Gladstone at Royal Lighting would agree that he too has thousands of satisfied customers. Adding a floor or ceiling fan to your dream home or condominium not only improves the décor – it moves the air around too.

Artwork for the Walls

In [Home Decor](), [Writing (all kinds)]() on **March 13, 2009** at **12:08**

The Stuart Jackson Gallery opened in the mid-1970s and is nestled under a hair studio called Fiorio in Yorkville. Carol Dorman has been working along Stuart Jackson for 11 years in January of 2009.

"What we carry is unique and it is special in that way," says Dorman. "There is no other gallery in Canada that we know of that exclusively specializes in Japanese prints."

People ask Dorman what her favourite print is and it is really hard for her to say. Due to the fact that they are all antique they are in their different conditions. There is one that was done in the mid-1800s and that stands out for the beauty of the condition and was done in 1859. It is a head and shoulder shot of a woman holding some beans, like soya beans.

"She is leaning on a counter and holding some beans," says Dorman. "I got interested because I was student of anthropology and I'm interested in the ones that show me about life at the time."

The prints that we carry are from the 18th and 19th century. When Dorman sees prints that show her something really interesting about the period, she likes those prints too.

Dorman likes working at the gallery because it gives a chance for her to tell people about the artwork.

"This is not the type of artwork that is usually taught in art classes," Dorman says. "A lot of people do come in and really like it."

A lot of dealers that would sell this type of art would do it privately, however having a gallery gives people a chance to come in without any pressure to buy.

In terms of décor and fitting this type of artwork into your home, some of them are quite suitable to a Japanese design in furniture at your home. Many of the prints include landscapes and nature scenes that can work in any type of décor. For the antiques…there are things that are under $100 and one thing over a $100,000, however there is quite a range in prices.

"There is a lot of nice stuff that is really affordable for the average art collector," Dorman says.

Dorman started as a collector when she was in university and bought her first print. She was a student at the University of Toronto when she bought it. Dorman bought her first print from the Stuart Jackson Gallery, however they did not become friends until the 1990s.

She was buying prints for seven years before she even knew Jackson and started working there in 1998. Jackson and his wife were running the shop before Dorman came. Jackson took out a license as a dealer in 1972. The intent was prior to that and using his own name for the gallery happened in 1975. His wife passed away in the 1990 and he ran the gallery on his own for many years.

"My wife and I were interested in getting into the arts and thought about it and it evolved into exclusively Japanese prints," Jackson says. "It was kind of a hobby that went berserk."

The concept of the Stuart Jackson Gallery began when he was in university and bought his first print. He got jobs in various museums and that slowed down the development of opening the gallery.

Jackson says a lot of people do not hang the prints, they just buy them to have them.

"We get two very distinct type of customers," says Dorman and Jackson. "We have the home decorators that hang them on their walls, and the serious collectors. The concept of possession…" as Jackson closes off.

Dorman says she collects many of them of things she likes. Jackson's collection was almost exclusively landscapes and sold off some of them. As it has been rebuilt it has become more eclectic for Jackson.

"Either really nice or really rare," says Dorman.

Dorman says she likes some that are old and they are antiques and they are in really good condition.

"The one I was talking about looks as though it could have been yesterday," Dorman says.

Jackson is interested in the beauty and the interplay of line and colour. Dorman loves the beauty of the art and showing the life of 18th and 19th century Japan and what she learns about the people. Jackson is interested in the poety and Dorman is interested in the story.

To find out what might interest you about the Japanese prints at Stuart Jackson Gallery, you can visit them 108A Cumberland St., lower level in Yorkville. They are also on the web at: www.jacksonarts.com.

Beautiful Bedrooms

In Home Decor, Writing (all kinds) on **March 14, 2009** at **00:21**

It is where we start our day and where we end our day – the bedroom. Making your bedroom a beautiful place to be in, something more like a haven, a refuge or a sanctuary may be pivotal to getting good sleep and enjoying special moments in that room too.

Diane Fotheringham with Titus & Louise located at 677 Dupont St. specializes in creating beautiful bedrooms for her clients. After retiring from her former work training people on computers with an airline, she started sewing. Designers in the city liked the work she did, so she opened up a store at Christie and Dupont. The store has been there for about 15 years.

"First of all I think people should keep in mind how much time they spend in the bedroom and they should consider what they really, really love," says Fotheringham. "They should think of the experience as an inexpensive way of having some wonderful luxury. They should be thinking of the experience of sleep, and the luxury of the experience of sleep and the time before and the time after and the practicality of it all."

Fortheringham says your bedroom should be, "a haven or a refuge, because today I think it's becoming less and less an experience of that, it's becoming less of a haven."

Titus & Louise carry many products to help change all that. Your bedroom can be the haven, the refuge or the sanctuary you want it to be. Giving you the chance to sleep soundly and enjoy your time there.

"Well bedroom-wise we carry about 15 different companies and the lines of the different companies," Fortheringham says. "We select what we think is best, but we still select what we think is best. In a large capacity the products are coming from Europe, Israel and China. The quality has gone way, way up in China and the pricing is low so it makes it more affordable for clients. In the past five years there has been a huge escalation in quality and design. And the price has remained quite low. The European fabric that is assembled in Canada has high quality and they have more fabulous colours and are more innovative."

Titus & Louis has duvets, silk duvets and bamboo sheets. They have bamboo blankets and silk blankets.

"In addition to all of that, we also make and we can custom design bedding," says Fortheringham. "We also manufacture and make what people need custom-wise, such as if people need decorative cushions. We do coverlets as well. We also do window treatments. We can coordinate the window treatments to go with the bed linen, we also do blinds. I also do the service of going out to people's houses and telling them how to do the entire thing – floors and carpets too. I can do the whole thing. I have a consultation service – what they should go with, what they should get rid of, if they want to keep certain things."

The initial consultation service has a charge where options on how to work are decided. Fortheringham then can come in for subsequent meetings to create a bedroom you would really love.

"Other people like being part of process," says Fortheringham. "Other people are curtain challenged. We probably have one of the largest and eclectic variety of collections. Sometimes we do not have a large showroom, we work from hangers and bedding. They come one place and see lots of stuff. If people need to do a whole change in their bedroom, we also design headboards for the bedroom. Bed linen is a huge thing here. I think it's really, really important that people think of what will bring them happiness and it's really little way to make life lovely."

Creating beautiful green (Originally Published in New Dreamhomes and Condominiums Magazine)

In Environment, Home Decor, Writing (all kinds) on **March 16, 2009** at **00:22**

Helen Mills, vice-president of Green Gardeners, says that when you are inside at night and you hear a rustling outside, you may think it is the leaves in the wind. It is not the leaves, actually it is an earthworm and they are helping to decompose the leaves to help create the garden of your dreams.

"The ideal thing for leaves would be to let them decompose if you have a lawn," Mills says. "This turns them into a beautiful mulch that is good for the lawn. You know your garden is trying to get there. If you copy nature as much as possible then you would have a much easier garden to get there."

Mills helps homeowners create their gardens. Many times she will go into a home and see what is going on with their garden space. She believes in following nature and got this idea from the Natural Garden Book.

She advises that homeowners do nothing with their gardens during the first year they live there. That way they can discover where is the shade to sit in for warmer weather. They can also find out where the sun beams for cooler weather.

"I work with the client to find out what are their needs, their dreams their lifestyle," says Mills. "Then you work with the space, so if there is a place with water, then use that place for water."

Mills also recommends the use of plants in a garden that are native to the area.

"In Toronto there are some native plants that are almost extinct like the Oak Savannah ecosystem and it is in High Park and the Beaches. If you live in those areas you can grow a beautiful native garden."

She says you can preserve biodiversity not just by growing native plants, but heritage plants too. You can save yourself some food miles as well. Even a little container saves in culture crops. There is more information on growing from seeds at Seeds.ca. Green Gardeners shares information about what they do with their clients.

"We do a lot of education as well," says Mills. "We also go in for a quick visit and work up a little action plan. We do a lot of work. We actually put the garden together as well. We grew out of a north Toronto visit. It was a real barrier that some people did not have a lot of help and we started Green Gardeners out of that need."

A big recommendation Mills has for homeowners who want to start or improve their garden is to use mulch.

"It's a great way to control weeds. Smothering the lawn with newspaper and then covering it with mulch saves tons of water and backbreaking work. The mulch breaks down and goes into the soil. This helps to replenish the nutrients in the soil."

Claire Suo-Cockerton, director of Aesthetic Earthworks agrees with using mulch to start or improve your garden too. As an organic garden care company, Suo-Cockerton says they try to produce sustainable products.

"We recommend using ground cover and natural stone covers with sustainable cover techniques. Mulching with shredded pine is an excellent way of protecting the microorganisms in the soil. It deters weeds and pests. A great garden starts with good soil amendment. Not contaminated or chemicals or foreign substances. Bringing in rich soil. We would recommend, getting rid of your grass. It is one of the hardest aspects of landscape to maintain and tends to need mowing, fertilizing and weeding. It is the cause of so many herbicides and pesticides that run into our lake."

Suo-Cockerton also recommends using local providers that preferably grow organically. There are many native plant sources available at all sorts of major nurseries.

"You need to consider how it will look like in the winter time, the summer and the fall. It is good to have your vertical growing and wispy shapes in grasses. I think a good garden reflects the spirit of the house and the functionality of the space. Under planting should be complimentary and not compete and be able to survive among the magnificent root systems of these trees."

Aesthetic EarthWorks began as a one-woman show. They are about 16 people now. They do landscaping and stonemasons and organic garden care.

"We maintain gardens people build," says Suo-Cockerton. "We do above-ground gardening for urns and plant urns and this is important in urban environments where people do not have access to soil. We have an exhibit at Canada Blooms, 'Literally Green' an example of a balcony gardening."

Aesthetic EarthWorks will also be at the Green Living Show, Fall Home Show and The Sustainable Building Show. Suo-Cockerton also says they are an affordable company.

"We work with a variety of budgets and we're not a 50-grand plus type of budget. We welcome all sorts of budgetary challenges. We do not limit to a specific income bracket."

Cultural home design (Originally Published in New Dreamhomes and Condominiums Magazine)

In [Culture](), [Home Decor](), [Writing (all kinds)]() on **March 17, 2009** at **11:47**

Many people enjoy accenting their décor with accessories and furniture pieces that reflect their cultural heritage. An Inusktut from Aboriginal culture, a painting of a Spanish village or a bonsai plant from Japanese culture can be reflected in a home by people of that culture and also by people not directly from that culture.

Susan Fowlie is the founder and owner of Hollace Cluny. Her company specializes in ethnic home design.

"Cultural home design, for me, refers to the skillful introduction of ethnic art and artifacts into a contemporary setting," says Fowlie. "The textures and earthiness are a perfect complement to what can otherwise be a very stark environment, yet one must be careful that the end result is neither contrived nor overdone. When you look at the work of designers such as Kelly Hoppen, Vicente Wolf or Clodagh you realize how the proper balance of modern and ethnic can bring soul to a space."

Kelly Hoppen is recognized around the world for her inspiring contributions to cultural home design. She is a British designer who recently won a Euro award for women. Some of her books on design include Table Chic, In Touch, Close Up, East Meets West and Kelly Hoppen Home was published in 2007.

Vincente Wolf has 30 years of experience in cultural home design and he has designed such places as hotels on Rodeo Drive, stores in Hong Kong and stores in Chicago and New York.

Clodagh is based in New York and originates from Ireland. At the age of 17 she left high school and dropped her last name. She is inspired by the countryside of Ireland in her designs.

With Hollace Cluny here in Toronto and in business for 11 years, Susan Fowlie says she gives warmth to décor with ethnic touches.

"The juxtaposition of the rough-hewn stool carved from one piece of wood placed beside the pristine sofa demonstrates the inherent beauty of imperfection or as we sometimes term it, wabi sabi," Fowlie says. "By combining these different elements and cultures you give a space interest and life. Diversity creates the magic. I am not talking about displaying souvenirs but rather tastefully selected items that stir the soul and make the environment yours.

"During our eleven years in business we at Hollace Cluny have tried to demonstrate in a very understated way, how to integrate the two - contemporary and ethnic. I always describe what we do as "soft contemporary" -design without the hard edges. We accomplish that with texture and form and a combination of materials that bring a softness to what could otherwise be a very sterile setting. Our clients have come to count on us for just the right accent and we are constantly searching for appropriate and meaningful accessories."

Each piece at Hollace Cluny has a history.

"I think it is important for the client to know the story behind the piece and we do our best to provide as much history and information as possible."

Fowlie and her store Hollace Cluny are often seen in the home decorating media business as the "go to" spokesperson when it comes to questions about cultural home design. She is a much sought after guest on various design programs.

"We have received very favorable press and stylists use our product in photo shoots constantly," says Fowlie. "We were particularly proud to be included in the Wallpaper City Guide to Toronto."

There are many other local Toronto designers that specialize in cultural home design for every ethnic group you can think of. One of them that now sells online is the Ashanti Room at: www.ashantiroom.com. They focus on African-Canadian art and design and carry many things such as books you would need for home too.

Sometimes even visiting places like the Chinese Cultural Centre can give you ideas of how to infuse your environment with ethnic touches. Just remember, it is more than about souvenirs.

Disability and Homes (Originally Published in New Dreamhomes and Condominiums Magazine)

In Disability, Health, Home Decor, Living, Writing (all kinds) on **March 18, 2009** at **00:01**

Open House signs for dream homes and condos are all over the city for most people who can get to them. What about if you cannot get to them? What happens when you are looking for a dream home and your sight, your hearing, your chair, your cane...prevents you from climbing those stairs or even reaching the newly renovated cabinets?

Don Barrie, an Independent Living Consumer knows this experience well. Currently he rents and when he first moved into his downtown apartment, the entire bathroom had to be remodeled for Barrie and his chair.

"Where I live is a rented apartment," says Barrie. "I remember six months after moving in, the whole bathroom needed to be refurbished because it was not accessible. There was a tub and people had to be very careful about transferring me from my chair to the shower stall. I moved out of the tub to the shower stall from the left side of walking in there and the sink was moved to the centre of the room. It required me to leave the unit for a couple of days."

Barrie has experience with how important it is for people with disabilities to live independently. Living in a comfortable and accessible home can really make a difference.

Five years ago, Barrie would help people with disabilities find homes and condos that were accessible by working with the Centre for Indepdent Living in Toronto (CILT).

"Sometimes we would get accessbile houses and condos up for sale," Barrie says. "They would not come up very often. When they did appear, what I would do is help publicize them on the web and the 24-hour phone line called the "News Line. It was very rare though."

So what makes a home accessible?

"If it was a bungalow, or with another level there would be an elevator installed. Even if it was a basement. Many years ago I had a friend who lived in Scarborough and there was an elevator to take him to the basement when it was installed upstairs."

Focusing on the fact that accessible dream homes and condos were rare to find in Barrie's position with CILT, he thinks there needs to be more of them out there.

"The ones that do exist they do not get publized that much and most people do not know about them. Five years ago when I worked at CILT I knew about them. I know about somebody that had a condo and it was newly built when it was purchased and there were a lot of things that he could access himself like furnishings. Might still need someone to come and assist you though, does not mean you can do everything by yourself, but it makes it easier."

Barrie also notes that finding an accessible dream home or dream condo is not just about the home itself. There are other factors that make the dream come alive.

"Right now you want to be able to find a place where you are integrated in the community, that goes without saying. Where I live for example, the friend I talked about earlier, he lives with his family with the elevator."

Don feels a part of the community he lives in and he lives downtown.

With the majority of people with a disability requiring affordable housing and the cost of home ownership in Toronto is high, many issues need to be faced to ensure that this group of Canadians can have their dreams come true through owning a home. Without stable incomes and sometimes having to rely on government support – this makes home ownership a distant goal. Barrie knows people who have done it…like many dreams – they can be possible.

Safety and Your Home (Originally Published in New Dreamhomes and Condominiums Magazine)

In Home Decor, Living, Writing (all kinds) on **March 19, 2009** at **01:52**

Now you have bought that new dream home or new condominium. You may not know your neighbours and the neighbourhood well yet. You need to make sure that for all the time you will live there – you will be safe.

This is where security comes in. Who does not want to feel safe in their home?

Robert Saxe works with Intelligent Building Concepts. He has been in the business of helping homeowners feel safe in their homes since 1993.

"I was initially installing security systems for condominiums," Saxe says. "In about 1998 I saw a need for security reports and audits for how to improve the security systems found throughout the GTA."

Saxe works with the board of directors and the managers throughout the condominiums to see how to improve security. He does a lot of work with a number of developers as well. Some of the more notable ones are Brookfield, Del, Monarch and Context.

"The most important thing is the resident's awareness of not just the security features and how to be more secure in the building," says Saxe. "Whatever we do to secure the building is only as good as their behaviour in the building."

Saxe gives many tips on security. The first tip is do not hold the door open for a stranger.

"If someone wants to visit your daughter in the back bedroom and they came to your door and you didn't know them – you wouldn't let them in," Saxe states. "So don't hold the door open in a condominium to a stranger. We want the resident to be more security conscious. Often simply by going through the process of upgrading and looking and spending money on the security – this improves that."

Saxe says that once he has worked out a plan for security with a property owner for a condominium, he jumps into action.

"We may end up improving the camera system or the card access system or the lighting and all these reflect on the aspect of the building. So that both residents and their guests realize they are in a building where security is a feature and they modify their inappropriate behaviour and a crook looking to break into a building may go elsewhere."

At the request of the management and the board of directors Saxe provides them with a report that indicates the security features around the building. Even the signs saying that there is a camera are as important as the camera itself.

"The first thing we want to do is to deter the activity," says Saxe. "The second thing is to record it. We deter it, we detect, record and act."

Many of the buildings around town may have partial or 24-hour man security. Although many of the security control officers are highly qualified, this will improve over the next year because the Ontario government has introduced a new bill that will improve the quality of the security guards. This is Bill 159 that replaces the Private Investigators and Security Guards Act. This bill will help to improve the credentials of security guards. The bill has been passed and will be enforced next August.

Saxe also mentions there is an underlying principle of crime prevention through environmental design. This is also known as CPTED – crime prevention through environmental design.

"How you trim the trees so you can see what you're doing, fix the broken window, clean up the garbage," says Saxe. "If a space has a defined purpose it is less likely it will be used for a crime purpose. It is practiced strongly out in Brampton. It's an underlying principle of what I do."

Light up your life! (Originally Published in New Dreamhomes and Condominiums Magazine)

In [Home Decor](#), [Writing (all kinds)](#) on **March 20, 2009** at **13:23**

There are experts out there who are inspired by light. Not just the light coming from the sun, but the kind of light that makes your home a beautiful place to live in. Clint Gage is one of these people. He is the sales and marketing manager of Creative Lighting and says colour charges everything he does.

"Every time I go to a home it comes up – let's get some colour in the garden – let's get some fibre optics," says Gage. "There's a nice birch tree, let's put some red on it. There's a nice pool cabana, let's put some blue on it. It's come such a long way that now we're not the moon ray guys. We have solid bronze – they cast it in sand and they're bulletproof. The pricing is good."

Gage's work with Creative Lighting focuses on landscape and architecture. He is inspired by famous places in Toronto when he thinks of light and colour.

"Look at the CN Tower…what is wrong with a little colour? I was out in Burlington the other night and you're seeing more and more buildings with purple and blue in them. I would like to see more of that into the residential. Different temperatures of white and colours do that. I would like to take it one step further, go with the blue, the red, the green."

Some of the work he has done with condominiums includes the underground parking lots.

"It is obviously exterior," says Gage. "[We] light trees. The landscape lighting is what I really love about it is creating effects and setting moods. There is a lot more technical into it. They use the same techniques. Every client is different. I love it when the client says here is the canvas and lets me go with it."

Gage has lit up many yards and through trial and error knows what works and what does not.

"I have placed fixtures over the years," says Gage. "A couple of years ago we did a nice project and I am really, really happy with, the clients that we have dealt with I don't mind going the extra mile. I do not mind giving back. Our calibre of clients are more than excellent."

Michael Gladstone, general manager of Royal Lighting, is also an expert. He says he is a little bit biased, but he finds lighting the most important thing in any home.

"Lighting will finish off a room," says Gladstone. "Lighting will help you to have the proper light so you can function. Especially like in the bathroom, you need lighting to put your makeup on or shave properly to see properly. The bathroom, the cooking area in the kitchen and the laundry room. In the home office you need good light. Dining room you should have good light, but should have a dimmer light so when you want to change the mood you can do so without it being a big deal."

Gladstone says the rules of interior lighting for homes and condos are the same.

"When you get into houses you need good exterior lighting so people do not trip and sue you. A well-lit house will not get robbed as often as a dimly lit house. People can see when they are walking up your porch where to light. It also adds a beauty there to that, despite the functionality. It adds to the whole décor of the house. A lamp here a lamp there."

With condos, Gladstone mentions that 15, 20 years ago there were not as many as there are now. The explosion of the condo market has created specialized lighting.

"What is available now is like mini-fixtures. There are fixtures specifically made for these smaller condos."

The Future of Furniture Design (Originally Published in New Dreamhomes and Condominiums Magazine)

In Home Decor, Technology, Writing (all kinds) on **March 21, 2009** at **01:06**

The future has a lot in store for furniture design. Christopher Wright is a designer with Figure 3, an interior design practice based in Toronto. He is also a member of the Association of Registered Interior Designers of Ontario (ARIDO). Figure 3 specializes in corporate office, retail and hospitality design and a small bit of residential. He has thoughts on where furniture design is going.

"Minimalizes and mondernism have had a huge impact on the aesthetic of furniture and prices of modern furniture," says Wright. "The ability of making furniture less expensive in China has had a huge impact. Furniture in Italy and Europe was beautiful but out of people's range. It's also gotten people to live with modern design."

Wright mentions that technology has a huge impact and new materials used in furniture production are enabling designers to be even more creative. It's also become quite a fashion industry as well with a plethora of HDTV and Women's TV programs and TLC programs and all the programs that specialize in interior design and trends.

"I'd like to think that out of all the rooms in the house kitchen design has become very sophisticated and I would like to think that could spread into other rooms into the house," Wright says. "The same sophistiation and design into other rooms of the house based on function. More open plan living, instead of people living in a bunch of different rooms, where the kitchen, dining, living and entertaining will be in one big space and that will change the way furniture evolves."

With the growth of condo living there is an upswing in multifunctional products that are designed for small spaces.

"Emotion is creeping back into design where it's almost sculptural in qualtiy," says Wright. "One designer I really admire is Patricia Urquiola. Google her images."

Monique Le Ray with Le Ray Design has been a designer in Canada for 27 years. She agrees with a lot of what Christopher Wright has to say.

She was trained in Paris, she worked in Dubai at the start of her career. She came to Canada in 1981. Le Ray is also a member of ARIDO. She is third in a generation of people in her family in the furniture business and designed a restaurant with her Dad. She does residential and commercial spaces in her design business.

"I think we are going to go more towards the trend that we went with Wenge, the dark espresso wood," says Le Ray. "It's a type of furniture that is a wood veneer. Darker than a walnut. See a lot of that furniture in the stores with a very, very simple lines. It is very easy to copy and lots of furniture is coming from China now. In a Paris show in January there is more accent on ormentation. Like when people bring overscale objects and overscale patterns as a way to dress up the simple lines. See that more simple style but with more presence."

Now there is more of an executive look in furniture design. In future, Le Ray thinks the trend will be to stay away from that.

"If I furnished my own room, I would go with a chair of a different style and a table of a different style. Ultra suede is very sophisticated in look. That is a common fabric that we use lately. The buffet would be an exotic piece. It becomes a very personalized interior. Even in a bedroom of the same thing I would not buy the whole set. I would find something for the side of the table and a chair. It becomes a one-of-kind result."

Le Ray also says that furniture pieces will continue to be lower to the ground and technology also plays a big role in the change towards the future. Functionality will be key. As well as having furniture that goes with artwork and photography.

"Each client is different that I would not push the furture look on someone who likes the classic materials. The revolution in furnishing is also technology and also people live differently. They live less formally than their parents and the furniture design has a different use. People can even do without a dining room. Have a fireplace to create more an ambience. The kitchen is changing tremendously as well….becoming very clean looking and the gallery for entertaining. People do not buy furniture for the sake of buying furniture…they choose the best way for furnishing a place. The need brings the design instead of the other way around."

For more information about Le Ray Design you can visit the website at www.leraydesign.com.

Working with Wallpaper (Originally Published in New Dreamhomes and Condominiums Magazine)

In [Home Decor](#), [Writing (all kinds)](#) on **March 22, 2009** at **02:56**

That paper you can put on your walls is a lot more than what it used to be when it was so popular back in the 1970s and 1980s. The times of designers encouraging homeowners to tear it from their walls and all the struggle in stripping it from your walls are over. Wallpaper is making a comeback.

Tara Ford is one of the owners of West Toronto Paint. She says masks that are used in artwork are coming back and this translates into wallpaper designs.

"It's coming back," says Ford. "It's not coming back where people are doing their entire house. Often times they are doing their powder room for a more dramatic feel, a more elegant feel. In our store we are featuring furniture items and wall vignettes with wallpaper and the wallpaper is selling, it is doing really well seeing it. People can visualize a lot better. Wallpaper is definitely more popular and like I said it is coming back and the old style is being contemporized. Even a steel gray going into the blue tones."

Ford says a lot of the impact wallpaper is having on home design is being inspired from fashion design. Fashion design is one stage of being that is also merging with trends in home design.

Bob West is the general manager at West Toronto Paint. He has spent decades working with wallpaper and he agrees with Ford that it is definitely making a comeback.

"It's actually a logical progression of the big craze that hit the market 10 years ago," says West. "Everybody was pulling it down. The design of today is so current. People instead of doing the full finish, they are looking for more impact of that. We're finding people are using much bolder prints and prints that make much more of an impact in a room."

West says wallpaper becomes even more necessary when you think of what some people do with their homes with just painted walls.

"I think the idea of just plain painted walls is a little dated," West says. "They are looking to go in a different direction. There are lots of new products that have come on the market. We have paper that is totally not difficult to remove. Everybody has the memory of damaging your wall when you are trying to remove it. There is actually a company out there that will make a wallpaper that is reusable. You can re-wet it again and hang it again."

This type of reusable wallpaper is something that West saw from a salesperson in Arizona. He has not seen it in Canada yet. Canada still does have a lot to offer for people who are interested in designing their homes with wall coverings.

"Wall coverings are being aimed at a younger and hipper audience…seeing a lot of IKEA inspired designs," says West. "A lot of designers we find are actually using it in the designer industry. Ten, 15 years ago, designers would be talking people out of it. Now they are promoting it."

West also notes that you can see wallpaper coming back even by watching television. Many TV shows are decorating their sets with wallpaper.

For many, if you are thinking of the environmental impact of introducing wallpaper into your décor, there are design options that answer this dilemma.

"There are also a lot of natural fibres," says West. "Grassclass, it is natural fibres, with bamboo and this was huge in the 70s and you see it in many different applications. It is a wonderful textural backdrop. It works well in a modern type design and something quite traditional."

West also talks about some of the products that are selling well at West Toronto Paint.

"What we are doing really well with as well is paintable wall coverings [is] anaglypta is the proper British name. It is a wonderful way to create a wall that is in bad condition to make it brand new again. You actually apply the paper, apply it to the wall and let it dry out and lay a coat of latex paint over it. We have geometrics and it has been in use in Europe for centruries because the old stone walls would be covered and this would keep it together. So you could keep papering over top. We have a lot of interest in wallpaper murals. Not like your palm tree…we have an extreme close-up of a field of poppies. There are wonderful commercial uses for that too."

Your hi-tech home (Originally Published in New Dreamhomes and Condominiums Magazine)

In [Home Decor](), [Technology](), [Writing (all kinds)]() on **March 23, 2009** at **00:55**

Kevin Haber who drives to many dream homes to fix people's computers sees technology creating a whole new communication universe for a homeowner.

"In the future, people will access their communication device remotely and they can adjust the temperature in their home, run a bath, change the lights, have pre-set schedules for everything to take place so when they get home – everything is going to be ready for them," says Haber. "There will be pre-set schedules as to their liking. And everything is going to converge. Now you have touch-screens where you don't need to type or click anymore."

Tony Wright is a writer who formerly worked with Time-Warner in New York City. He agrees with Haber.

"At my age, it's amazing the advances that have been made," says Wright. "I know people who have basically movie theatres in their home. There's TiVO and Rogers Direct. There are so many different things for cleaning, like self-cleaning vacuum cleaners. You can clap your hands and turn on the lights or the TV."

Wright says the way things are now are similar to the kinds of things many of us grew up watching on the "Jetsons" or "Star Trek."

"The newer houses, they're even more technologically-advanced," says Wright. "The condo market up here that is a real selling point for real estate agents. The young people want the gadgets. A friend of mine got an iAquarium. They come in different sizes and you program the setting of the aquarium so you can have a Caribbean, African, Mediterranean or certain islands motif – any kind of aquatic life that you desire you plug it in and there you go. It's like having an aquarium without the work."

Kevin Haber does technical support for 24/7 Tech. They service the need for emergency computer response for residential homes and commercial businesses 24 hours a day, 7 days a week. They have been in business for nine years.

"A very successful insurance broker came to us with his hard drive that he had accidentally formatted and it was his entire financial history and accounts," says Haber. "His whole financial life was in that hard drive. We kept working on the data recovery. He came to us I think by word of mouth or from the yellow pages, I cannot remember. It was kind of referral or advertising that he saw. We were the only ones that were open. We responded right away and we recovered all the information back. We got most of it, we got the exact data he needed back – he was thrilled. There are tons of stories like that. We did another data recovery after that for his daughter for a laptop that crashed, actually two of them where we recovered the data. He lives in an upper class home."

Haber notices that a lot of homes are implementing wireless networks. When wireless networks first came out, the security was less. Over time the companies that supply these wireless routers have implemented stronger security.

"It's all converging, it's all trying to converge to having Internet on the television having long distance on Internet," says Haber. "People are buying these home phones, using services like Skype and Vonage and SIP phones – those are special phones that you use with your computer, they can be USB or cordless and people are saving a tremendous amount of money by using these phones with a headset and an earpiece and microphone and using that to talk all over the world for a fraction of a penny. You can buy these things for $20 to $30 for unlimited calling all over the world."

Haber also says Fido came out with an unlimited plan, if I have my Fido plan people are getting rid of their home lines.

"A lot of people have eliminated a land line and they're using their cellphones, or blackberries and IPhones to communicate and able to text message people in real time. Everybody from high school kids and up have cellphones or PDAs or instant messaging. They're actually using them to communicate with their parents, cheat on tests. Now there is an instant messaging language. All converged into these mini-computers."

Everything is becoming inter-connected in almost a real-time fashion. All this technology is converging into an all-in-one appliance.

Music, video, pictures, cameras are being built into phones now and those cameras can also take movies as well. A lot of them can be sent via wi-fi or blue tooth. Then there also GPS navigation system to get to and from home in a more efficient manner.

"Robots that clean the floors, cut the grass are really becoming more prevalent," says Haber. "It will be a clean home and it's all part and parcel of automating the home now and it's just going to get more and more."

Watch and learn (Originally Published in New Dreamhomes and Condominiums Magazine)

In [Home Decor](), [Technology](), [Writing (all kinds)]() on **March 24, 2009** at **02:41**

It's a life journey renovating a house. Anke and Kirk Simpson saw their Edwardian house in Riverdale only twice before everything was finalized with the sale. They knew for sure it needed work. A house that had two apartments inside, with a boy and girl under three they wanted a house the whole family could enjoy.

The work began in November of 2007 and they started blogging about their renovation on 247reno.ca. The site gets about 6,000 to 7,000 visits a month. They also get about 15,000 to 20,000 page views a month.

"We get about two or three comments a day," says Kirk Simpson, vice-president of sales of Green Living Enterprises. "There are a lot people asking questions about certain questions or contractors. We plan to keep up with it."

Anke Simpson contributes the interior design knowledge to the blog.

"We started the blog and we wanted to share our experience with other people, it's a great way to document the journey ourselves. See how we progressed and what we learned along the way."

Keeping a successful blog while renovating a home is enough of a challenge. The Simpson family moved from a semi-detached to a home that now has about 2,500 square feet with an open space concept. Anke Simpson who is director of buying at Indigo designed their new space and helped to make it livable in time for Easter.

"Our last house was more cosmetic fixs," says Anke Simpson. "This one was more structural. We had a very very short amount of time and we knew we didn't want to live in it the way that it was. We gutted the main floor as soon as we moved in. We had only seen the house two times on very, very quick visits to figure out what to do."

The Simpsons knew they wanted a family room, a powder room and an island in the kitchen. It was also really important for them to have a lot of light. Coming into the space, it is an older home and it had a lot of interior walls.

"It's all open concept with the exception of the front foyer that has a powder room and a large closet," Anke says. "We're really happy with it. Again, we had to sort of jig things on the fly. We had intended to put things in different places. You start to understand that things can't happen for a certain reason, the powder room has to be a 4 by 4 space. You have to change your plans very quickly. A lot of compromises."

Anke Simpson is not an interior designer by profession, although in her former job she worked with Caban, part of Club Monaco. She mainly learned how to decorate her new home by reading and learning.

"From the moment we got the house and even with our old house, I tend to go through a lot of magazines. A lot of features that I really love about a home. Just for future reference, if we ever do move, just to keep great ideas on file. I would often refer back to things and the kind of materials that I really love. When you're going through a new build or a rebuild, at least if you know the direction that you love and the materials and the style, even down to window casings and baseboards and floor finishes and the style of window. You have to make all those decisions so if you have something in your mind to put together it makes it easier."

The Simpson family learned how to sleep through hammering. They had to reinforce the main floor, the structure, that took three and half weeks to get it down. They ripped up old carpet and put down hardwood floors and painted.

"It's nice to create a space that is functional for you and your family," says Anke. "It is critical to know that we can go into the kitchen and have the kids right in front of us. That is something we didn't have in our old house. We saw potential."

Anke Simpson says there is still a lot more work to be done.

Anke's husband Kirk contributed to the renovation before the contractors came in.

"Over three days we had a garbage bin brought in that was changed and there were upwards of eight of us demolishing the main floor and literally bringing down the ceiling and there were studs [two-by-fours] everywhere," says Kirk Simpson. "Lathe and plaster with the house. Thin strips of wood that run horizontal across the two-by-fours. Then it was constructed before the drywall. We wanted to go down to the studs so we could then replaster. This way you get a more modern and less cumbersome way of maintaining your walls."

Kirk says contractors came in and they basically took it from that to a finished product as it relates to the wall and the trim and the new windows.

"There were basically two things we focused on with the do-it-yourself, we did the demolition and Anike designed the whole layout as well as the whole kitchen. We were down to an open space and needed to reposition the powder room and the functionality of the kitchen room and she handled all of that."

Kirk says he is lucky he knows how to deal with ceilings, walls and floors because a couple of his friends are knowledgeable about that and told him. Coupled with a little bit of online research and a little bit of trial and error and he was able to get the job done.

"In our old house we had done a lot of the work ourselves," says Kirk. "For this house we needed to rely on professionals for the most important parts of the renovation. Painting outside and landscaping outside we relied on the professionals.

"It's really the fact that Anike had the vision to see what she wanted in the space. We have a really large space here that is pretty open concept."

Urban Women at Toronto Street Festival Review (Originally Published in Pride Newsmagazine)

In Culture, Events, Music, Writing (all kinds) on **March 25, 2009** at **02:29**

Juno-nominated Jully Black kicked off the presence of the African-Canadian women performing at the Toronto Street Festival on July 8th to 10th. Black rocked the big crowd at Yonge & Dundas with jazzy R&B sounds.

To add that club feel, Black even had her own DJ who is featured on City-TV's "Ed the Sock." But, it was Black's voice, singing live, not like Ashley Simpson, which kept it real.

Her second live song from her new album, "This is me now" merged a twang of reggae with DJ scratching. She segued right into a slower beat that was more like grooving music, singing "To hell with you." Her fourth song was for her mother.

The song is called "I travelled" and it was a ballad that got the audience snapping. She also got the audience screaming out "love" after she said "peace." The crowd seemed happy, and on Saturday the 9th a diverse group of Torontonians came out to see Juno Award winner Sonia Collymore at Yonge & Dundas.

Collymore did a fantastic job – putting on a show that I'm sure most people would have paid for. It's amazing it was free. At one point, she pulled a young man out of the audience on stage with her. Her song "No cash flow" got everyone dancing, including her four Baby Boy dancers. The dancers showed the audience some dancehall moves – getting everyone ready for their afterparty. This song and more is on her new album "WYSIWYG" which means "what you see is what you get."

Collymore put on a great performance, dressed in a gold bustier with a jean skirt with fringe. The unexpected surprise to her stylish onstage presence was her comfortable white tennis shoes.

One would need comfortable shoes to catch all the action at the Toronto Street Festival. The venues were being held at sites from Yonge & Dundas to Yonge & Lawrence from the mid-town areas of Yonge & St. Clair and Yonge & Eglinton. The Yonge & Eglinton spot is where Andreena Mill and the Honey Jam Alumni performed on the 10th.

Mill, who was on first and has been compared to Alicia Keys. She is a classically trained pianist. Her sound had a definite funky vibe which was also expressed in the bright yellow jacket and knee socks with stripes she had on.

It was a hot day on Sunday and Mill did a jamming tune to heat up the crowd even more. Mill did a ballad she wrote after a bad relationship. One of the highlights was a song called "Rewind" where she also showed her vocal talent by singing without the band for the beginning. Her debut album will be out in 2006.

After Mill was the Honey Jam Alumni. This was a rare performance of all-female African-Canadian talent. The alumni included Kelly Lee Evans, Jocelyn Mercer, Andrea Lewis, Joy Lapps, Queen Cee, Lori Nuic, Black Pearl and Motion.

End Piece: an uplifting experience (Originally Published in Concordia University Alumni Magazine)

In Education, Media Writing, Writing (all kinds) on **March 27, 2009** at **00:19**

Since I was seven years old I knew I wanted to write. My master's degree in media studies from Concordia helped me reach that goal — and much more. When I entered the master's program in 1997, I was quite depressed. I had been living and working in Uganda, but health problems had forced me to return to Canada earlier than expected. I was staying with friends I knew from my undergrad years in Ottawa. The only place that came close to providing me a sense of home was Toronto; I just hated Montreal. I wasn't doing any writing, the medication I was putting pounds on and I was generally unhappy with myself.

In my first year of the master's program, I didn't even have enough confidence to handle a full course load, so I slugged through two courses in the first term. I started exercising at the YMCA at my doctor's suggestion, and the only writing I did was the essays for my Communications Theory and International Affairs classes. Thank God I had that.

If it wasn't for those essays, I wouldn't have been doing any writing at all.

Slowly I built my confidence up, and I started doing some volunteer work at a radio station. There, I met someone who linked me with Radio Canada International, where I had an opportunity to do freelance radio stories. My first story was on an international radio conference in Montreal — and it was awful! The show's producer gave me a fair and balanced critique; more importantly, he let me do another story. By this time I was taking a full course load at Concordia and I was a teaching assistant with comm studies professor Marie-Hélène Cousineau, and my confidence started to build. My second piece was much stronger.

While I spent the summer in Montreal, I even wrote a short story, "Church Sunday," that was later published in Concordia's creative writing anthology, Headlight.

By my second year I learned the art of independent study, and my depression started to fade. That year was one of the best times of my life. Early in the school term I was at the reception for Headlight with two friends and colleagues from my program. I was saying that I didn't know what to do for my master's thesis. The conversation turned to hair, and they suggested that I do my thesis on the politics of black hair. At first I thought they were joking, but I soon began to take them seriously, and that eventually became my thesis topic.

The suggestion went one step further when professor Kim Sawchuk suggested I do a website and a project as part of the thesis. I hesitated at first because I thought you had to be a rocket scientist to do a website, but soon learned otherwise. The hands-off style of my advisor, Martin Allor, was just what I needed. His input was invaluable, and when I was having difficulty coming up with bibliographic material, he directed me towards Michele Wallace's Invisibility Blues. This book became like a Bible for me — Ms. Wallace had also gone through a depression while doing her academic work.

I eventually finished my thesis, Afro Forever. When I presented it to Dr. Allor on my birthday in 1999, he gave me as a gift a book on hair. I probably didn't show it, but I was deeply touched, and really felt that I had come a long way during the two years completing my degree.

It's now six years since I've graduated and I've had lots of writing jobs — including one with a team of other media studies graduates. Thank you, Concordia.

Taking the stress out of your move

In Living, Writing (all kinds) on **March 28, 2009** at **05:34**

Making the move to your dream home or condominium can be a stressful one. Toronto City Movers is an independent company that has seven years of experience specializing on both local and long distance relocations. As well as providing safe and secure storage facilities. Dmitry Amialkovich who owns and manages Toronto City Movers has some tips on how to make your move less stressful.

Choose your moving company carefully. Decisions based on price alone will likely place your goods and belongings in the hands of clumsy and careless mover "Your chances for a damage-free move are much greater when the movers do the packing," says Amialkovich. "They're experienced and they use only the best moving boxes and packing supplies. However, you can save a lot of money if you do the bulk of the packing, though you should limit yourself only to highly replaceable and non-fragile items such as books, linens, clothing, inexpensive plates, dishes, and small kitchen appliances. Keep in mind that the movers are not liable for the items they didn't pack, however, these items will be cheaper to replace in case of damage as opposed to hiring workers and purchasing their supplies. Let the movers pack your furniture, mattresses, and heavy appliances."

Amialkovich also suggests that you should purchase the proper moving boxes. Wardrobe boxes save you valuable ironing time later on. Although you can pack T-shirts and jeans in suitcases and regular boxes, you do not want to pack your fine clothing such as suits or dresses in the same place. Mattress cartons protect your mattresses from filth, grease, and rips and tears during the transit. Padded dish boxes with dividers help protect your fine china.

For your replaceable and non-fragile items, you can save money by obtaining free boxes from the supermarket and wrapping the items in old newspaper.

"Take the time to pack your items carefully, especially if you are packing your fragile items on your own," says Amialkovich. "It is recommended that you purchase the professional packing supplies for these items. However if you use regular boxes, it is important that you buffer and separate the fragile items with plenty of old newspaper, bubble wrap, sheets, blankets, pillows, or towels. Fill in empty spaces to minimize movement during transit. Wrap each item separately. Pack plates and glass objects vertically, rather than flat and stacked. Fully secure the bottoms to prevent fallout."

The heavier the items, the smaller the box it should occupy. Do not toss everything into one huge box. It will make the hauling much more difficult. Keep the weight of each box under 50 pounds. Remember to lift with your knees, not your back.

You should never let the movers pack your jewelry, family heirlooms, hobby collections, or other priceless items. Should they be lost or damaged, the insurable value will not come anywhere close to the value you would place on them. Pack these items personally and take them with you, either in the car or as carry-on luggage if the size allows.

"Do not pack hazardous materials," says Amialkovich. "These items include: paint, thinners, solvents, oils, varnishes, firearms and ammunition, bottled gas, propane, lamp oil, anything flammable, explosive, or corrosive, motor fuels and oils, nail polish remover, bleach and aerosol cans. Also note that spilled sesame oil leaves a terrible stench."

Facilitate and organize the loading process by designating a room in your home, preferably the one closest to the door, in which to place all of your boxes. This will also help keep the area to and around your large pieces of furniture open. Group related boxes since they will end up in the same room.

Corporate advertising to blacks (Originally Published with Suite101.com)

In Business, Culture, Media Writing, Writing (all kinds) on **April 4, 2009** at **02:51**

Many companies do not feel it necessary to create advertising aimed specifically at Black communities. Sometimes Trevor Campbell, president of Porter Novelli, is asked in his public relations practice whether he has experience in ethnic media outreach? He says it is hard to measure the media that reaches ethnic communities.

"There's media monitoring companies and they do not necessarily track those papers, there may be language barriers," says Campbell. "You're seeing in some ads that it's not just a white person, you're seeing people of all shapes of sizes and people are recognizing that the city is diverse. Ads are a bit easier. The thing with PR is that a spokesperson is interviewed by Sway Magazine by ex-product; many people are going to use that product. We're looking to target Torontonians that drive fast cars. Perhaps it's more inclusive that way as well."

Although the way advertising, PR and marketing work right now are more inclusive, Campbell says that perhaps the black man that drives the fast car has different needs than the white man, but there are many similarities. There are some groups that feel marketing to the black community or having blacks represented in their advertising is important.

"I think this conversation five years from now, 10 years from now, the conversation would be different. Sports, Hip Hop and Stevie Wonder...so many people listen to him [Wonder] people from all walks of life are being impacted. Without having to divide along black and white lines. Looking forward may see more companies focusing on different communities because it may be because of a public service perspective. You also want to connect with the influencers as well and you may see smart advertisers and marketers doing that. Community leaders are important as well, could be the church pastor to the star of the football team. If you have a black person who is a survivor it makes a difference."

Campbell says that overall he sees corporations or businesses viewing the black community as a larger community – this is how they focus on them and that is how they target them.

"That is how the community is focused along gender, age, educated versus uneducated."

Sandy Johnson who is currently a recruitment consultant with WWWork, but has a previous career in advertising for television agrees with Campbell and adds that things are different in Canada than they are in the United States.

"I do not know that in the advertising streams that I have been involved with that it is as narrow a stream to target that kind of market," Johnson says. "The print media that is targeting a specific market that is that kind of way. In television, the message is not targeted to any one group. The fact that there is an effort to represent the groups, it shows there is a more inclusive message, rather than targeting different groups."

Johnson says that when television commercials are being cast, advertisers have a corporate responsibility to make sure their advertisements represent the Canadian population.

"There is an effort to find the best actors in a television commercial regardless of their ethnicity. If the best actor is black, then that is the way you go. I have never worked on behalf of an advertiser that has felt it is targeted to one group to another. I do not feel the Canadian market targets ethnic groups as much as it is in the United States that may happen because of a bigger population base."

Johnson notes that in print and web advertising, it is a more selective and targeted style of advertising technique,"the advertising channel and the different groups will dictate more who the market is. Canada also does not have the kind of financial and population base to do targeted marketing. California has a huge Hispanic base, they have the population base to support it."

Corporate advertising being more inclusive even affects the homes that are targeted to ethnic communities. Amit Kalia who is a real estate broker is marketing City Condos in Mississauga and the multicultural community that surrounds it.

"It has a lot of mixed cultures and communities together," says Kalia. "There is a festival hosted in the South Asian community. They have something called Carassauga. It is the largest cultural festival in Ontario – it's called the festival of cultures."

The condo has all the amenities and features that can be expected in the higher end condo market aiming to attract professionals.

Quoting from a website called Electronic Village, data compiled by essayist and retired patent attorney Richard Everett, African Americans are projected to have spending power of approximately $1 trillion a year by 2010. That will be a significant increase over the roughly $800 billion Blacks are believed to have spent in 2006. If one only takes about 10 percent of this number to determine how much blacks in Canada are spending, those are some powerful purchasing dollars that very well may change the way blacks are targeted in advertising. As Campbell said, advertising has more to do with money and education. The more educated and the more buying power blacks continue to have, advertisers may have to respond to this change.

Adjusting to a new place

In Home Decor, Writing (all kinds) on **April 5, 2009** at **08:54**

Your months, or even years of searching for your dream home is over and now what? You have to adjust to this new place and make it your home.

Monique Le Ray of Le Ray Design and also a member of the Association of Registered Interior Designers of Ontario have some tips on how best you can get comfortable in your new surroundings.

"Somebody who just moves into a new place there is the excitement of a new place and changing homes is a big step," says Le Ray. "There is a lot of emotional stuff that goes into getting a new place. They go with their instincts and there is a lot of emotion. You hope that you are going up in your life not down. For me when you go into a new place…a lot of my designs are more emotion than rational."

Le Ray says that the rational mind has to come into play when you settle into your new home and the emotion of the new buy has settled.

"Move into your new place like you was a renter, not like you were the owner," Le Ray says. "If you own the place, you want to do everything at once. If you want a new kitchen, or a new garden, if you look at your place and you want a little bit of this and a little bit of that…chances are you will be more rational."

With the renters mind you would move the furniture that you already have says Le Ray. After six months of living in a new space, you would take your time and rebuild.

"Renting a place, you do not go right away to get a contractor working on the basement. No, you do not want your office in the basement; you want it on the third floor. You want the space to work for you and the space is your own and your moving and you do not have to show all your friends how beautiful your space is right way."

Le Ray says prioritizing is key.

"You do that powder room and nothing else," suggests Le Ray. "I had friends of mine that had friends come in and they posted things on the wall and when they would come for coffee they would put writings on the walls so people would write with magic marker their comments about the space in the room. They would go for a coffee and get the opinions of their friends. After a while this is something that has grown up and it is fun to have parties to redo the kitchen. A tacky basement – you can have a tacky party."

The money goes so far that it is never to the liking of many homeowners for the money they plunge into adjusting to a new place right away, says Le Ray.

"I wish I can extend the family room and extend this and that. If you do things immediately, chances are you are not doing the best you can. The old family room in the old place, you can think of what you liked before and bring it into your new home. You find that emotionally. You get what you like about the past and what you want to bring inside. You find out what you like about the new home or new neighbourhood. You can look at the garden. If you know that your kitchen is going to be 50-grand plus, you want to have the right feel, the right back splash, you should take your time to make it happen.

"If you are going to bring up your children in that house…you want to take your time and remember why you bought that house. That is the feature you bought the house for and you should take your time and the rest of your house will grow to accommodate that."

Le Ray recommends that when you first move into your new home, you should wait about six months before making major changes. This will give enough time to get used to the environment and the unique qualities of your home.

For more information about Le Ray Design, please visit www.leraydesign.com.

Organizing 101

In [Home Decor](#), [Writing (all kinds)](#) on **April 5, 2009** at **08:57**

Whether you are looking for your dream home or looking to organize your existing one – Nada Thomson, former founder and chief consultant of Artful Organizers has some tips for you. She starts off with people who are looking for their dream home.

"I would want them to plan how long they would plan to be in the next place," says Thomson. "If they are thinking that this move would be for five years would there be space, would there be children, would it be just themselves. They really have to see the place they are in right now and see what they love about it. Their closet space, and a room they really like – those qualities stay…that is something you want to be looking for in the new space. The place – did it have a lot of shelves? Did it have a lot of storage space? They do not want to lose the things they love about the place they are in right now in the new place."

Thomson also says that if you have just moved into a new place, it would be important to take a geometric view of the new surroundings.

"Looking at spaces, rather than rooms. Looking at cubes and circles. Know they are also going to be doing a little bit of yoga in there, or a little bit of office space in there if it is open concept – if they categorize those compartments then they can see how to function in that space in an attractive way. If they have end drawers, it may be a good place to pop in their laptop. Or spaces for candles or yoga equipment. This is thinking of condo spaces."

Thomson has some tips for huge open areas as in a house.

"Not everything needs to be against the wall," says Thomson. "Having toys that are ready and structuring the closets that are nearby to accommodate what is happening in those sections, and finding the right furniture for that."

Thomson has a special way of working with her clients. She does not want them to clean up the house as though she was an average visitor to their home.

"I want to see how it looks on any given day," Thomson says. "I ask my clients what is not working for you. Usually it's the area near the front door that is always a mess. They cannot clean up, I need to see what is happening. Rather than try to train them, I try to help them see the ways they are dumping their space as more attractive. Putting a nice rattan bowl catcher. Maybe the front door closet is crammed full…we organize a closet so not all four seasons need to be in the closet. It can be done with colours, each hanger with a different colour for each season. Some people have extra closets in their home, some people have extra storage racks in their home."

Thomson recommends a good quality garment rack for clothes that can be found at most organizing stores or department stores so the clothes do not get dusty.

"You just want somewhere else to hang these things, have a canvas box with a zipper on the box or each thing goes in a garment bag. The idea behind it is to be aware of what you are using on a daily basis, why you are dumping and it and where you are dumping it."

Thomson says organizing is like a puzzle, all of a sudden everything comes together and works.

"Ninety percent of the time the reason why things are not organized is because there is just too much stuff. Not to say that they need to get rid of the stuff, just that they need to relocate the stuff. It is also important to decide that this closet is just for A, B and C, and this drawer is for D and E, and this cupboard is for F. And you know where to get it and it is always that way."

Now, Thomson is working with a non-profit organization in Toronto. Her years of experience in helping people get organized have many uses.

Gaiser Construction (Originally Published in Canadian Builders Quarterly)

In Business, Writing (all kinds) on **April 10, 2009** at **04:16**

Bruce Gaiser got into a pinch back in the late 1980s and 1990s when he started doing business with Native reserves in Manitoba. The cash flow of the business dried up, "I decided I would work for more credible companies, like school boards, government, provincial boards, municipalities, cities, now we're getting more into the design build," says Gaiser. "You solicit the general contractors which is what we do, this is how the owner decides which builder to go with. Competitive build is what it is called. Back in the early 90s you would get 10 and 11 guys bidding on a job, now you would get about three. You can be more selective about who you deal with. Honing in on what we are good at."

The company does about a dozen to two dozen projects a year. Currently two of their projects include grocery stores in Shore Lake, Manitoba, "looking at Esther Hazey, Saskatchwan," says Gaiser. "They mine for potash and they use it for fertilizer, it's a huge commodity because they use it for ethanol so they just upgraded to one of the mine sites. Real estate in the town overnight jumped to over 25 percent."

When it comes to marketing, Gaiser says the company is not big on it. They work with Goodon Industries and they manage the excavator, the plumbing, the heating and the drywaller, "so we've developed a strategic alliance with them in Aylmer, Ontario. The guy who started the facility they grew tobacco."

Gaiser finds it hard to keep his best people when it comes to human resources, "well that's a tough one because labour is so tight right now. It's a tough market right now and the availability of trained skilled labour is tough to find. The people we do have with us we are giving them incentives, we are giving them wage incentives and we are bumping them two to three times a year. Hospital districts we work for too. They poach our people. We give our people training and we give them opportunities."

Gaiser says he had one woman with their company who they trained and she did well. She did so well that the federal government hired her. Another man was traveling miles and miles to get to Gaiser Construction Specialists. The company did some projects in his hometown and came to know about the work – soon he was hired on in his local town.

"We pick a volume, we can only do so much work because we only have only so much resources available, we look at subcontracting and we have to be very careful about the projects we are going to work on," Gaiser explains. "The economy improves and then people are getting poached to bigger companies. The strategy changes to how you can do well and give customer service because in the end that is what is important."

To keep the Gaiser Construction Specialists going so they can continue strong customer service, their recent strategies in investment are important. They buy land, not gold. Their concentration is on commercial properties, although they do have some residential properties as well. Bruce Gaiser invests in his company, "we look at buying revenue properties and that's our strategy and that's where we have got to be. Real estate is going up. Where the ceiling, I do not know."

In terms of development, they are in a busy market right now where it is easy to find customers, "you want to keep your level of customer service substantial," says Gaiser. "The people who are kicking tires and looking for the best bargain, once you give them the price, they either see the value or they don't. We're working with companies like Wyeth Organics [pharmaceutical company]. Basically pick the customers and get in with those people who have lots of work and develop those strategic alliances."

Some of their strategic alliances include working with the school boards on rooms for children with disabilities. This is a project worth $75,000.

"We're doing a hospital of 4,000 square feet and that's about a $6 million job," says Gaiser. "It's all soup to nuts…it's all based on the customer and what they need. Customer service, that is really the foundation of what we do. We as contractors build on an understanding and a set of drawings. We are always building on the understanding of what they need us to do. You have to understand how the process of the training and the education is going, like on Extreme Makeover it's a makeover with Ty [Pennington] and motivating people. You need that inner satisfaction when you're doing a project. That's the customer service side of things.

"We build on your on your ideas. Have that on the side of my truck."

K2 Contracting Ltd. (Originally Published in Canadian Builders Quarterly

In Business, Writing (all kinds) on **April 11, 2009** at **02:20**
Kevin Fairweather manages the business K2 Contracting Ltd. that does about $3.5 million to $5 million dollars a year.

"We do some residential homes and light commercial work," says Fairweather. "We're in the construction area so our number of employees fluctuates depending on what we're doing. We have about 30 employees, have had up to that. Now we have 18. Most of them are apprentices, they are finishing their last years of apprenticeship."

In a small community such as Rossland, BC where they are based, their recent strategies towards marketing are different than most. They focus on the bigger houses and higher end homes that the was something smaller-end people cannot even look at.

Customer service is important to K2 Contracting Ltd., "try to look at your clientèle's best interests, and try to develop a good rapport with your suppliers and subtrades," Fairweather says.

It is the people behind K2 Contracting Ltd. that really make it happen. Fairweather tries to keep his employees happy. He gets guys coming in who want a day off and he makes sure he helps them out so they keep wanting to come in on a daily basis.

"We're in a modern age here where your employees do more of the driving of the boat than an employer would like," says Fairweather. "There is a lot of give and take."

To beat the competition coming from bigger cities, Fairweather employs a plan, "we may take the heat of the financial burden to employ a few more people that is deemed necessary, it gives you the ability to grow instead of to staying stagnate in one place. The same for tools and equipment. We'll just leverage something so that we have it when we need it."

K2 Contracting Ltd. just landed a $3.5 million contract at the base of Red Mountain. They are building phase one of a complex of 10 townhomes.

K2 Contracting Ltd. works with what their clients' needs, "the more information you can give your clients, the more educated people are going to be to your questions. It's important to view what they're doing through their eyes, not necessarily through yours."

Fairweather also says that safety is an important part of the job.

"It's important that everyone enjoy themselves. Not to a state where you are going to be unsafe or harmful to themselves. Everyone having a good time, having knowledgeable staff definitely helps. Honesty and being able to live up to what your demands and what demands you said you could meet.

"Customer service, we're in a small town. You could rip people off, take months to do things, that would take work. Unethical. We're at a day and age as well, where someone would want to do a little bathroom reno a homeowner could do that. We're in a day and age where a homeowner should not try to build a house without a contractor with them."

Good Luck for Your Home (Originally Published with New Dreamhomes and Condominiums Magazine)

In Home Decor, Writing (all kinds) on **April 13, 2009** at **11:40**

Here is a treat for you instead of a trick for Halloween. Zeny Maninang is a sales representative since 1985 with HomeLife, Bayview Realty. She has learned a lot about developing your luck through your home. Paul Ng, philosopher and geomancer who also specializes in feng shui, was able to bring good luck to her home that helped her business and personal lives.

"What he did is he took the birth date of everyone in the family," says Maninang. "Because my house is facing west and he thinks it is not suitable for us, he felt it was better to go south exposure. Usually it is not a good sign to have a post. He asked me to get six turtles…three turtles on the right hand and three turtles on the left hand side of the house as you are facing the house. They have to be exterior ones and they are hard to find."

The turtles are meant to promote good energy to flow into your home.

"You have to make an island in front of the house to block whatever comes into the house," Maninang says. "He asked me to put rounded leaf plants instead of pointed leaves for more flowing energy for the house. [He also said] not to have a mirror by the bed."

Maninang has a king size bed in her master bedroom. Right beside that are mirrored closet doors.

"The way to go against the draining of energy is to close [the doors] or have a vase with flowers. My house is a bungalow, you cannot move around the bed because it is a small bedroom."

Ng also asked Maninang to remove the aquarium because the fish are always dying. He asked her to put a fountain outside the front door to welcome the flow of the water.

"After he did that…everything went smooth with my deals," Maninang says. "I did my own feng shui. Everything I did was all wrong…sometimes it is worth getting someone who is a specialist for that."

Ng also made other changes to bring good luck into Maninang's home. He changed the way her desk was backing the window. He said she was going to make a sale after that.

"And I sold the last lot the next day," Maninang says. "I do not know if it is superstition. Maybe that is why the Chinese believe in that. I believe in feng shui, it works for me. People will advise you whether you should buy that lot or not. We do a lot of changes in the houses and that is how I learned a lot about feng shui." Maninang says that she has also discovered that the master bedroom bed should not have a stove below it.

"It means that you are always on fire," Maninang says. "The bathroom you should not see through it. So many things… Stove should not face the sink, so it has to be moved around. You do not want the front door, facing the other door. Going to the backdoor. If you have money coming in, it just goes out."

Maninang says when she is dealing with clients, if they like the floor plan, or they like the layout, you have to put a French door, so the flow of the money does not come out right away between the front and back doors if they are facing each other.

She also recommends to put a money area in the house.

"Even my clock was placed forward and facing outside the house. He does not want that [Ng], it has to go towards the money area."

Maninang says this is the reason why some people lose money. When it comes to your romantic life, there should no live or dried plants in the master bedroom. It affects your relationship.

Maninang also says that the front of house should be clear and have no clutter. There should be a black or dark blue carpet in the front, this slows down the energy. Plants with rounded leaves should be at the front. Plus, putting a water fountain in the summer outside and bringing the water fountain in for winter is good luck.

"Viney plants do not let grow down to the floor," says Maninang. "You want to keep it neat and it should not creep. Rounded not too overgrowing. Lucky bamboo in the office and to have a crystal hanging in the room. It gives out reflections."

Maninang says that when she started working with the new homes and she was experiencing so many rough times, she asked Paul Ng to come over and move things and it really helps.

"Get rid of clutter, bathroom too. Nice to have a plant too in the bathroom. Bathrooms drain the energy in the house. I put the lucky bamboo, you do not have to maintain it."

Maninang also says that even her car is dark blue because Ng said she should drive a dark blue colour of car.

"Before people would complain to me and there would be problems. Now everything is fine."

For more information about selling or buying your home with Zeny Maninang, contact: zeny@sellhomestoronto.com.

Home staging

In Home Decor, Writing (all kinds) on **April 14, 2009** at **18:10**

You have been looking around for that perfect dream home or condominium and you are constantly astounded by the beauty or the décor and how clean the environment is. It helps you to picture yourself living there. Who helps to design this space you are dreaming of living in?

Well, there is a special name for creating new home spaces through cleaning and décor so you will want to live in them – it is called home staging. Colleen Palmer with Distinctive Nest is one of the people who creates these beautiful spaces you see when you are out house or condominium shopping.

"We've been around for a couple of years now," says Palmer. "Officially a year old. We usually try to work with real estate agents, but that is not always the case. Usually the real estate agents phone us up and we go in for a consultation. Sometimes the home owner phones us up."

Palmer, working with her partner Nancy Durelle, goes into a space to assess what needs to be done.

"Usually it's some basic, basic simple things," Palmer says. "It's basically de-cluttering. Little things like family photos, buyers want to see artwork. Sometimes it's just the colour, if it's really wild then we change the colour. Plus furniture…there is too much furniture in the room. And we place that in storage as well. It's sort of like house cleaning and decorating combined."

She says her favourite places to work on are the new developments.

"We have also done some model homes as well, some homebuilders and that is even more fun because you have a blank palette to work with," says Palmer. "We rent the furniture and we stage the house so it looks like it is lived in. If a homeowner loves the house the way it is, they will buy all the furniture in there. Usually it's the drapes whether it be blinds or fabric drapery…it's made to fit that window. Windows are not always a standard size, so it's made to fit that window and goes with the house."

Home staging is an acquired art that comes with training and experience.

"I've got a certificate from Sheridan College and I'm a certified in interior decorating…the two things are house cleaning and decorating at the same time," says Palmer. "Yeah…I can see myself living in this home and that is why it's called a stager."

Palmer says home staging is basically a new phenomenon.

"It's only been about the last three to five years that it's been around. The housing market really took off, the houses that were staged would sell faster and usually you get more money for them. What is it about my house that people would find attractive? If people don't like my house then they'll go 'whiffle'…but they will, they'll go down the street and they'll buy. I think because the market took off that this staging of houses has become so popular."

With Distinctive Nest, Palmer also offers other services besides just cleaning and decorating that go along with the home staging.

"We also do flower arranging that for staging is good as well. A nice decoration on a hall table or a dining table. We can do artificial and real flowers and it really helps to decorate a house."

Palmer has some tips when it comes to home staging.

"When you do stage a house, you certainly will help to sell the house faster because I will buy house number 37 because it has neutral colours. Down the road it's money in your pocket and you can move down the road with whatever changes in your life that you want to make."

Distinctive Nest normally charges $100/hour for a consultation to see what needs to be done in order to launch the home staging. After that, once they have gone there for the first hour then it is a $100 for every hour.

"You are getting two people for a hundred dollars an hour so I think people are really getting their money's worth," says Palmer.

For Distinctive Nest, when it comes to home staging, business is good all year round as the housing market continues to boom. For more information about Distinctive Nest, you can visit their website at: www.distinctivenest.ca.

Bayshore – March 26, 1993

In Culture, Education, Writing (all kinds) on **April 25, 2009** at **07:54**

Sitting on a couch in her living room, 10-year-old Michelle Lucien points to a bruise on her left ankle. Her crutches sit in a corner of the room.

"My ankle got sprained when this boy at school kicked me and me trip," says Michelle. "He called me a black bitch."

Michelle is a grade 5 student at Bayshore Public School. Her mother, Girlsen Lucien, says Michelle has experienced racial discrimination at school for over two years.

Every day since November 1992, when Michelle returns from school she writes in her green journal. She writes that classmates have kicked her and tried to push her down stairs, called her "queer" and "black bitch" repeatedly, lied that she choked them to get her in trouble with the principal and screamed intimidating words at her like "Klu Klux Klan."

"Every day of our lives we worry that Michelle will be safe," says Lucien, holding her husband's hand. He finds Michelle's situation so upsetting he cannot talk about it.

"We're trying to deal with it," says Lucien. "I always encouraged her to tell the teacher when she's hit."

Michelle says the teachers and administration at Bayshore don't help her. She says they call her a liar and blame her for every fight she's involved in. Lucien says the school administration is racist and treats her child unfairly.

"The school never believes her," says Lucien. "They have suspended her four times since September without giving equal punishment to the children who fight with her."

In her green journal, Michelle writes that when she's in a fight, the teachers and school administration punish her severely and the other children mildly or not at all. She also writes they harass her by grading and yelling, label her a liar, call her down to the office every day to accuse her of things she did not do and call her names like "fat" and "stupid."

Lucien says the school administration denies allegations of racism towards them or the school. The school's comment on Michelle's situation requires the permission of her parents under Bill 49 in Ontario legislature. The school administration had not received the parent's permission in time to make a comment for this story.

In a seven-page report, the principal of Bayshore Public School, Valerie Wright, summarizes the incidents Michelle was involved in since September 1990. She indicates that Michelle disobeys principals and teachers, called two teachers dummies and one a liar, caused parents to frequently complain about Michelle harassing their child and instigates fights with other children.

The principal also writes that Michelle's parents are unable to be specific about charges of racism, except to say the school is being unfair to Michelle.

Lucien sent back a rebuttal to the principal.

"This is nonsense!" she writes. "These adults should make an effort to be honest in their recordings of their interaction with a 10-year-old black child in their school."

Bayshore Public School is in the region of the Carleton Board of Education. Superintendent of school operations at the board, John Beatty, says there have been two cases of racial conflict he knows of over the past year, which have come to the attention of the board. Michelle's case is one of them. The board does not keep statistics on how many racial conflicts occur across the schools.

"When the situation involves parental complaints, suspension, or media coverage, it comes to our attention," says Beatty. "Many go unreported, many are only the knowledge of the principals."

"Between the Luciens and Bayshore, I've never seen such a bitter and long conflict," says Ray Sunstrum, a social worker and chairperson of the education committee at the National Capital Alliance on Race Relations.

Sunstrum, at the request of the Luciens, is attempting to resolve the conflict. He attended a meeting in January with the Luciens and the school administration.

"I've been actively involved in dealing with racism in schools for seven years," says Sunstrum. "For things to get better, there needs to be a willingness to recognize the problem."

The school administration has made attempts to resolve the conflict, which include:
· Transferring Michelle to a different grade 5 class.
· Transferring a girl who fights with Michelle out of the school.
· Suggesting Michelle has behavioural problems and should seek counseling.
· Suggesting Michelle leave the school, according to Girlsen Lucien.
· Having various meetings with the Luciens the superintendent of the Carleton Board of Education, and outside mediation agencies.
· Seeking outside mediation, which the Luciens denied.

Lucien says she doesn't believe that the school wants to resolve the conflict.

"Their attitude is so bad," says Lucien. "I see them screw up their faces at Michelle whenever she speaks. They always see her as the problem. The principal even said she had behavioural problems."

Last fall, the Luciens took Michelle to see two psychiatrists. In November, Dr. G. I. Kambites at the children's Hospital of Eastern

Ontario wrote a letter to the Luciens, that Michelle was not by nature a disobedient or delinquent child.

He wrote, "she is a child who has suffered from quite abundant stress and an inability at times to properly ventilate her anger as a result of factors beyond her control." In the letter, he also encouraged the school to deal with the issue of racism.

June Girvain, education officer with the Ministry of Education in Ottawa, says the conflict has not been resolved, partly because the education system is not set up to deal with racial problems.

"This sort of situation happens too often," says Girvain. "The school is a socializing place, with the idea that children should be obedient, the school is not designed to deal with assertive children, especially assertive black children."

Michelle's older brother Deleon, 13, graduated from Bayshore and Michelle's younger sister Natasha, 8, is in grade 3 at Bayshore. Lucien says her other children have had problems, but not as frequently as Michelle.

"Deleon and Natasha are much quieter than Michelle," says Lucien. "Michelle always sticks up for herself. She doesn't think anyone should treat her badly, no matter who they are."

Michelle says there is another black child in her class who never gets picked on by the other children.

"I don't know why they (her classmates) always bother me," says Michelle. "Maybe because I talk back and I hit back and I know I have rights."

Sunstrum says the situation has not been resolved because the school administration is not recognizing the problem of racism.

"Racism is a taboo subject in schools, but it is there," says Sunstrum. "In my experience, when racism comes up, schools always deny that it could be there. If you don't recognize the problem, you can't find a solution. The school system doesn't deal with racism."

Sunstrum says he has witnessed school psychologists telling racist jokes and guidance counsellours using racial slurs to describe children. He says educators must learn how to deal with racism. He's planning workshops for principals in Quebec for April and May.

"The workshop will help principals to understand what racism is and what it does to those who experience it," says Sunstrum. "Hopefully, training like this may help in stopping problems before they happen."

Girvain says part of resolving the conflict may come from the child. She says often the child's point of view is not sought in resolving the situation.

Michelle says she thinks that if her classmates were taught that racism is wrong, she wouldn't be called so many names.

"We never talk about racism in class," says Michelle. "When there are posters and stickers at school saying 'Let's Stop Racism,' the kids always pull them down, and I find them in the garbage. I tell the teacher and they do nothing about it."

The school administration of Bayshore said they are too busy to comment on the issue of antiracist education and the number of racial incidents in the school.

"I am inundated with report cards right now," says Margaret Pimm-Dupuch, presently acting principal.

Girvain says that resolving the conflict is vital to the well being of the child in these situations.

"The troubling question is, how does what's happening now surface in the child in grade 8 and 12?" asks Girvain. "When this happens to some children, they internalize it. Others like Michelle fight it and get a reputation. By time I hear of the situation, it's often too late to help."

When the alarm clock wakes Michelle up in the morning, she tries to pretend to her mother that she didn't hear it and is still sleeping.

"I try to get up as late as I can, because maybe I won't have to go to school then," she says.

Lucien says despite all the days Michelle has missed from school because of suspensions and doctor appointments to check her bruises, her grades include some B's.

Michelle hates school. She says the only reason she even goes is because she likes her new teacher. She also says that not everyone picks on her. She does have good friends.

Michelle says the greatest part of her day is when it's time to leave.

Michelle says she only feels safe at home. Sitting on a chair in her living room, she pulls up her pants. Her legs are covered with scars and bruises. Michelle gingerly fingers a bruise below her left knee.

"This one is still sore," she says.

Michelle's mother is very concerned with all the bruises her daughter is getting from her school experiences.

"We know that those bruises aren't just skin deep," says Lucien. " I just hope one day all the scars from this will heal."

Up to Us

In Creative Writing, Media Writing, Writing (all kinds) on **April 26, 2009** at **14:59**

Scene 1 – (Sun is setting and Jake Watkins sits at his dining room table snorting fine white powder into his nose. When he is done, he clears away any remaining traces of the powder and sits back in the chair and waits to feel good. Soon a smile appears on his face and he knocks over the chair when he gets up).

Jake: (screaming to an empty room) I need a par-tee, man! (Jake starts dancing around, swinging his arms, and knocking over a pot of flowers and a sculpture that were in his way. Then he grabs his car keys from the dining room table and leaves the house, wit h the door left wide open).

Scene blacks out

Scene 2 – (After midnight, Mrs. Watkins is packing across the floor, while on the telephone, in the kitchen.)

Mrs. Watkins: I wouldn't be so worried if he would have at least left a note…(pause)…Well, Jake has been acting very strange lately, I just don't know why. He fights with Rikki all the time, he's always disappearing like this. I just don't know what to do with him anymore…(pause)…OK…thank you Wendy, I'll call you if I go into another frenzy. (Mrs. Watkins hangs up the phone).

(Rikki and Clyde enter the kitchen).

Rikki: Hi Mom, what's up?

Mrs. Watkins: (glaring disapprovingly at Rikki and Clyde) Where have you been?

Rikki: Clyde and I went to see a movie. Is something wrong? Where's Jake?

Mrs. Watkins: Your brother is missing again. He wasn't at school all day. I was just talking with Milo's mother. Milo isn't at home either. Mrs. Redmond doubts that Milo is with Jake.

Rikki: (sounding nervous) Have you tried calling his regular hangouts? He might be at the Pizzaplace or Walt's Bar?

Mrs. Watkins: No, I haven't, but he should be home by now. I think it is time that I called the police.

Rikki: That's not a good idea, Mom. Jake hasn't been missing for 24 hours yet. If he's at some party with people we don't know, and we get the police after him, he'll be embarrassed.

Mrs. Watkins: (frustrated) Then he should have told me where he was going. Why is he doing this to me? Why does he think he can do whatever he wants?

Rikki: Why don't you give me a chance to find him before you involve the police?

Mrs. Watkins: Fine, Rikki. I just hope that you do find him. I had to cancel a date with Richard tonight because of Jake. Let him know, if you find him, that I am very upset with him.

Rikki: Yeah, anything you say, Mom. (Rikki grabs Clyde and steers him out of the kitchen).

(Rikki and Clyde exit the house and enter Clyde's car).

Clyde: Your mother really hates me, doesn't she?

Rikki: Honestly, yes. (Rikki laughs at the horrified look on Clyde's face). Don't worry about it though. It really doesn't matter to me what she thinks. She knows I hate her boyfriend Richard, but she doesn't let that bother her. My mother hates to let anything bother her. That's why Jake is really going to get it when he comes home.

Clyde: What's wrong with Jake anyway? He seems to be throwing his life away. I remember the days when he was just like Milo, nauseously nerdy. Football hero, a brainer, Mr. Popularity. Now his name gets called to the vice-principal's office almost as much as mine does.

Rikki: I don't know (a distracted look appears on her face). He used to tell me everything that was on his mind. All he ever seems to enjoy anymore is being by himself, or with all these scummy people who don't go to Leabay. Half of them look like high school dropouts. I don't know what's going on, unless, it has something to do with…

Clyde: (He turns into the parking lot of the Pizzaplace) Something to do with what?

Rikki: (Lowering her voice) When I was looking for my Beatles album in his room, I found a bag of cocaine under his bed.

Clyde: (nervously) Cocaine? (He parks the car and turns the engine off).

Rikki: Yup. When I asked him about it, he got really upset and told me to mind my own business. I decided to try and forget about it. My brother is not the type to do drugs. If he was doing them, I would know.

Clyde: I'm sure that Jake wouldn't be mixed up with the drug scene. (Rikki and Clyde looked for Jake at the Pizzaplace with no luck. Next they check Walt's Bar also with no luck).

Clyde: I guess your mother is going to call the police (he pulls away from Walt's Bar).

Rikki: Just stop at a pay phone. I want to at least try Milo. (They go to a phone and dial Milo's number).

Voice through the phone: Hello, Redmond residence.

Rikki: May I please speak to Milo?

Milo: Rikki, it's me. I'm really glad you called. Jakes' here and he's in pretty bad shape.

Rikki: Where has he been? My mother almost phoned the police.
Milo: Well, tell her not to worry anymore, but don't tell her where he is. Your mother shouldn't have to see this.
Rikki: What the hell is going on, Milo?
Milo: Besides a few bruises, some which I think he did to himself, he's alright.
Rikki: (yelling) What happened, Milo?
Milo: Rikki, shut up and get over here. (Rikki hears a dial tone and hangs up the phone. Soon she enters Clyde's car).
Rikki: Step on it, Jake is at Milo's house.
Scene blacks out.
Scene 3 – (Clyde's car pulls into the Redmond's circular driveway. Rikki hops out of the car).
Clyde: Rikki, I hope you don't' mind, but I should really get home now.
Rikki: Bye, Clyde. (Rikki keeps running as she sys be to Clyde. Before she rings the doorbell, Milo opens the door and grabs Rikki's hand to pull her inside).
Milo: What took you so long? He's sleeping now. (Milo leads Rikki up to his bedroom. There, Jake is lying face down on Milo's bed with a bucket next to him).
Rikki: (Frightened) My God, Jake! (She runs over to him and cradles his bruised face in her arms). Who did this to his face?
Milo: (He grabs Rikki's arms). Let him sleep, Rik. He's been having a lot of nightmares. Come on. (Milo leads Rikki out of the bedroom and into his living room). He was here when your mother called my mother for the second time, but I promised him that I'd pretend I didn't know where he was. (Milo sweeps away the hair out of Rikki's eyes) You look terrible. Should I get you something to drink? A scotch on the rocks, maybe?
Rikki: (Shouting) No, I don't want anything to drink, Milo. Just continue the story, asshole.
Milo: OK…calm down. I felt bad to lie to your Mom, but I promised Jake. When he came, he was shaking badly. He was sweating all over the floor, he was so pale. From what he was trying to tell me it sounds like he owes some guy a lot of money, and when he didn't have it, the guy beat him up.
Rikki: (Confused) Why would Jake have money problems? Mom gives us more than we need. Jake doesn't even spend money. He seems to just wear the same old things all the time.
Milo: He spends his money on drugs, Rikki. Don't you know that?

Rikki: (Defensive) He's not addicted or anything, Milo. I know he has tried it a couple of times, but that's only at parties. It's not like he's…

Milo: Rikki, when is the last time you've seen Jake in school?

Rikki: So, his grades are slipping. Jake can afford to goof off. He's always gotten good grades.

Milo: When's the last time you've seem me at your house, or Jake over here in the past few months? He's my best friend and I hardly hand out with him anymore.

Rikki: I know that you and Jake haven't been as close as you used to be. That doesn't prove anything.

Milo: Rikki, remember when Jake almost got run over because he roamed out in the streets in the middle of the night?

Rikki: He was sleepwalking.

Milo: (Shouting) He was high! Remember the last time he was in school? He was sent to the office because his nose started to bleed.

Rikki: (Screaming) So what! My brother is not some fucking druggie. I would know. He tells me everything.

Milo: (Screaming) He used to. Does he still? I bet he doesn't. He used to tell me everything too. He doesn't do that anymore. He's a different person now. Stop denying it, Rikki.

Rikki: (Bursts into tears) How did this all happen? Could anyone just answer that for me? How did my brother get this way?

Milo: I don't know, Rikki. (Milo puts his arms around her). It's been so long since the old Jake has been around, so long. (Sighs) I remember the first time I started to notice the change in Jake. He was getting so obsessed with his future. Maybe the pressure of always trying to be perfect was too much for him to take.

Rikki: (Mumbling) I know, he has change. I guess he does have a drug problem. (Getting angry) We can't just let it keep happening. We have to get Jake some help.

Milo: (Sighing) I don't know what to do.

Rikki: (Wipes away the tears and says sarcastically) Should we throw away all of his drugs? He won't be able to use them, then.

Milo: No, Rikki, he's only get more, I know that. He should be in a rehab centre.

Rikki: Sometimes they don't work.

Milo: They don't work when the person addicted doesn't want them to work.

Rikki: Maybe we should go after the bastard who beat Jake up.

Milo: That's the police's job.

Rikki: Are they doing it right? I think not. They obviously need some help. (Rikki walks over to the bay window in the living room). My father always told me that if you want something done, it has to be done yourself. Even on his deathbed he would tell me that if you have faith in yourself, you don't need to have faith in others. I've always believed, anybody can do anything that they really set their mind on doing.

Milo: (Shaking his head) I don't think you're making much sense. What are you saying, Rikki?

Rikki: (Serious) I'm saying that if we really want to help Jake, we have to do it ourselves. It's up to us. We can help Jake by eliminating one his major problems, the drugs. We an deliver to the police the drug dealer.

Milo: That is a stupid idea, Rikki! It will never work, and it's far too dangerous to get involved in.

Rikki: Do you have a better idea, Milo?

Milo: Yes, I do. Jake should go into a rehab centre. The only way we can help him is to notify the police, and give him all the love and support he will need to combat his problem.

Rikki: Fine, Milo, I agree with you. However, just because we go with your idea, doesn't mean that mine couldn't work. We can still get the police on the case, but we'll just do a bit of our own investigative work.

Milo: We don't have the right to interfere, Rikki.

Rikki: My bother and your best friend is addicted to drugs. Leabay is swarming with drugs, and there's a code of silence that police officers would find difficult to break. However, we could do it Milo. Detective work isn't that hard. All we have to do is come up with a good plan, follow it through, and be happy. It's that simple.

Milo: We don't have the right to interfere, Rikki. Drug dealers handle their business in a way that is out of our league.

Rikki: The scum that's helping to destroy the people at Leabay, people like Jake, has to be stopped. People die from drugs every day and all the time. If we can do anything to help the situation, let's go for it. Do you want to help Jake or not?

Milo: Rikki, I really don't think…

Rikki: Milo, I'm going to help my brother with or without you.

Milo: (Staring into Rikki's eyes). I guess I have no choice then.

Rikki: (Throwing her arms around Milo) You won't regret this.

Milo: I already do.

Scene blacks out.

Scene 4 – (Milo's bedroom next morning – following scene plays out with music) Jake awakes and instantly wants more drugs. Milo and Rikki urge him to admit that he has a problem with drugs. When Jake takes a good look at himself in the mirror, he admits he has a problem, but refuses to go into a rehab centre. Jake promises to go cold turkey with drugs from then on. He lasts for a week. He crashes up his car and almost kills a pregnant woman in the other car of the accident. The woman has a healthy pre-mature baby, and Jake enters the Carry Crescent Drug and Alcohol Rehabilitation Centre. Milo and Rikki try and get information from Jake about who was selling the drugs to him, he's not much help.

Scene blacks out.

Scene 5 – (At Rikki's locker in Leabay High) (Clyde gives Rikki a goodbye kiss by her locker. Milo watches in the distance, and waits until Clyde leaves to approach Rikki).

Milo: (Agitated) You spend way too much time with that clown.

Rikki: His name is Clyde, now clown. He happens to be a very nice guy.

Milo: (Looking at the diamond on Rikki's finger) Did he give that to you?

Rikki: Yes.

Milo: How can he afford that? Actually a better question would be, how can you accept that?

Rikki: When my boyfriend gives me such a generous gift, I accept.

Milo: Well, he's definitely not rich. I'm just wondering how he manages to shower you with diamonds.

Rikki: I don't know. He works a lot, that's why I hardly see him. But you know, absence makes the heart grow fonder.

Milo: Or buying love makes the heart seem bigger.

Rikki: Got to hell, Milo. Do you have anything interesting to say?

Milo: Actually I do. I have come up with a brilliant plan.

Rikki: Well, what is it?

Milo: What better way to get in deep with drug dealers then to buy their product. Or, at least pretend to buy it. The regular users are easy to spot. All we have to do, or me…

Rikki: If anyone is going to pretend to be a buyer, it'll be me. You're too visible in this school. The minute anyone found out that you were interested in buying they wouldn't be convinced, and it would be the talk of the school.

Milo: Must I remind you once again about the danger of the situation, there is danger.

Rikki: The point I'm trying to make, Milo, is that if I am the buyer, people would believe it. I am considered the bad Watkins kid around this school, at least before Jake started messing up.

Milo: Rikki, you're not Nancy Drew, OK? What we're about to do is not some adventurous plot line to some fictitious book. This is the real thing. There might not be happy ending to all this.

Rikki: Just because I'm younger than you Milo, I don't deserve to be treated like a child. In my 17 years of living I have learned a lot of things about myself, one of them is that I'm not stupid.

(The bell rings for class).

Milo: Fine, Rikki, I'll give in to you once again. (Milo turns on his heel and heads towards his class).

Rikki: (Quietly to herself) There's no time like the present. I should start putting my Nancy Drew impression to work right now. (She puts her books back in her locker and takes her jacket out. She heads outside of the school to the tennis courts. She spots who she's looking for and approaches the girl).

Rikki: Hey, Pats, what's up?

Pats: (Getting ready to light a joint) The sky's up, Rik. What do you want?

Rikki: Is that any way to talk to your long lost friend?

Pats: Long lost is right! Ever since you've been going out with Clyde, you don't even have time to blow your stinking breath in my face.

Rikki: Sorry, Pats.

Pats: Don't sorry me, just try and remember who introduced you to him.

Rikki: Of course I remember, pats. Why do you think I'm here now, I'm craving for your company.

Pats: (Surprised) Really? (She hands the joint over to Rikki) After what happened to your brother, you can probably use this more than I do.

Rikki: (She takes the joint, turns her head, and pretends to take a drag). How do you know about that? My brother is confidential information.

Pats: Everything that happens in Leabay never remains confidential. You have to be pretty crafty, or dangerous to keep secrets in this school.

Rikki: (Handing the joint back to Pats) Where could I get this stuff, Pats?

Pats: (Laughs harshly) If you only knew.

Rikki: What do you mean by that?

Pats: Nothing, Rik. Why do you want to know anyway? Drugs aren't your scene.

Rikki: Well, I've had a lot on my mind lately. My mother's dating a major league loser, my brother's going to court for driving intoxicated, and I've been having horrible nightmares about my Dad. Is that enough reason for you?

Pats: That sounds real rough, Rik, but I don't know. My supplier is real picky about who he sells to.

Rikki: Pats, I don't see the problem here. I just need a little to help me feel more up. Just enough to get me through the times I'm having now.

Pats: (Reluctantly) OK Rik. I'll see what I can do. I'll you tonight.

Rikki: Thanks, Pats. You're a true friend. (Rikki starts heading back to school).

Pats: Only when you need something, Rikki.

Scene blacks out.

Scene 6 – (Rikki's bedroom – scene plays to music). Rikki gets the phone call from Pats. Pats gives her a time and location to meet the dealer the next afternoon. Rikki fills Milo in on what's going on. Rikki gets to Walt's Bar at 3:00 p.m. to meet the dealer. He never shows up. Next day, Rikki tries to find Pats to ask her what happened, but Pats won't talk to her and she also has a black eye. When Rikki questions Pats about the eye, all she says is that Rikki better find another dealer because hers won't sell to her. Pats warns her that if Rikki keeps trying to get drugs from her dealer, Pats is the one that will get hurt. Rikki and Milo both discouraged, question Jake some more about who his supplier is. Jake tells them he never got a good look at the guy's face because he was always wearing a hat and sunglasses. Rikki, Clyde, Milo and Mrs. Watkins all go with Jake for his court trial for driving under the influence of drugs. Jake gets his license revoked for three years, has to stay in the rehab centre for at least three months, and is on probation for six months after that. Jake takes the verdict hard. In a long conversation with Milo after the trial, Rikki confides in Milo that she is really worried that they'll never find the drug dealers in their school. Milo encourages her that he has a strong suspect in mind, and if he's right, then they can call the police. The next day, Milo skips school and follows around a guy, dressed in a hat and sunglasses, the camera never focuses on his face, but Milo knows who it is. Milo witnesses the disguised man selling joints to Pats.

Scene blacks out.

Scene 7 – (In the school's library. Rikki comes in to look for Milo. She finds him trying to get some homework done).

Rikki: Milo, I've been looking for you. Why weren't you in school yesterday?
Milo: I had a little investigating I had to do.
Rikki: Did you find out anything?
Milo: Yes.
Rikki: (Angrily) Don't be an asshole, Milo. What did you find out? Is it time to call the police or what?
Milo: You might not want to that anymore.
Rikki: What the hell is going on, Milo?
Milo: (Looking Rikki directly in the eye). The drug dealer we're about to throw in jail is Clyde.
Rikki: (Confused) Clyde who?
Milo: Your boyfriend, Rikki. (Rikki stays silent for a good minute).
Rikki: I can't believe that, Milo.
Milo: It's true, Rikki. I've had this funny feeling for a while now that Clyde isn't what he appears to be. I thought maybe if I tapped in the gossip grapevine I could find out something about him. But no one has anything to say about Clyde Allen.
Rikki: I can't believe it.
Milo: The description that Jake gave us about his dealer, the height mats Clyde's and the build. The way Jake says that the guy had such a strong jaw, it sounded like Clyde. That only fueled my suspicions.
Rikki: I can't believe it.
Milo: I followed him all day yesterday. I saw him selling drugs to Pats. When he gave the drugs to Pats, he took off the sunglasses, I could make a positive ID.
Rikki: If Clyde was a dealer, especially Pats' dealer, she would have told me.
Milo: Not if she thought it was going to get her another black eye, or worse.
Rikki: If Clyde was a dealer, Jake would have recognized him.
Milo: Not with the hat he wears. It covers any trace of his hair. Plus, the sunglasses cover half his face, and he puts on a fake earring and moustache.
Rikki: How could it be Clyde, he's just not like that. Clyde is not like that.
Milo: (Grabbing Rikki's finger with the diamond ring on it). How did he afford this, Rikki? How does he afford that flashy blue convertible of his? How does he afford to take you out all the time? He spoils you, you love it, but he's spoiling you with drug money.

(Rikki jumps up and runs out of the library. Milo follows her. Rikki heads towards the empty tennis courts straight towards Pats, who is smoking a joint).

Rikki: Pats, I need to ask you some questions, I need the truth.

Pats: Leave me along, Rikki, Every time I talk to you, trouble starts.

Rikki: (Tears staining her cheeks) Is Clyde a drug dealer?

Pats: (Shocked and frightened) Who the hell told you that, Rikki?

Rikki: Never mind who told me that, I'm asking you to tell me now.

Pats: That's ridiculous, Rik. Clyde would never…

Rikki: Pats, if you don't tell me the truth, I'll go to Clyde and confront him. I'll also tell him that you told me. If he's the one that gave you the black eye, you'll be lucky to be alive once I…

Pats: Fuck off, Rikki, just leave me along. Clyde's not a dealer.

Rikki: (Angrily) I meant it pats, either you tell me the truth, or Clyde will.

Pats: (Taking a deep drag on the joint) Oh shit, please leave me alone, Rik. None of this is my business.

Rikki: Tell me Pats, I need to know.

Pats: Leave me alone, bitch.

Rikki: Fine. I'll have to talk to Clyde then. (Rikki starts walking away quickly towards the school).

Pats: Wait! (Pats catches up with Rikki).

Rikki: What do you have to say, Pats? I'm in a hurry.

Pats: (Hesitatingly) Clyde is a dealer. He doesn't use the stuff himself. He just does it for the money. Makes him feel like a big man to act rich. And he enjoys impressing you with all that shit he's always giving you. Don't be so hard on him, Rik. Just pretend you know nothing.

Rikki: Pats, he was knowingly selling drugs to my brother. He's probably the one who beat him up. He's kept this all a secret from me, and has done nothing but lie to me. He told me that he's a dishwasher at some diner along the highway. I admired him for being so hardworking.

Pats: Rik, do you really think that a rich girl like you would have stayed with a poor ass like Clyde for long? If he wasn't constantly flashing his money around you, you would have said 'so long' a long time ago.

Rikki: I don't care, Pats. He's a drug dealer, a liar, and a fake. He's going to get what's coming to him.

Pats: Rikki, I beg you, don't do anything. (She clutches on to Rikki before she almost falls. He'll kill me, Rikki. He'd kill you too if it kept him from jail).

Rikki: (Surprised) He would?

Pats: He wouldn't do it himself, but he'd get someone else to do it.
Clyde: Who would do what?
(Both girls turn around shocked to see Clyde approaching them).
Pats: Nothing, Clyde.
Rikki: Clyde, I was just about going to look for you. (Acting sweet).
Clyde: (He tries to kiss Rikki, but gets her cheek instead) I've been looking for you too, but I didn't expect to find you here.
Rikki: I just wanted to say hi to Pats. We haven't said much to each other in a while now…(awkward silence)…Clyde, I wanted to make sure that we were still going to that Spanish restaurant tonight?
Clyde: Definitely, I've already made the reservations.
Rikki: Good, I'll be waiting at 8…(awkward silence)…Pats, I have the car today. Why don't I give you a ride home?
Pats: (She notices the expression on Rikki's face) Sure.
(Rikki and Pats say goodbye to Clyde and head towards the parking lot).
Scene blacks out.

Scene 8 – (Rikki's bedroom – scenes under music) Milo already knows what happened because he was watching the whole thing behind some bushes. Rikki tells Milo her plan over the phone, and how she had to threaten pats to be a part of it. The plan is that Pats will call Clyde for a buy to be done while he's having dinner with Rikki. That's when Rikki would call the police. Pats will be a little late, to give the police more time to arrive. Hopefully they'll be on time to catch Clyde. Rikki uses her acting skills to be with Clyde that night. The plan was put into action when Clyde left the table saying he had to go call his mother. Pats shows up, then the police. Clyde takes Pats as hostage to save himself from the police. His getaway is interfered with by Milo. Milo uses a knife to try and get Pats away from Clyde, Clyde has a gun and shoots Milo to get out of his way, the bullet hits Milo in the arm. Rikki runs after Clyde and begs him to let go of Pats. Clyde lets go of Pats in return for Rikki. Rikki begs him to give up. The police thinking that Rikki is an accomplice with Clyde, threatens to shoot both of them. Clyde decides to give himself up.

Last part of scene is of Jake, lying still on the floor of his rehab centre room. A nurse finds him and calls for an ambulance. When the paramedics come they pronounce him dead of a drug overdose.
Scene blacks out.
Scene 9 – (After Jakes' funeral, Milo and Rikki sit silently by Jake's grave. Milo's arm is in a cast).

Milo: (Sadly) I'll never be able to understand any of this. He threw away his life. Then he had a second chance, and he threw that away too. I don't' know if I'm mad or sad.

Rikki: I know, you almost lost your life for him, and he decided to throw his life away. (Rikki laughs sarcastically). What good has come out of this?

Milo: (Shocked) What are you saying, Rikki? Clyde's in jail now. Maybe he'll start choosing an honest profession from now on. Pats realizes that she needs help, she's getting it.

Rikki: My brother is dead. I miss him so much already.

Milo: (Putting his arms around Rikki) So do I. Don't ever forget that I'll be there for you, Rikki. We'll survive this together. OK?

Rikki: OK.

Scene blacks out and a list of statistics of how many people are addicted to drugs and die from every year appears.

Miracle Makeover

In [Beauty](), [Business](), [Writing (all kinds)]() on **April 28, 2009** at **07:27**

On my way to Urban Textures Salons on 44 Gerrard St. W. I lost the hat that was covering the recent and awful weave I had received. It was an afro weave, done with synthetic hair, but I came with great expectations to put my head in the hands of Urban Textures's owner Christos Cox and his team.

He's come a long way from his first salon in Glendower. The décor of the place is welcoming, down-to-earth and warm.

"Everyone comes in here and they feel comfortable. We put a lot of effort into creating the atmosphere of the salon – everything from the colours to the logo on our shirts," said Cox.

Rose Hibbert, the weave specialist, took out the synthetic hair so fast; I barely knew what was happening. My hair has not been chemically-treated in more than a decade, but I have been wearing synthetic extensions of and on and five wigs – one of them which claims to be human hair by the woman who sold it to me.

During my consultation, Cox's analysis of my hair is that based on what he could see is that I'm a natural, an earth lover; I have a love for the natural. But, he said my vice could be colour. (My natural colour is jet black)

"You could go two, three textures and it would look softer and something that matches your undertones. The mahoganies the reds, the dark, dark blondes would all be good," Cox said.

He approved of my image to stay true to myself in the industry I'm in. He promised me I would leave that day with "bouncing and behaving" hair.

The problems I have with my scalp are water-based type funguses. The synthetic hair is material and contributes to this. He said he could also see scaring from relaxers and perms I have had in the past. He did say the damage was nothing major.

"They're working with worse chemicals than the sodium hydroxide [with synthetic hair]. We're not magicians, we can't solve it first time off, and we're practicing to get better, but not practicing what we've done forever. That's what Urban Textures is all about"

Now I knew that Urban Textures wasn't cheap – and I'm on a budget – so one of the first things on my mind was how I could maintain the health and look of my hair without going broke.

"You could buy home-care products that we recommend. Come in on a week-to-week basis, we sell packages, loyalty packages you can get 30 per cent, 40 per cent off," said Cox. Since colour is done best on dirty hair, the colour specialist did a great job. We decided on auburn and chocolate with highlights that would look good when I wear it in an afro.

"You need to deposit a lot of moisture on the hair if you have colour," said the colour specialist. "Make sure you moisture, moisture, moisture and it will be okay"

Cox says that cotton is a big moisture stealer. "A lot of people don't know that you can have bouncing and behaving hair with super curly hair. You can absolutely condition it to do anything. I have several clients that people don't know they have an afro."

"We respect relaxers, we do them every day. It is damaging the hair – relaxers damage the hair. But, we do them with respect. We do them to the most integrity. We do not relax to the extent it becomes bone straight."

Cox added that they try to take 65 per cent to 75 per cent to the maximum of straightening. "Curly hair is prone to be dry because there is a lot of protein that makes up that hair. It tends to be dry, dehydrated, and less porous. We have to do what we can to retain the moisture. That's the biggest issue. As Puffy would say, 'we try to moisturize the situation and preserve all the sexy.' That's something we would like to share with the industry. Our people are taught to feel the difference in the hair. It's stuff I was taught by mentors of mine. One of my mentors was a gentleman at Omari's [in Montreal] who is now a pastor in Halifax and is still doing hair. Literally God told me to hire this man and assist him. He taught me everything I know about hair and finding the moisture. I had to look for that squeaky clean. It's about making your hair canvas [like an artist]. All hair requires that to make it a canvas."

There are a lot of great hairdressers that share the same philosophy. André Walker who does Oprah hair shares the same philosophy.

"I have an addiction, and it's to making people look beautiful," says Cox. "I have an addiction to smoothing hair." He's even like that with his jeans which had a stain probably from the Oragina drink that he's also addicted to.

Urban Textures is specifically designed to target the multi-ethnic demographic of today and of the future.

"Our target is to be the multi-ethnic salon – just based on the fact of the paradigm shift in the population. Unless Canada commits to developing the designated groups Canada will not have the pool of trained resources to compete in the world market. Places like Eaton had forgotten the market of XXX clothes and this in part is why they went under. We're not going to be caught blind-sided like Eaton. By 2010 the Chinese and Indian community will represent the largest portion of the population and whites will be in the minority. Each and every person that works in the company needs to be sociologically sound."

Cox runs a shop where there will not be telling of Muslim jokes.

Pictures were snapping to capture all the beautiful moments in the salon that evening. I hadn't felt that good about my natural looks in a long time. Thanks to everyone at Urban Textures.

There are two locations in Toronto: 44 Gerrard St. W. at Bay, across the street from the Delta Chelsea. They're also in Scarborough at McCowan and 401 – across from CTV.

Lofty Living (Originally Published in New Dreamhomes and Condominiums Magazine)

In [Home Decor](), [Writing (all kinds)]() on **April 28, 2009** at **09:12**

He's young, hip, running a raw food and vegetarian restaurant downtown and owns a couple of properties for rental. His name is Chris Italiano and where he calls home is a two-storey loft at 1029 King Street West.

"It's a nice open space, that's what the advantages are," Italiano says. "It has bright high ceilings, big windows. It's an open space you can do pretty much what you want to it."

The loft development went up six years ago. Italiano is the original owner.

The loft has a brick interior, stainless steel appliances and big windows. The floors are hard-wood and there are tiles in the washrooms and downstairs in the kitchen. One level has the kitchen; the washroom is on the same floor, plus an open space. It goes upstairs with a bedroom and a big walk-in closet with a balcony railing to look over.

Italiano's sister Jennifer is a new mom and took over the space for awhile. Chris Italiano will be moving back soon. He first bought the condo six years ago because he needed a change from renting.

"I was tired of renting and it was my birthday," Italiano says. "I was tired of paying people $1400 to live and it was just cool living and it was trendy at the time. It still is."

Tony Griffin a real estate agent for Re/Max has many satisfied customers in loft/condo homes. He would call the kind of space Italiano is living in as the "warm and fuzzy" style of a loft/condo, out of two types.

"When you're talking in terms of lofts…there are two distinct styles, but they can take any of a variety of forms," Griffin says. "One of them is concrete. The merchandise building is an excellent example of that. Ceilings of 12 feet and the walls and ceiling left bare. As compared to the Candy Factory, that has exposed brick and large beams that dot the ceiling and support structures. [They have] wood floors and large impressive beams that have been (built) years and years ago."

Something like the Candy Factory and Italiano's loft is called "warm and fuzzy." The style of the merchandise building and those loft/condos that have concrete is called "cool."

Griffin says the condo market itself is really a big part of the housing market. The loft is a boutique area of that kind of market.

"We'll call it the loft craze," Griffin says. "That's the way it evolved in the mid to late 90's and early part of the new century. It really started with a focus on one of the most popular projects in the downtown area and that was the Candy Factory. That was kicked off, about 1994 when Harry Stinson kicked off the Candy Factory project. It was like a pent-up demand. People who had heard about lofts were just dying to find out what it was all about."

Griffin says lofts have been built in Toronto since the 1980's, but they were a secret.

"The Candy Factory spawned these other developments and possibly the largest in Canada is the merchandise building," Griffin says. "[It's] located on Dalhousie and Jarvis and Dundas area. It's an enormous project. The merchandise building has something in the order of

600 residents varying in size from about 700 square feet to well over 2000."

Griffin says the loft/condo market is a strong part of the housing market, but a small part.

"It will probably continue to be very popular in new construction projects," Griffin says. "Not the conversion of an existing building, but new construction of loft-style condominiums."

Italiano says his six-year-old loft/condo at King and Strachan is a good home to have for now. He says when he thinks of a "true" loft, he thinks of the one in "Flash Dance," the movie.

"My dream would be to have the floor of a warehouse."

Is Journalism Education Becoming Obsolete due to Citizen Journalism?

In Education, Opinion, Writing (all kinds) on **April 28, 2009** at **10:40**

It seems as though anyone can pick up a video camera, a microphone and start a blog today and call themselves a journalist. What does this mean for journalism education?

Journalism education does not have a long history. Actually the first journalists, such as Ernest Hemingway were not actually trained in journalism. Journalists like William Zinsser were not trained in journalism either. Journalism education is a fairly recent phenomena especially in places such as Canada, where Carleton University was the first journalism school back in the 1940s. Before that, the newspaper men and women who delivered the current events were trained in other areas.

It seems as though things are coming back to those early days. The Internet is drastically changing the access that anyone can have to producing journalism. This is known as citizen journalism. Ordinary citizens are starting to pick up video cameras, a microphone, and start blogs, as well as posting information on YouTube to get their voices heard – just like journalists. In many ways this is a good thing, however – does it continue to make journalism education relevant?

I would argue that journalism education is still relevant. Many of the successful blogs that exist today are actually about mainstream news events. This shows that the mainstream news, filled with journalists that have graduated from such schools as Carleton University, Columbia University, Northwestern University and Ryerson University are still being put to good use by adding to the blogosphere. As well, because we still live in a paper driven society where the credentials one has are extremely important in landing paid work, journalism education continues to be important for the purposes of people with interests in the media to find and keep a job. It is a reality that many people who have their own blogs do not make a lot of money from it. It is possible, although people like Matt Drudge of the Matt Drudge Report are more an exception rather than the rule.

The Internet can actually be used to help improve the level of journalism education. There is more information on the web about what journalism is about and understanding media – this information can be used by professors to make the classroom a more vibrant place.

When it comes to journalism education and getting a job in journalism, it is also important about the contacts you have. Going to a credible journalism school ensures that you will have access to people who can help you to find a job. This is something that will surely help journalism schools not to become obsolete.

When I look back on my own journalism education it was one of the best things I could have done. Most people that get into journalism do so because they want to write. Going to journalism school gave me the chance to do this and make my mistakes while I was in school so I could perform better in the job market. I received many opportunities while I was school, such as traveling to Germany, Belgium and Holland and co-producing a documentary that is now in the library of the city where I went to school. Producing that documentary helped me to be involved with other documentary projects. Just being at the school started a long working relationship I had with the public broadcaster in my country where working there was like an education on to itself. Later, when I went back to school for a graduate degree, this is what helps me to know about journalism education today and to work in the field, as well as media in general. I teach at the college level and am able to continue working as a journalist to keep current in the field.

A journalism education is important, however, it is true that for anyone that has talent they will do will in the field. Many times this talent can come through work experience that can be honed by doing citizen journalism work. Equipping yourself with a studio environment right in your home can make a difference in getting your name known and out there, making all the difference in the world when you do apply for a job in mainstream or even alternative media.

I teach at a number of schools and have taught at a number of schools in the past. I have seen great success coming out of the students I have taught. Success levels higher than what I have heard from people who did not go to journalism school. Even people that went to school, however did not study journalism is still a viable option for breaking into the field. Many people do become successful this way too.

In conclusion, I would say that although citizen journalism, web based journalism or Internet journalism is a huge phenomenon that is challenging the meaningfulness of mainstream media outlets, many mainstream media outlets are actually combating this situation by "jumping on the bandwagon." Places such as CBS plans to have many of their programs go online so they take advantage of the power of the Internet. The real answer that journalism schools need to do to find a solution to the challenge of citizen journalism is to make sure they are offering courses and programs that answer to the power of the web. Their students must be prepared to work in the virtual world and prepare to potentially receive employment that is completely web based. This is future; things will not change any time soon.

Does Online Education Pack on the Freshman 30?

In Education, Technology, Writing (all kinds) on **May 4, 2009** at **07:42**

Distance education can be seen as quite a sedentary act. If you are sitting at the computer for hours on end, without any exercise…this could be something that could help someone put on weight.

Even for people who go to school that is not online, reports have shown that many young people are gaining 15 pounds from eating cafeteria food in their first year at college or university. What happens if you are studying by correspondence? Does online education pack on the freshman 30?

Many students who are young people and older people who chose to sit at their computer to take their courses lead busy lives. Many times their reasons for not physically going to college or university is because it is simply more convenient for them to study and to take classes from home. They have the advantage of being part of a social network with education at its focus. It is easier to squeeze in the time to do the lessons.

Many of us also know that as we spend a lot of time at home in front of the computer, it is much easier to reach the refrigerator, order a meal or take time to cook a meal. The urge to get hungry could happen often and there may be no one around to manage our eating habits. A student who studies from home could be eating just as badly as some of the food in the cafeterias on the campuses of colleges and universities all over North America. The virtual campus is accessible by computer, plus a bag of Doritos to munch on while you are doing your homework.

Doritos, added with too many servings of Kraft Dinner, plus some french fries ordered at Swiss Chalet could end up doing more damage – if coupled with inactivity. At least the freshman student on a college or university campus gets the opportunity to walk around.

The question still remains unanswered though. Does online education pack on the freshman 30? At the end of the day and at the end of your semesters, that may be more a question of how active virtual students are in their lives when they are off the computer. Are they making time to go to the gym? Are they taking time to have breaks so they can go on walks? Do they have children that are helping them keep fit by having to chase after them? Do they work in physically strenuous employment? Are they meeting with other online students to study the course material? Is the act of typing alone an exercise more physical than it is mental?

With these questions answered by each student who is studying over the Internet, it would be easier to determine if online students would actually gain more weight than students who actually have to get up and go to classes. I will attempt to use my own experience as an example.

When I was doing my undergraduate education, I lived a fair distance from the school. It would take about 40 minutes to walk there one way. Due to the fact that I did not have a lot of money when I was in school, I would walk to school to save on bus transportation costs. So I did receive exercise walking to and from school. This was different from when I was in my first year of university when I lived on campus. At this time, I avoided eating the cafeteria food and lived on Hickory Sticks and Skor bars in fear of gaining weight. I would walk through the tunnel system and spend as much time walking as I could. I also spent a lot of time in the first semester going out dancing at clubs in a city not far from the school.

In my second year though, and subsequent years, I would walk 80 minutes a day, plus work out at the school gym. This kept my weight down low. As well, when I was in graduate school, my weight was higher than it was in my first experience with higher education, however I would still take time to exercise.

Studying online is similar to working many desk type jobs. Once I got into the world of work, I would spend a lot of time at the computer and exercise became less important to me. I have found over the years that a lack of exercise is one reason why I am not even close to the weight I was at during my school days. I would imagine that the same would happen to a student who was studying through distance education and lived a non-active lifestyle. Perhaps it would be possible to gain more weight through the experience of a virtual classroom compared to studying on a campus.

OK, now it is time to discuss solutions to the potential of packing on the freshman 30 through a web course or program. Now that the problem has been presented, it would be important for anyone who is studying in a virtual classroom to also make sure they are doing physical exercise. It would also be important to make sure your food choices are healthy ones, because everyone has to eat – at least most of us. Choosing fresh fruits and vegetables, versus a bag of Doritos or Lays would be the first and obvious choice. Reducing one's amount of coffee intake to a maximum of one a day would be ideal for your health. Coffee is known to stimulate all kinds of things such as diabetes. If you cannot dream of living without coffee, try tea instead. There are so many varieties out there, I am sure whether it is herbal tea or black tea, you would be sure to find one you like. As well, it is important to minimize the amount of meat you eat. It is always better in general and as a rule for even ruling out illnesses such as cancer that you try to choose fish and chicken over beef and pork.

I know these things are hard to do. I am hardly saying I am perfect at it myself even though I know what the right things to do are. Truly the key is exercise. If you can at least get a half hour walk in every day, and I mean on the weekends too, this would really help you to be healthier. If you do not enjoy walking, you can always choose an exercise that truly suits the kind of person you are. As long as you are keeping active…this is the key. This way you can prevent putting on the freshman 30 and continue to have the convenience of studying online.

A Hair Peace (Broadcast on CBC Montreal)

In Beauty, Culture, Education, Health, Media Writing, Opinion, Writing (all kinds) on **May 6, 2009** at **12:21**

My first hobby was playing hairdresser to my Barbie dolls. I had my childhood in the 1970s and 1980s but I was not much different from Black children in the 1940s who chose White dolls over Black dolls in a landmark study that lead to the desegregation of American schools.

It was not that I liked chocolate skin over the cream of white colour; it really came down to the hair. I wanted straight, long, blonde, brunette or red hair, hair that blew in the wind and that I could toss over my shoulder. And when I could not wish it on my head, I used a towel instead.

Get a group of Black women together and the conversation usually turns to hair. If I had an American dollar for every time I've heard a Black woman's hair story, talked about my own hair, seen a hair reference in a movie or read about hair in a book, well I could buy a lot of hair, I could pay to have my own live-in hairdresser. I thought I was the only one who changed my hair just about every week. But I have found that many other women have permed, straightened, coloured, cut, lengthened and shortened their hair as often as I have. My hairstyles have been a sign of the times inside and outside of my head.

Over the past few years I have come to stop wanting Barbie doll hair. I spent many years in hair salons stretching out my super curly hair to dead straight and walking out of the salon with the wind blowing through my hair, and being able to toss it over my shoulder. Who says wishes do not come true – for a price. Although straightening Black hair is known as perming, there was never anything permanent about it for me. There was a war happening on my head, if my hair represented a people, straight strands with the use of chemical warfare were ethnically cleansing the curly strands.

Despite the chemicals, I have always loved the atmosphere of a salon. In this predominantly White country, Black hair salons create a Black world. During the civil rights movement, in North America barber shops and hair salons became town halls for discussions on race relations. Even now, a hair salon in South Carolina is used to educate about AIDS. Places for hair are no strangers to political activity. And it is in a salon where I came at peace with the politics happening on my own head. Hairdressers looking at my natural hair and not ready to open up a jar of Bone Strait has made me rejoice in the hair God gave me.

Professor and author Gloria Wade-Gayles once said, "my hair would be a badge, a symbol of my pride, a statement of self-affirmation. "It has taken me a long time, but I finally agree.

Don't Minimize Children's Anxiety about Pandemics, says Psychiatrist

In [Health](), [Writing (all kinds)]() on **May 13, 2009** at **12:35**

By Gail Bergman and Indira Tarachandra

It takes longer for children than adults to get over traumatic experiences; fears must be addressed to avoid development of more serious conditions

Newmarket, Ontario – May 8, 2009 – The spread and severity of the Influenza A (H1N1) virus may fluctuate as the days go on, but for many children, the anxiety of contracting the mysterious flu remains constant. As a result, parents would be wise to educate and communicate with their kids to calm their fears and avoid the development of more serious conditions later on, says a Canadian psychiatrist.

"Children's anxiety from crisis situations, such as a pandemic, can last one to two years, whereas the average adult may be affected for only a matter of months," says Dr. Rasiah Paramsothy, a psychiatrist at Newmarket-based Southlake Regional Health Centre, explaining that this lag is due to children's limited life's experiences, level of understanding and maturity. "Even for children who are healthy, whose family and classmates are healthy, and who haven't come into contact with anyone who has travelled to Mexico, the fear of contracting the H1N1 flu can be very real."

Parents must be open with their children about the facts and encourage them to express their worries, says Dr. Paramsothy, adding that the next step is to empathize with them and accept their feelings. "Considering the constant flow of media reports, and the fact that H1N1 is a new stream of virus with many unknowns, it's understandable for adults to feel anxious, let alone children," he says.

Brigette Boaretto, a mother of three children aged 8, 6 and 4, knows first-hand about calming young fears about the H1N1 virus. Boaretto is Manager, Infection Prevention and Control at Southlake Regional Health Centre, who has been overseeing the surveillance of patients who have contracted the virus – a situation that has created anxiety in her eight-year-old daughter.

"In addition to having anxiety about me going to work, my youngest son's friend went to Mexico and my daughter is concerned about him going to school," Boaretto says. What has worked best to calm her daughter's fears, says Boaretto, is explaining to her how their whole family can stay healthy by washing their hands often and coughing or sneezing into their sleeves – and encouraging others to do the same. "I gave all three kids a brand new bottle of hand sanitizer and they were all very excited about it. They carry it with them wherever they go and offer it to their friends."

Dr. Paramsothy offers these additional suggestions to manage your child's anxiety:

Share the facts: Allow your child to have full access to information. While parents should act as the sole information source for younger children, older children should supplement their parents' education by reviewing public health pamphlets or visiting their websites. Keep in mind that it's better for children to learn the facts at home rather than hearing half-truths or rumors from friends at school.

Talk it out: Probe, ask questions and encourage your kids to express their thoughts and fears so that you can better understand what's going on in their minds. Be empathetic, but challenge automatic negative thoughts. It's easy for kids to let their imaginations create a worst-case scenario, so do a reality check. Without getting emotional, ask: Is anyone sick around you? Are your friends sick? Have they or their parents been to Mexico recently? and so on.

Use art therapy: Encourage younger children or kids who are withdrawn to communicate using a paper and pencil. Ask them to draw how they feel when they are both healthy and sick. Parents can in turn use art to educate their children about the virus, how it is spread and what it's all about.

Reassure: Keep things in perspective. With one exception, the cases identified in Canada have been mild, and those who have contracted the illness have recovered, largely at home with only bed rest and fluids. Discuss the symptoms of the H1N1 virus with your child, explaining that the illness is similar to a common flu but with a high fever.

Manage stress: If your child is still anxious in spite of your best efforts, try using relaxation techniques as a way to distract the child and regulate his or her emotions. Seek professional help if needed, and speak to your child's teacher or guidance counselor who can carry over your efforts at school. Remember that children will observe adults' behaviors and emotions for cues on how to manage their own feelings, so maintain a positive outlook at all times.

"If a child's fears are not well-managed and persist over time, this may trigger obsessive-compulsive behaviour pertaining to germs and cleanliness, so it's important for parents to take their children's anxieties seriously and address their concerns early on," Dr. Paramsothy says.

More information is available through your local public health office or by visiting www.southlakeregional.org.

About Southlake Regional Health Centre

Based in Newmarket, Southlake Regional Health Centre is a full-service hospital with a specialized focus on cancer, cardiac, arthritis, pediatric and perinatal care, child and adolescent eating disorders, and child and adolescent mental health care. Serving more than one million residents of York Region and South Simcoe, Southlake is in the midst of transforming into a teaching and research centre.

Amanda and her Big Sister (Originally Published with Young People's Press)

In Education, Writing (all kinds) on **May 25, 2009** at **17:23**

A typical preteen girl, Amanda enjoys going to the mall, socializing with her buddies and chatting long distance about life's trials and tribulations with her Big Sister.

The Cambridge girl and her Big Sister, Lindsay Serbu, who works in Windsor, have chatted regularly online since being matched in Big Brother Big Sisters of Canada's (BBBSC) new Digital Heroes program.

"I have a six-year-old brother and my mother wanted me to have a Big Sister. We talk about school, our weekend plans and we are getting to know each other," says Amanda, 12, who cannot be identified under Big Sister policy.

"I'm glad I can support a girl who is approaching her teens," says Serbu, 25, who works for a psychological counseling office and runs a cake decorating business in her spare time. "I can offer her my guidance when she may want it or need it."

Amanda waited five years for her Big Sister. Currently, more than 6,000 boys and girls are waiting lists with Big Brothers and Big Sisters agencies in Ontario. Digital Heroes, an e-mentoring program, is an extension of the traditional mentoring relationship and links a young person via E-mail to an adult mentor.

The program matches volunteers with Internet access to children, allowing a Big Sister Little Sister relationship to develop and flourish online. It not only bridges distance and geography but time constraints on adult volunteers. Instead of committing to two to three hours a week to a face-to-face relationship, volunteers only have to commit to one hour that they can do from their home or office.

Digital Heroes hasn't only given Amanda a non-judgmental friend with whom to share thoughts and concerns, but helps build familiarity with technology and improve literacy skills.

"The program has allowed Amanda to have increased responsibility. E-mailing her Big Sister several times a week has kept her focused," says Amanda's mother, Renee.

Youth matched in Digital Heroes, which is administered by BBBSC and Frontier College, receive a computer with Internet access and training on how to use it. The program, currently available only in Ontario, is expected to expand across Canada.

Computers for the project were contributed by RBC Financial Group and CIBC and upgraded by reBoot Canada. The Ontario's Promise initiative launched the program and formed the partnership.

The major sponsor of Digital Heroes is AOL Canada. John Hamovitch, vice-president of human resources at AOL, says Digital Heroes is a true example of what can be accomplished through partnerships.

"This program brings together technology, innovation and human spirit to benefit children and youth," Hamovitch says. "I applaud Ontario's Promise for their ingenuity and determination to make this program a reality."

Mentoring has far-reaching and beneficial effects on participating youth, says a BBBSC official.

"We know that mentoring works and has a long-term positive impact on a child's life. Using the Internet to link up more young people with mentors allows us to serve more children and create those caring relationships," says executive director Mike McKnight.

Big Brother Little Brother (Originally Published for Young People's Press)

In Education, Technology, Writing (all kinds) on **May 26, 2009** at **07:03**

Charles may not see his Big Brother often, but he talks to him a lot – online that is.

The 13-year-old Barrie youth started to E-mail and chat online with his Big Brother, Darryl Ingham, about sports, humour, video games, family life and his favourite Web sites after the two were matched in a new Big Brother Big Sisters of Canada (BBBSC) program, Digital Heroes.

The program, available through the Big Brothers of Barrie, matches volunteers with Internet access to children, allowing a Big Brother Little Brother relationship to flourish online.

"The program is fantastic in that it allows the interaction to happen over the Internet," says Ingham, a 35-year-old insurance company executive. "Since I work in Toronto and travel a fair deal, the Internet has allowed Charles and me to communicate from anywhere. For example, we chatted while I was in Calgary on business."

Instead of committing two to three hours a week to develop and maintain a face-to-face relationship, adult volunteers only have to commit to one hour a week that they can do from their home or office.

Charles's mother knows about the importance of having a Big Brother.

"Growing up, my brother had a Big Brother. Many years later, they are still friends. Most importantly, I felt that Charles needed a positive male role model in his life," says Michele.

Charles had been having trouble in school, playing the class clown and getting detentions and extra assignments, she says.

Charles had been on the waiting list for a Big Brother for three years when he was matched in the Digital Heroes program. More than 6,000 boys and girls are on waiting lists with Big Brother and Big Sister agencies across Ontario.

"We know that mentoring works and has a long-term positive impact on a child's life. Using the Internet to link-up more young people with mentors allows us to serve more children and create those caring relationships," says Mike McKnight, BBBSC executive director.

Having an e-mentor has been good for him, Michele says. Charles enjoys receiving Ingham's undivided attention and praise, and Ingham's positive support and perspective have increased his self-esteem.

"Darryl never puts Charles down or disrespects him. He is always positive. I have seen a huge change in Charles' self-esteem. As a mother, that means the world to me," says Michele.

Youth matched in Digital Heroes, which is administered by BBBSC and Frontier College, receive a computer with Internet access and training on how to use it. The program, currently available only in Ontario, is expected to expand across Canada.

Computers for the project were contributed by RBC Financial Group and CIBC and upgraded by reBoot Canada. The Ontario's Promise initiative launched the project and formed the partnerships. AOL Canada is the major sponsor.

"E-mail is one of the easiest and most effective ways for people to keep in touch, but many at-risk kids in Ontario don't have access," says AOL Canada president Steven McArthur.

"Our goal with this program is to provide kids with the technology to stay in touch with their Big Brother or Big Sister, to ensure they can communicate instantly using E-mail or AOL's Instant Messenger service whenever they need advice or just want to chat," McArthur says.

Digital Heroes allows for a meaningful and lasting relationship between youth and adult, regardless of conflicting schedules and geographical location.

Ingham has a supportive and significant role in Charles' life, Michele says.

"One Saturday, Charles beat his own personal best average in his bowling league. He told me that he couldn't wait to go home and E-mail Darryl," she says.

Brantford Boys (Originally Published with Young People's Press)

In Education, Writing (all kinds) on **May 26, 2009** at **10:13**

The greatest challenge to Big Brothers of Brantford and District is attracting volunteers, says executive director Pam Blackwood.

"It's hard getting the volunteers to commit," Blackwood says. "And they're hesitant to work with the teenagers."

But the agency may have found a solution in Digital Heroes, a new e-mentoring initiative by Big Brothers Big Sisters of Canada (BBBSC).

In Digital Heroes, volunteers with access to the Internet are matched to children, enabling a Big Brother Little Brother relationship to flourish online through E-mail and online chats.

Instead of committing to two or three hours a week, volunteers only have to commit to one hour a week – and they can do so from their home or office.

The kids in the program receive a computer and training on how to use it effectively.

It's a new spin on the traditional one-to-one matches for which BBBSC agencies are known.

Blackwood says Digital Heroes attracted the Brantford agency because it's easier to match older children through e-mentoring, and the more flexible time commitment may make it easier to attract volunteers.

Many Digital Heroes volunteers are business people already on computers, she says.

Brantford is one of nine agencies piloting the program. Although Blackwood admits they have been slow getting it off the ground, she has high hopes for Digital Heroes.

"I'd like to see it continue and build, and I'd like to see this sort of mentoring across Canada," Blackwood says.

Digital Heroes is being administered by BBBSC and Frontier College. The program is expected to expand to different parts of Canada in 2003.

The Ontario's Promise initiative was responsible for launching Digital Heroes and formed partnerships among various members of the corporate and non-profit sectors. Computers for the project were contributed by RBC Financial Group and CIBC, and upgraded by reBoot Canada.

AOL Canada is the major sponsor of the project. Jon Hamovitch, vice-president of human resources at AOL says Digital Heroes is a true example of what can be accomplished through partnerships.

"This program brings together technology, innovation and human spirit to benefit children and youth," Hamovitch says. "I applaud Ontario's Promise for their ingenuity and determination to make this program a reality."

As for Blackwood, she says she'd like the kids in the program to be positively influenced by their mentors.

"I'd like kids to see what they can possibly do with their lives," she says. "Thirteen and 14 are very formative years for deciding what they want to do with their future."

You Can't Clap With One Hand (Originally Published in NuBeing International)

In Education, Writing (all kinds) on **May 26, 2009** at **12:00**

Five-year-old Heather Keogan smiles at the reflection in the mirror. Pushing her blonde hair off her face, she touches her blue nose and red cheeks. BOOM! BOOM! BOOM! The sound of African drums draws Heather's attention away from the mirror.

Heather goes to a corner of the room in the YMCA-YWCA in Ottawa [Ontario, Canada]. She joins about 14 other painted faces that were also lured to the same spot by the drums. The rhythms touch the children's feet and slowly they begin to dance. The children shake wildly, trying to follow the beat. Some children hold hands while dancing. White hands hold yellow hands, brown hands hold red hands and black hands hold white hands.

The children, aged 5 to 10, are part of a workshop called African Cultures: Multi-Media Workshop Series. The workshop explores the history, culture and social organization of specific ethnic groups in Africa through performing and visual arts. Music, dance and mask making are a few of the techniques used to explore African culture. The workshop is focused to broaden children's awareness of Canada's diverse cultures in order to prevent racist behaviour. "Some 16- and 17-year-olds are racist because they weren't taught to prevent that behaviour at 8- and 9-years-old," says Susan Ship, a coordinator of the workshop series. "You can't confront racism if you don't' know other cultures. We give children a chance to do things and be things in another culture."

In February of 1993, the children spent their Saturday afternoons at the YMCA-YWCA. With prompting from a workshop volunteer to remember the names, 7-year-old Elizabeth Cummergen says she has learned about Somalia, Ghana and Tanzania. On a Saturday in March of the same year, 15 children learn about Zaire. "Hello every," says Taki E'bwenza, pointing to his nametag. "My name is Taki and I'm from Zaire."

"Hi, Taki!" the children shout.

A coordinator of the workshop series, Gifty Serbeh says contacts with the African community get culture specialists like Taki to teach the children. "The kids also get to look at the inter-cultural aspects of Africa," says Serbeh. "They get to discover that people within Africa are not all the same."

The children follow Taki to a slide projector in the corner of the room and crowd in front of it. Taki talks about each slide in French and a workshop volunteer translates in English.

"How long does it take for a hut to be built?" asks a girl, point to the slide of a hut resting on hard, brown earth. "With lots of help, two days," replies Taki, ready to take another question.

The slides are meant to give children a chance to see Zaire and learn about what life is like there, says Ship. In one slide, a Zairese girl, about 10-years-old, wears a festive costume at a ceremony that would initiate her into womanhood. Five-year-old Anna Cummergen remembered the slide. "In Zeer," she says, meaning Zaire, "girls have separate dances and sometimes boys get together with girls to get dances."

After the slides, Taki brings out several pictures of masks he has recreated on his computer. He gives one to each child. The children colour the masks with scented markers. The smells of orange, grape and chocolate fill the air. "I'm going to put a string on my mask and put it on my face," says Heather, grinning at her mask. Heather brings her orange, purple and brown mask to Taki. "This is a Kakungu mask," Taki tells Heather, encouraging her to pronounce "Kakungu" correctly on her own. "It's the name of a group of people who live in Zaire."

After the kids paint masks on paper, they all sit in a circle. Pictures of painted masks on faces of Zairese people are passed around. Ethnomusicologist John Rudel begins to play the drums in the corner of the room. Taki goes to play the drums beside Rudel and the sound fills the room.

The children disengage themselves from the mirror images and start to dance and clap. The adults who organize the workshop dance and clap with the children.

To increase the effectiveness of the workshop, Ship says the adults get just as involved as the children and try to set examples of good behaviour. The adults are from different races. Ship says she hopes the interaction among the adults has a positive effect on the children. "It's hard to measure the success of something like this, on preventing racist behaviour," says ship. "You don't see the results right away. The influence that it has on the children comes through observing the interaction among the children here, who are from many different races. Also by things children do at home."

Heather runs to her mother, Beth Keogan, after the workshop. "Look at my face," she says. "It's an Africa thing." Keogan, who has two children in the workshop, says she's pleased her children enjoy it and hopes they learn a lot. "I want my children to dislike people because of their character, not because of their colour or culture. I want them to experience multiculturalism and not be ignorant of other people."

Michelle Sewanuku says she wishes more children were involved in culture workshops. "When I was in the third grade, kids would ask me if my parents were monkeys. They didn't seem to know anything about Africa except that monkeys lived there. They made me feel bad about coming from there."

Ship says, in the upcoming sessions, the workshop will teach the children about the experiences of Africans who live in Canada. Depending on finances, she would like to see a larger project with more children involved in exploring other cultures. The Panicaro Foundation, a non-profit foundation that gives money to charities and pilot projects, contributed $6,000 to the program and the government gave $5,000. "We've been working on a shoestring budget," says Serbeh. "Kids' can't get treats because we don't' have the money."

The workshop had space to register 25 children, although the demand was greater. The workshop costs $10.00. Bill 21 amended the Education Act that required that all the boards have a policy on anti-racism, says June Girvan, a former education officer of the Ministry of Education office in Ottawa. Girvan is now working with a group of young people on celebrating the 200-year anniversary of the anti-slave bill in Canada. The commemoration will take place Black History Month in 2001. Among her other projects are working with a group in Quebec to develop an anti-racism policy. She has also set up an endowment fun at Carleton University to help young Canadians of African ancestry to become more attached to their identity as Canadians. This scholarship will begin for first-year graduate students in the fall of 1999.

One way that schools began practicing the anti-racism policy that Girvan spoke of is through programs like the Multicultural Arts for Schools and Communities, a program that is still running today. The program brings creative artists from different cultures into the classroom.

Ship says she wants to see the workshop expanded into the school system. Serbia says the Ottawa Board of Education doesn't like organizations that are not a part of the school system to do activities for the children. "We'll keep trying," says Serbia.

Epilogue:

The African Cultures: Multi-Media Workshop series continued until 1995. The focus turned more on some of the racial tensions around Somali children who make up a large population of the area around the Centre. Obtaining funding to continue the program because difficult, but the Panicaro Foundation continually supported the project and encourages and would support any future efforts.

As Heather smiles at her reflection, she also smiles at the other faces of the children in the mirror. "Your face is different than mine," she says, point to the painted face of 5-year-old Adam Sarumi.

When the drums play, Heather grabs Adam's hand and they dance together.

In a Strange Land (Published in NuBeing International)

In Writing (all kinds), travel on **May 28, 2009** at **03:52**

In Berlin, 11-year-old Leli came running to her home, digging her nails in her flesh so hard that blood was almost drawn. Tears were running down Leli's face as she fell into the arms of her mother, Tsion Letta-Teferra, an Ethiopian woman who had lived in Germany for 16 years.

"My daughter had just come from the house of the old lady who lived next door," says Letta-Teferra. "The old lady told my daughter that she is dirty, and that's why she has brown skin. Leli was trying to scratch her skin off."

In July of 1993, Letta-Teferra packer her things, closed the door to her Berlin home for the last time, and moved to Canada with her daughter and her husband.

"I left Germany because of the racism, because of the feeling of hatred from the Germans," she says. "I feared the Neo-Nazi violence, and how the racism all around us was affecting my daughter. I didn't want her growing up there."

Letta-Teferra had gone to Germany in 1978 and had studied psychology at the University of Maryland in Berlin. The university was an escape from the dangers of war in her home country of Ethiopia.

"In my country, they put you in prison easy," she says. "Walking on the streets you would get shot. We had bullet holes in our home."

Letta-Teferra always saw living in Germany as a temporary situation. After one week there, she says, she wanted to leave.

"People are always pushing you, [they] don't looking in your eyes," she says. "Human touch is not usually there. They are always complaining. I think they have everything. They are lucky they live in a safe place."

She lived the first 11 months in Bonn, and then 15 years in Berlin. Letta-Teferra says Berlin is better because it's more accepting of those from other cultures. She says this is because "Berliners are from all over."

Despite this, Letta-Teferra was never able to make Germany feel like a second home to her.

Every year someone would tell her, "Next year you will go." Her neighbours and people who worked in stores would ask her, "When are you leaving?" When she came, she didn't need a visa but had to report to the Foreigner Police, also known as the Auslander Police. This branch is designated to deal only with foreigners. Auslander is the German word for foreigners. Letta-Teferra says she thinks auslander only refers to those who are of colour and from third world countries.

"Auslander has a negative connotation," she says. "The Germans prefer black Americans to black Africans. They don't call black Americans auslanders. You definitely get the message that it's bad to be black and from 'dirty' Africa."

In Berlin, a German cab driver that did not want to be named says Germans don't consider Scandinavians or Dutch people to be auslanders.

"They are more accepted, Germans like them because they look more like them," he says.

Auslanders now need a visa because of a change in the law a month after Letta-Teferra went to Germany. Without a visa or papers that are in order, auslanders are sent to prison.

"Everyone's like the police here, even the neighbours," she says. "They ask you questions."

Letta-Teferra says the laws of the country tell the Germans that they can do anything to auslanders. She tells a story of an African girlfriend that was a friend of a German man who was married but separated. The estranged wife of the man found out about the relationship and was angry.

"The wife went to the Auslander police and told them that her husband and the girl were having an affair," says Letta-Teferra. They put this information in the girl's file so when her visa is needed to be prolonged, it wouldn't happen."

Letta-Teferra says that, while she wasn't happy in Germany, circumstances kept her in the country longer than she wanted. She married a man she had known in Ethiopia who was also living in Germany. His work as a civil engineer kept them in Berlin. After getting her BA in psychology, Letta-Teferra completed an MA in social sciences. After graduation, she did an apprenticeship in a church and taught about other cultures at the German university she had graduated from.

Letta-Teferra still found life in Germany difficult. She says that when she would leave on holidays to the United States or Canada to visit relatives, she would realize how bad her life was in Germany. "I needed a month to get adjusted to Germany again," she says. "I would get sick to be back there."

In a briefing at the Federal Foreign Office in Bonn, a government official spoke of "everyone is living together" as one of the objectives of the German government. However, there was not talk about the rights of the non-Germans in elections. Letta-Teferra says the laws for auslanders need to be changed by the government then perhaps the attitudes of the Germans will change. There are still no anti-discrimination laws in Germany concerning race, says Marina Roncoroni at the commission for Foreigner's Affairs in Berlin.

Letta-Teferra says the situation is also bad for those who are German but don't look like other Germans. "Many of the black people in Germany are half-German so they are German, but not everyone thinks so." The Commission does not keep statistics on how many black Germans live in the country, says Roncoroni.

Letta-Teferra says she feels sorry for black Germans. The children are growing up between two cultures. They are German but no one accepts that, she adds. "I was waiting for the train and I saw this boy, he was about 8-years-old and half-German, half African. Other kids were asking him where he was from," she says. "When he told them he was

German, the kids were denying it and saying 'that can't be, no.' This kind of thing is very common."

Sometimes rejection of black Germans comes from their own families. Twenty-three-year-old David Zacharias, who lives in Berlin, was abandoned by his mother because he's black. "People asked her, why do you have this black child?" says Zacharias. "She told me that people would call her a n*gger-lover and should feel shame." His mother lives in a spacious apartment in Berlin but her son lived in a boy's orphanage.

Living in the former East Berlin, Zacharias has been beaten up three times by neo-Nazi skinheads. "They jumped on me as I was going home one night," he says. "They kicked me in my stomach, in my back, everywhere. They put white spray paint in my eyes and told me to 'go home to Africa.'" Zacharias says he was born in Germany and has lived his whole life there. He doesn't know of any other home.

In Germany, police reporter 2,285 acts of rightist violence in 1992, mostly against foreigners, including seven murders. On May 29, 1993, a neo-Nazi firebomb killed five Turks – three young girls and two young women. There have been many other violent attacks on Turkish refugee hostels, homes and restaurants, according to Z Magazine.

"All you have to do to see what is wrong in Germany is to come out of the railroad station of any big city and look at the crowds on the streets," Michael Petri, a 26-year-old militant, was quoted as saying in an article in the New York Times. "Sometimes you wonder if there are any Germans left at all. Everything's in foreign hands."

Germany has a population of 80 million with more than 5 million foreigners. Since the fall of the Iron Curtain in 1991, many people have entered Germany. The German government's rules of citizenship create anti-foreigner attitudes in the neo-Nazi group, says Ian Kagedan, director of the B'Nai Brith Canada. In a briefing at the German Embassy, Jurgen Hellener, deputy ambassador, said Germany is not a "country of immigrants." He also said German-born immigrants, such as Turkish people, are not considered Germans.

German citizenship can be acquired after living in the country for eight years and giving up any other citizenship. Auslanders who are not citizens pay taxes, says Ronconori at the Commission for Foreigner's Affairs. "Someone born outside Germany who can trace their ancestors back to the Nazis can become a German citizen faster than a theirgeneration Turk." Roncoroni is of Italian background.

Zacharias's experiences in his home country make him feel like he's been treated like an immigrant, he says. Letta-Teferra says that the laws of Germany encourage everyone, whether they are neo-Nazi or not, to have racist attitudes towards they don't consider one of them. In World War II, definitions of who was and who wasn't German resulted in the death of millions of Jewish people. Adolf Hitler's rise to power came with the promises that he would keep Germany for Germans.

Germany has come to terms with its history, says Kagedan with B'Nai Brith. He says the racist attitudes of Hitler are reflected in the government today.

Zacharias wants to leave Germany. He sees a better life for himself in the United States or Canada. "I'm not treated any better than an auslander," he says. "This is my home but I feel like an auslander."

Letta-Teferra says she feels happier and more welcomed in Canada. She works as an employment counselour at the YM-YWCA. She says that in her first month in Canada her daughter Leli was hugging everyone, especially black people. "I think she's starting to feel better about who she is," says Letta-Teferra. "I don't think she's starting to feel as alone."

The strict definitions of what German is affect the lives of immigrants and German-born people who aren't entirely of the Aryan race. The racism that results occurs at the level of old women who make little girls cry and neo-Nazis who beat up young men. "The German government needs to change its laws about auslanders, about citizenship, and most importantly its definition of what a German is," says Letta-Teferra. "To me they think Germans can only be blonde and blue-eyed. When the government and the country become more accepting, maybe neo-Nazi violence would decrease. Maybe I never would have left there."

Not Just the Baby Blues (Originally Published in Today's Canadian Black Woman)

In [Disability](), [Health](), [Writing (all kinds)]() on **May 30, 2009** at **07:50**

When Halima Ali, an immigrant from Somalia living in Toronto's west end, was 20 she decided that she wanted to get married and have a baby.

She did just that. However, her decision came with some unanticipated problems.

Three years later while pregnant, Ali had morning sickness like many other normal women. She kept getting sick and so weak that she had to stop working and was hospitalized.

"Immediately I got jaundiced, but I felt better after coming out of the hospital," says Ali. "Once home, I was still throwing up and losing a lot of vitamins. The doctors said I had a salt deficiency. I went home again and one morning woke up confused."

Ali had a burning sensation in her brain. She did not know her name had difficulty remembering things. Again, she was taken to the hospital, at seven months pregnant, and stayed there for two weeks.

She was in the hospital several times during her pregnancy. Ali thought that when she gave birth, everything would go back to normal.

"I had my son and returned home to become mentally confused again. I went back to the hospital where they put me on medications. Not only did my life change because of my son, my health changed too."

Ali has not been completely diagnosed, but the doctors think it is postpartum depression.

Christine Long, executive director of Postpartum Adjustment Services Canada (PASS-CAN), a non-profit organization helping postpartum mothers, says that Ali is an atypical situation.

"She still has not recovered, and there may be other disorders like thyroid problems or anemia," says long. "We need to acknowledge in our society that having a baby is a major life event. Symptoms can appear during pregnancy and after." Long does not like the word "postpartum depression" to describe all situations. This condition is often called "the baby blues," and is much like the flue. Eighty per cent of pregnant women experience this.

With a prenatal mood disorder, the major disorder is anxiety before the child is born. Long says that the literature on the subject and diagnoses from psychiatrists rates the problem at about 10 per cent for postpartum mood disorder. Through meeting women at conferences and the increased knowledge on the subject, according to Long that number has jumped to between 20 to 25 per cent. She also notes that postpartum mood disorder does not discriminate against any group of women.

"The major symptoms we see are anxiety, panic attacks, unable to swallow. Women feel they have electrodes to their scalp, pain in the chest, heart racing, and numbness of limbs. Many women think they're having a heart attack," says Long.

PASS-CAN tries to train people in the health field about these symptoms because some women go through cardiology when in hospital.

"I couldn't take care of my son so he is being taken care of by my aunt, who is really like another mother," says Ali. "My son is 6-years-old now and he knows I'm sick, but he doesn't fully understand what it is. I lost my job when I first got sick. I also lost my husband. He didn't understand what I was going through so he left."

Long says what Ali went through is the severe end of the disorder. "Many women also have obsessive-compulsive behaviour. Overly concerned about the baby's health, scary thoughts about the health of the baby. Thoughts become repetitive and intrusive. The most common one is seeing the babies' head crashing open and falling down. Eighty per cent of pregnant women will experience some kind of scary thought," says Long.

Long says the path to help is to talk to a doctor. If a woman is not feeling like herself during or after pregnancy, they should let someone know.

After the baby is born, there is a visit with the doctor. PASS-CAN is advocating for these questions to be asked:
- Are you able to sleep when the baby sleeps?
- Are you eating, and if so what are you eating?
- Are you able to get out, other than to the doctor's?
- Are you having any scary thoughts about yourself and the baby?

"If there's a problem with the woman, by question number two, there are tears. With the questions, what you're doing is humanizing the experience of being a new mom."

Women get better knowing about it, being educated, trying to prevent it through knowing their medical history, being able to talk and having good healthcare professionals, says Long. The other part that really helps is western traditional and alternative medications.

"If it goes untreated there can be family breakdowns, suicide, and in some cases infanticide when it comes to postpartum psychosis," says Long. "We have a tremendous amount to gain by treating this. These are some of the most in-tune, powerful, sensitive women I have ever met. What's happened is that their experience has made them stronger." With a combination of traditional medications and prayer, Ali has been better. She is now 29 and sees her son often. Caseworkers at the Canadian Mental Health Association helped her to find affordable housing and get back to work. Although Ali's first love left her, she is dating again with a new boyfriend.

"I dream to be able to raise my son and further my career, I just want to be regarded as normal as anyone else."

Low Flying: Island Wings has promise, but never takes off (Originally Published in the Hour in Montreal)

In [Writing (all kinds)](#), [book reviews](#) on **June 1, 2009** at **13:23**

As many Canadian children were being told fairy tales of mystic lands where houses were made of candy cane and gingerbread, where glass slippers and a mere kiss could turn girls into royalty, the magical tales told to a young Cecil Foster were about joining his parents in the Land of Plenty: "We would sit around the fire with Grandmother enthroned on the big rock, her dress or skirt lapped between our legs, while she told us stories. She taught us about our family history and painted glowing pictures for Stephen, Errol and me about the great life awaiting us, when we joined our parents in England." This is the story Foster tells in *Island Wings: A Memoir*.

A journalist who's worked with the *Toronto Star*, the *Globe and Mail*, CTV and CBC, Foster is probably better known for his novels such as *No Man in the House* and *Sleep On, Beloved*. *Island Wings* follows Foster's awarding-winning *A Place Called Heaven: The Meaning of Being Black in Canada*. *Wings* is set in Barbados, the place where Foster's "navel string is buried," and is an attempt by Foster to come to terms with tangled relationships, principally with his parents and his homeland, both of which are so inextricably linked.

The book begins when Foster's parents leave him and his two older brothers on the island and head off for the mother-isle of England: "My mother cried that day on the Bridgetown Wharf as she walked off, leaving her three sons: Stephen, Errol and me, still a baby. My brothers tell me they didn't cry, but how could they not? If they didn't maybe it was because they had fallen victim to the pressure of never openly showing emotion."

The quote seems significant considering that the book's primary weakness is its own reluctance to fully open up. As a result, Foster fails to engage the reader in his journey of disappointments and success. The writing is often bland and too much like straight journalism, lacking the fancifulness and use of metaphor that make for effective fictional writing. Granted, this is not a work of fiction, but memory is seldom pure fact. And seasoning the facts with some subjective descriptions would have enlivened these memories.

Yet *Wings* does raise some interesting questions such as: How do three little boys have such a distant relationship with two people whose intimacy created them and why do people who come from paradise (the island of Barbados frequently being an ideal vacationing spot for Canadians) want to leave? To his credit, Foster gives some answers. His story is one that is linked to those of many Caribbean Canadians who left what most Canadians see as paradise. In some ways Foster's story portrays the complex and dueling relationships between home, cultural identity and necessity – a reality well-known to many immigrants, not solely those from the Caribbean. Still, the best thing I can say of this book is that it's a good effort, one that may be a stepping-stone to more potent memoirs by Caribbean Canadians.

Association Helps Blacks (Originally Published in Centretown News)

In Education, Writing (all kinds) on **June 2, 2009** at **06:00**

What does a business of frozen cassava and fresh crushed peppers have in common with a business of permed hair and painted toes? It's the Black Business and Professional Association.

Black professionals and black-owned businesses have a chance to build contacts with other association members and in many communities, which will help them to succeed.

The association offers its members free seminars and lectures on information important to businesses, such as legal issues involved in signing leases.

"We're looking for people who are black," says Dave Tulloch, president of the association. "We feel we can offer them some kind of comradeship and information that we don't' normally get because we find ourselves on the fringe of many of the mainstream organizations."

This association gives black-owned businesses and professionals an opportunity to be in the spotlight and a support system they may not get from other organizations.

"What I get from the association is support," says Ottawa lawyer Hugh Fraser. "The contacts that you make are important. Networking is a very important aspect as you develop your career."

The association has provided its members a support system for three years in Ottawa. The association has been in Canada for over 10 years.

Statistics Canada does not keep figures on the number of black-owned businesses in Ottawa.

Tulloch estimates the association's membership is between 45 and 55 businesses and professionals. But, only 20 per cent of the businesses and professionals in Ottawa-Carleton belong to the association.

"The wider population is just not interested in getting involved," explains Tulloch. "Perhaps, they are too preoccupied or for whatever reason, we don't have them on our membership list."

But one restaurant owner says his is not even aware of the association. The Lion's Den at 399A Catherine St. is not a part of the association.

"It's not that I wouldn't get involved with the association, but I've never heard of it," said Robinson.

The owner of the year-old restaurant, Edward Robinson, does not advertise either.

Robinson does his own cooking, and the menu offers mainly West Indian food, like jerk chicken and curried goat.

Beneath the loud reggae music, the red, yellow and green décor reflects Robinson's Jamaican heritage.

Robinson's business is expanding. He has plans of offering more Canadian food for his younger clientele and adding a cultural boutique including information on Ethiopia.

"I'm sure the association could help me in my plans for expanding my business," said Robinson.

Perhaps, if Robinson were a member he would benefit from the business experience of Fay Campbell-Lenz.

Campbell-Lenz, owner of the beauty salon Head to Toe at 429 MacLaren St., is a board member of the association.

Campbell-Lenz, has owned the salon for 10 years. As an established business in Centretown, she says she does not benefit the same way younger businesses do from the information the association puts out.

"My work on the committee is to help other businesses," she says.

Campbell-Lenz shares her experience in business with less established association members.

She says one of the keys to her success is the support she gets from various communities, not just the black one.

"I have a multicultural clientele. I would not like to call my business a black business. It's a business that's owned by a black person. I am able to give service to anyone who requires service."

The association gives its members a chance to make contacts with other business communities. This widens the market of customers and clients for the members.

"We target organizations and institutions outside of the black community to get them sympathetic to our causes, and to get their assistance so they can help our members," said the association's president.

Last year, the association organized a black exposition. Business and professionals had a chance to expose the larger community to their services.

Negril, at 787 ½ Somerset St. W. has been in business for 14 years. Frozen fish and fresh crushed peppers give the place a scent of West Indian cooking.

"We couldn't survive with just the business in the black community," says the owner of Negril Tropical Mart Co., Lincoln Brown.

Brown is a member of the association.

"Our primary objective is to give our membership a way to access other people," said Tulloch.

Black History Gets a Seat in Classrooms (Originally Published in Centretown News)

In Education, Writing (all kinds) on **June 2, 2009** at **12:09**

Few people know that Matthew DaCosta, black fisherman and Micmac interpreter for Samuel de Champlain, played a role in Canadian history.

Historical information on black Canadians is almost absent in our classrooms and libraries.

"I'm on a hunt now to try and find information (on black Canadian history), but I haven't been very lucky," says Marva Major-Cosper, Connaught School. "That gives an example of the need that's out here because we don't' have a resource centre of information. It's so necessary."

If the efforts of the James Robinson Johnston committee are successful, professors, scholarships, and a resource centre in black Canadian studies will soon be available.

The committee will endow a chair for studying black history at a Canadian university.

"Almost everybody else has got a chair such as the centre for Aboriginal studies at Carleton University. I think there are 13 chairs across the country for the Ukrainians," says Carl Nicholson, a member of the committee organizing the Johnston chair.

"Almost everybody has an academic entity that is focusing in on their contributions and accomplishments in this country."

Paul Blackmore says the chair will not just benefit blacks, it will benefit all Canadians.

"It's just another type of knowledge and knowledge is wonderful. This is not just for black folks, this is for everyone who wants to know."

James Robinson Johnston was the first member of Nova Scotia's black community to graduate in law in 1898.

Johnston's community involvement, his beliefs that the interests of blacks would best be served through education and his excellence as a law practitioner are the reasons why the chair has his name.

Johnston helped start an orphanage for neglected black children in Nova Scotia. He also gained prominence in local politics.

The Johnston chair will create no a high profile university position sustained by the money put into it and its neither university-wide nor department based.

There are committees across Canada working on making the Johnston chair available in universities by September 1994.

The Johnston chair committee plans to build a resource centre with materials that will relate to black Canadian studies, including academic journals and literature.

Major-Cosper says this centre would provide information for a better view of historical contributions by blacks.

"If we had that type of institute, hopefully what we would see are teachers at the faculty of education having those resources at their fingertips," she says.

"No longer could they say they don't know anything about it can't be taught. The knowledge would be there, it would just be a need for it be tapped into."

The Ottawa committee began around September 1992, and there are 16 members. The committee developed through word of mouth and has attracted different people.

"There's no limit to our committee. Our committee isn't just built up of black people. It's a mixture of people who are from all over," says Naylor Ashley, heading the Ottawa Johnston committee.

Committee member Fran Lowe has a mixed European heritage, including Irish and Scottish, and is president of Fran Lowe Associates Inc., at 190 Bronson Ave.

But for the Johnston chair to work, it needs money.

The committee needs to raise $2.5 million.

The national Johnston committee is nearing their target. Close to $1 million has been raised.

Last year, the Ministry of Multiculturalism and Citizenship gave $400,000 to the chair. The rest has come from Nova Scotia's provincial government, private corporations and individuals.

Fran Lowe's experience with her fundraising-consulting firm, helps the Johnston committee form fundraising strategies.

A reception on Parliament Hill launched the fundraising on Dec. 2.

Lowe says the committee was trying to reach political and business sectors to raise awareness of the need for funds.

"It was to bring in some of the sectors that we had identified as good potential for wanting to support the cause, and give them a chance to hear from the people who were closely involved with it," she says.

The committee has raised nearly $5,000 in Ottawa since Dec. 2. But they are $200,000 short of their target.

The benefits of the Johnston chair to the black community are many.

Scholarships for three black graduate students selected form across Canada will also be given each year. A corporate fundraiser for the chair has already offered to personally put forward job applications submitted by scholarship winners.

"We need to see that our young people are coming up in a society that they can find a place in. It's through education of the general public that this is going to be done," says Ashley.

Knowledge of the committee alone is already encouraging some black students like Paul Blackmore.

Blackmore is a Centretown resident studying law part-time at Carleton University. He has been in Beachville, Nova Scotia, the first indigenous black Canadian settlement.

"If I'm still in school at the time the chair starts, I'd be interested in getting a third degree in black studies."

Committee member Carl Nicholson shares Blackmore's view on the chair.

"Many people look at black people and have some preconceived ideas about us. For example, very often, we are asked where do you come from? Generally, people don't know that black people lived in Canada for at least the past 395 years."

There are also plans for the chair to invite black scholars from diverse cultural backgrounds and areas of expertise to educate communities across Canada on black Canadian history.

Blackmore says black Canadian history needs to be known by all Canadians.

"Why should we learn about the Irish history? Why should we learn about English history? It's because it's all part of Canada. You also don't have to be black to learn about women's studies."

Black Professor Turns Negatives into Positives (Originally Published in Centretown News)

In [Education](), [Writing (all kinds)]() on **June 2, 2009** at **16:13**

In Greek, Bernice means "one who bears good news of victory." Bernice Moreau's life is a testament to achievement in the face of struggle.

When Moreau first came to Centretown in September 1991, she was called a "nigger" y three white youths at the corner of Bank Street and Laurier Avenue.

She walked away from the experience feeling great.

"Because I can walk as a black woman, and they have the problem. I don't, it's their problem, it's not mine. It's given me more power. They didn't know who I am," she says with a voice filled with the sound of the West Indies.

Black rights activist Rosa parks poses on Moreau's walls, along with other black and white photographs of black women.

At work, Moreau wears no makeup or any visible jewelry.

She's a natural looking woman who appears to hide nothing about her.

Moreau is the only black female lecturer at Carleton University on the tenure path. After certain specified conditions on length of service and performance, tenure will secure Moreau a permanent status in her job.

She teaches courses such as theorems of gender, race, and class and the history and philosophy of social work.

Moreau was born in Trinidad. She came to Canada to do a BA in sociology at Dalhousie University.

"When I got my first degree, I sent a picture home to Mom. She walked all through the community and showed it. It was a celebration. What I did, I did for my community," she says pushing her glasses higher on her nose.

"Social mobility, political or any kind of mobility was more by the way of education than any other route. As a black woman I could be the prime minister of Trinidad if I wanted to do it. "Being a black woman wouldn't have hindered me. Maybe in days gone by being a women would have hindered me, but not being black."

Moreau does not let being black hinder her in Canadian society. She is currently working on a PhD in sociology through the University of Toronto.

"For many white students, I'm the first black female professor that they've had."

She asks her class on the first day how they feel about having a black female professor.

"I deal with it head on. I know the society in which we live; I know that colour and race are major issues. Colour of skin equals intelligence. Worse again to society, I'm a black woman.

"I say here I am, if you have problems with me that's alright, you can talk about your problems and your difficulties. That is my way."

One of the first things Moreau does when she gets into a community is find a "PRO-tes-TANT" church, as she pronounces it.

"Spirituality helps me with the daily pressure, particularly in this society being far away from home. It gives me community.

"I drifted across this country quite a lot. From 1976 I've lived in Nova Scotia, Toronto, New Brunswick and here. Finding a church gives me an immediate community .I can share what I have, and they can share what they have with me."

She attends the Ottawa Church of God on Wellington Street, which is a mainly black church.

She teaches Sunday school, age's eight to 11. She plans to start teaching the history of black people to her class.

"When you know your history, you can stand proud."

Moreau is proud of who and what she is.

"I'm a model for black female students. I know for sure that in this department of social work the black women are encouraged."

Her victory as a black woman expresses good news of the victory others can also have.

Black Women Share Career Experiences (Originally Published in the Charlatan Newspaper)

In Culture, Writing (all kinds) on **June 3, 2009** at **07:09**

Nov. 6 presented a rare opportunity for five black women professionals to share their personal experiences, success strategies and encouragement with Carleton's black community.

"It's good to see someone there in the image of yourself succeeding," said Kathy Wilkinson, a member of Perspectives.

Perspectives, an African women's interest group at Carleton, host the career night, where a panel of five black women professionals talked about their experience. Four of the women are Carleton alumni and one is the only black female faculty member on the tenure track at Carleton.

Each woman had a different message to give the audience of more than 30 people in the Senate lounge.

Bernice Moreau is a lecturer in social work at Carleton. Moreau said black woman are strong and they were feminists long before the word was known. Moreau said she knows about strength from her own personal experience, which she shared with the audience.

"As a student (at Dalhousie University) I had to fight sexual harassment from professors because I was seen as exotic," Moreau said.

It has been a constant struggle in Moreau's life to let people know that she can be right. She said being the only black female faculty member does not give her any support system for her ideas.

"From 1946 to 1992 I've had to prove myself," said Moreau.

Dawn Armstrong is a graduate of political science at Carleton. Armstrong works at the Canadian International Development Agency.

Armstrong said she keeps herself in tune with future career trends and updates skills she needs for her job, such as learning French. She says achieving your potential takes strategy.

"I became really empowered because I had a lot of things that my colleagues didn't have. I had knowledge," said Armstrong.

Armstrong said she has been passed up for jobs that have gone to white people.

"I've never let myself get defeated," said Armstrong.

Jackie Lawrence, Marva Major-Cosper and Sylmadel Coke were the other panelists. Lawrence works with New Democratic MP Howard McCurdy and with *Beyond Black Magazine*.

Major-Cosper is a high school teacher. Coke started an immigrant abuse shelter in Toronto and works with Interval House, an abuse shelter in Ottawa.

The Women's Centre, the Funds Allocation Board and the International Students' Centre co-sponsored the event.

Yari Yari Conference (Originally Published in Panache Magazine)

In Events, Writing (all kinds) on **June 5, 2009** at **06:40**

An international conference in literature by women from African and the African Diaspora has been hailed an overwhelming success by its organizers. Held in New York and coordinated by New York University's Africana Studies Programme last fall, the conference brought together world-renowned writers to this first-ever scholarly conference that explored black female authorship. "Yari Yari – Black Women Writers of the Future," celebrated the creativity and diversity of black women writers. Among the 120 writers who attended were Ghanaian poet and novelist Ama Ata Aidoo, Maya Angelou, Gloria Naylor, Angela Davis, Sapphire, Haitian Edwidge Danticat and Maryse Conde from Guadeloupe. The conference also included notable filmmakers, artists, storytellers, journalists, children's authors, playwrights and publishing executives.

"The collection of writers who came from as far away as Africa, China and Europe led to a lot of important scholarship. People felt that they learned about the writers and about themselves," says Glenda Noel-Doyle of the NYU's Africana Studies Programme. The conference also involved male participants such as Walter Mosley and Richard Wesley.

"Yari, Yari," which means "The future" in the Kuranko language of Sierra Leone, could not have been a more timely forum to explore the contemporary role of black female writers. The conference was also co-sponsored by the Institute of Afro-American Affairs in conjunction with the Organization of Women Writers of Africa.

Universal Design is for Everyone

In <u>Disability</u>, <u>Writing (all kinds)</u> on **June 12, 2009** at **17:34**

Michael Lam, who did his undergraduate degree in engineering at McMaster University, is doing his master's degree at the Walter G. Booth School of Engineering Practice. This school is also affiliated with McMaster University in Hamilton, Ontario, Canada. His thesis is focusing on product design for people with disabilities.

"My project is revolving around designing art equipment for people with disabilities," says Lam. "I'm still narrowing it down and interviewing people. Maybe I will be focusing on easels for painters, or photography or large cameras, like professional cameras."

Lam started the program in September of 2008.

"One of the first things I've discovered is that there is a huge field of opportunity working with disabled people getting older. We've come a long way already, however there is not a lot of equipment and opportunities that are available for people with disabilities. For building accessibility."

Lam's program at McMaster is a year in length and he is under a tight three to four month timeframe to come up with his product design and report.

"I would come up with a design and a detailed report on it. All of the research I am doing now is identifying problems and looking at a wide variety of the things that need to be looked at. If there is time, then the design can be a prototype. We have a tight timeline so you have three to four months to actually work on the whole project."

Lam, being a dancer and not disabled himself, came up with some resourceful ways to find people he could work with to test out his product design. He emailed the organization Linkup that finds jobs for people with disabilities and asked people to volunteer to help him with his research.

"[The response has been] very positive. I've been meeting people about every other day for a good week so far. The response has been very positive."

After doing some more research, Lam is leaning towards focusing on easels for painting for his product design for people with disabilities.

"Universal Design is design for everyone, including people with disabilities. It is so people in a wheelchair can move in and anyone can move down a hallway. I feel it is important to be in constant contact with the people I am meeting with because I myself do not have a disability. For someone who has a vision impairment or multiple sclerosis they have trouble distinguishing contrast and universal design makes a big difference."

Hair Chat

In Beauty, Culture, Health, Writing (all kinds) on **June 19, 2009** at **04:18**

Four lovely women, a fifth one coming later, volunteered their time on a January afternoon in 1998 to sit down at Salon Utopia and chat about hair. Here are the details of their chat which will hopefully stimulate your own discussions.

LOCKS:

Naila (with locks): People ask me what is that…what you mean what is it…can you comb that out…I've had people from Jamaica asking me about my locks…what do you mean what is that?

Malene (with an afro): Have you forgotten what it's like when you relax your hair?

Naila: I've had Jamaican men ask me if I could comb it out – that's psycho! Dreadlocks started in Jamaica, well like Rastafarianism started in Jamaica. They know about Rastas, and they should know about locks, and they should know that you can't comb out locks, because you're hair is locked.

(Laughter)

Frank (with locks): It's down to about here (middle of back) so when I'm on the bus, it falls over on the seat, and they pull it. They want to know if it's extensions, if it's real. They want to feel how it feels. I don't know about you, but my dreads are clean, and I don't want your grubby paws on me.

REAL HAIR, FAKE HAIR, BLACK WOMEN:

Hirut (long curly hair that is hers): I get that from people too, is it real. I get that from Black people and White people too. It's my hair. I don't go around asking people if I can touch your hair.

Malene: Touch your ass, touch your balls, it's the same kind of thing. I don't know about you but for me this (indicating head) is a very sensitive area.

Frank: It's your face.

Hirut: Also, people identify me with my hair.

Frankie: Also, they look at you and they say she's a Black woman, Black people only come in these particular hues, and this particular kind of hair, it's really static.

Malene: They can't have long hair.

Frank: Right, that's the conception. You can only be one kind of Black woman. It's only this kind of hair, this kind of texture.

PERSONAL HAIR HISTORIES:

Frank: My hair history…I've been a dread for about 3,4 years. Before that I just had normal regular my hair, no chemicals, no anything. I just got to a point where I got lazy. I didn't want to comb it, I didn't want to coif it, I didn't want to spend the half an hour to an hour to make myself look presentable. I said to hell with it, I'm going to do it, I'm just going to let my hair dread.

Hirut: My hair has pretty much been the way it is right now for all of my life. The first time I really cut it in Canada was about 10 years ago. My Mom flipped. I wanted to cut my bangs. Bangs from hell. I didn't cut it for quite a long time, but then again it was so hard to handle. Very frustrating. I don't comb my hair; I comb it when I wash it once a week.

Malene: I first cut my hair when I was around 15 or 14. Before then, I was just using the pressing comb, doing that ghetto styles with my hair.

Hirut: I used to use the iron for my hair. My sister used to iron my hair for me. That makes it really straight.

Malene: I just used the comb, and I heard the sizzle. I was turning 15 and for my 15th birthday I was going to a salon and they cut it all off, and I was traumatized for about 2 months. But then I befriended my hair stylist, they also damaged it and I was going every week because they let me have free appointments until it gets better. It was terrible because I was there every week until I was 19 and a half. Every week…four years. After a while, they'd use me occasionally for a model, I was in the salon all the time, and one time I was there for 9 hours.

Frankie: What were you doing there for 9 hours?

Malene: I'd be waiting, then they'd condition it, and then I'd be waiting, then it would dry, and I'd be waiting for them to do what they had to do. I relaxed it, so they would be blow-drying it straight, sometimes styling it, colouring it. After a while I got frustrated wasting 8 hours a week, solely on my hair. I ended up having to buy lots of products. Black products…the good ones are really expensive and I was thinking I could be doing so much with this money. I could be buying a new pair of shoes, or books, something. And I also got into a fight with these guys. The relationship ended up being…they weren't just my hairstylist, they were like my gurus in a way. I became debilitated in a way.

Frank: Because of your hair…what a statement.

Malene: It's true. Many Black women don't know how to handle their hair and so these guys do and they would do such a good job with it that I didn't do anything with it, I just let them do everything.

Hirut: I've been 3 times to a stylist. All they would do is straighten it. This is a chance for them to do something creative, and they didn't, and I'm paying them.
Malene: They did really amazing hairstyles. Every week I had a new hairstyle, so the novelty wore off. I felt kind of off, I just wanted to stabilize myself, so I shaved my head. I was cutting my ties big time. I stopped talking to them. Going to the salon, spending 8 hours talking about hair, fashion, this, that, all these superficial things. I would sometimes have deep conversations with people, but I just didn't like who I was. So, shaved my head, and for the past 2 years, it's been like an afro. Every time it would start dreading out, I would cut it. But now I'm ready to go full dread, I'm just too lazy to actually do it. It's so easy because now all I do is wash my hair, towel dry it, and then I'm out the door, pick it, and that's it.

Naila: I went through the same pressing comb stuff when I was about twelve. It was kind of like a rite of passage, because when I was about twelve years old, all the women in my family, well my sister was getting her hair permed, and I was turning twelve, so it was my turn to get my hair permed. But my Mom had to wait until she was much older to get her hair permed. But she didn't really have a big issue with it, because I always used to get it pressed, but since it got humid (laugh) it was over. You'd go to school with this great style, these nice ponytails, and then it would rain. Then you'd walk home with an afro. So I got it permed. I remember being very concerned about getting my hair permed, why am I getting my hair permed. Everybody said it would be more manageable. It's a very odd idea that taking your hair away from it's natural state it can make it more manageable.

Malene: We've never learned to manage our hair, they've never taught us that. It's also learning to work with the naps.

Frank: We have been taught…if you came from the West Indies, you have been taught to manage your hair. You braid it, you cainrow it, you do wonderful things with it. But they're Black things. It's not the carefree White hair hanging down blowing in the wind. It's something different, but we want to get away from the cainrow and the beads.

Hirut: On Friday nights I don't go out, I do my hair. If I don't do it on Friday, I have like really bad hair for 2 weeks, because the schedule is all screwed up.

Naila: Yeah, so I got my hair permed. And I did the gel and the side parts and the buns and the bobs, and I had the curl and I had the styles and what not. And I had a really bad experience getting my hair permed because the next day there was blood on my scalp because the woman was having a conversation with someone while doing my hair. There were chunks of blood on my scalp. My scalp was just covered with blood, it was completely damaged. It was the first time I had gone to the salon on my own. Because Saturday, my Mom and sister and I, we'd go to the salon, there all day watching soap operas and listening to the salon talk. We'd go about once a month, but always on a Saturday. Then I was like no, this is not happening, so I cut it off. And I remember the guy in the salon was like, are you sure you want to cut it. I said sure, I want to cut it. He said if you cut it, you're not going to have any hair. He only cut it in a bob and asked do you want it lower, and I said, cut off my hair, keep on cutting until there's no more perm. He gave me this box cut hair, and people were insinuating afterwards that I was a Lesbian. What do you mean a Lesbian? If you have short hair. Then I had to go to a real barber to get it done right, with the fade, and then I was in business. And that was a real trauma for my family.
Malene: Well, that's another issue when cutting your hair. You're so-called sexuality and your family or whatever. It's like you're sexless if you cut your hair.

Frank: My Mom always says, a woman's hair is her crowning glory.

Malene: I was just thinking with the scabs on my scalp, I went through relaxers in my eye. Like he dropped relaxer in my eye. And it still has damage here a little bit. And you go back, and you say I'll forgive you for that. And the burns on the back of the neck.

Frank: It's torture.

Malene: Yes, it's to keep that womanly look. To have that bone straight look and have my hair on my shoulders and have it swing and bounce.

Frank: Womanly, that's a touchy issue. Because you're still womanly with a short cut.

Hirut: We understand that now.

Malene: It's also when you're 16, 17 years old…you can't be telling that to someone that age. That was my high drama.

Naila: That was really cool. For 2 something years I had it natural. My Mom and I got back into that mother-child, like daughter relationship, because she would do my hair for me again. And she hadn't done my hair since I was 8, or 9, or 10. And I would be getting the China bumps again and I learned to braid my own hair. And I would have this huge afro that I would just blow out and mind you this wasn't the 80s, it was like '94, and I was just like I don't care. The guys too that I knew, were like T-Boz (from TLC) has a great cut, Left-Eye (from TLC) has a great cut. You could do that to your hair. You could do what whatever's doing. And I was like, no, no, I'm happy. Then I went away and I came back, and I was stuck, I have to wash my hair. I don't have 3 hours to wash my hair, then oil it, then China bump it. And I was like Gail, my sister, perm it. And she was like are you crazy. And I was like perm my hair, I just did not have 3 hours to perm my hair. So just 2 hours later, I just threw it all away, I just didn't want to go through the whole thing of doing it. It just wasn't me, it just didn't look like me. So I cut it off again.

Hirut: You know what, when I cut off my hair it was in the summer, it was during exam time. My hair needed to be washed, and I hadn't washed it. I was like, I have to cut my hair. I went home and I just cut my hair. I didn't even comb it out because that would take time. Then I washed it, and it felt so good. The amount of shampoo it took to wash it was like half. And I got out of the shower and it took half the time. It was just very nice. It was very liberating having half the hair to take care of. It was the whole thing that I don't have time to wash it, comb it, and then style it. I've got other things going on in my life.

THE CHEMICAL-USING SALON EXPERIENCE:

Frank: I never understood that, you'd see these women go into the salon and they'd have this nice coif, and then the next day you'd see them in a ponytail.

Malene: That's because they slept on it wrong. They didn't prop the pillows up properly.

Naila: They didn't have the correct satin head wraps. (Laughs)

Frank: All that trouble to perm your hair, to relax your hair, and you go through the burning, and the scalp, and the eyes, and the money, but to put it in a pony tail.

Naila: But when you're hair is straight, you have the ponytail option. When you have a big afro, there is no ponytail.

Frank: My experience is so different from yours. I've been to a salon once in my life, and that was to cut off my dreads. That was all I wanted from them. My hair wouldn't do an afro. I would die for an afro, I would wish for an afro. It would do this; it would be flat on the top. And I'd tease it, tease it, tease it some more. I would try to get it to pouf, and just look at it, just limp. I braided my hair. I spent 10 hours braiding my hair; I wanted that so much, I didn't want the other stuff. I wanted it to stay, because it would unravel so much. It wasn't torture for me to deal with my hair. I liked going through those rituals.

Hirut: For me, it's like I identified with my hair. For me to cut my hair, I'm like scared. I want to cut it short, short, short. My sister's hair was to her waist, but recently, she's like almost bald.

Naila: The other thing is that you can't wash your hair before it's going to be permed, you can't wash your scalp. Because when that lye hits your pores and you scratch it, you'll be bawling. I've seen women in the salons with tears running down their eyes, but they're not washing out the perm for anybody, because they have roots, and they want the roots to be gone. They will stand and they will sit there and take it. They will take it, they will take it, take it, take it.

Malene: The good salons know that they would never put it down to the base of your scalp. They'll never put the actual relaxer on your scalp.

Naila: But that's what people want.

Malene: But the real salons, they won't do it, because they know that if they put it there, you can end up losing all the skin in that area, and all the hair there too.

Naila: What this is, it's just such a denial of how you come to this earth. There's one thing if you're doing it as a style and you're relaxing your hair because you want a certain hairstyle. But when you believe that's the only way you can wear your hair. If you sincerely believe that your hair can only be worn in the way other than how it naturally wants to be, then I just don't understand.

GETTING DOWN TO THE ROOTS OF THE MATTER:

Malene: What I find funny is that those women who believe this is my hair, and the extension. I laugh when people come up to me and they ask, how do you do that. I laugh and I say don't you remember, this is what happens when you don't relax your hair.(Laughter) I do have odd hair in a way, the way it's such a tight curl. And people come up to me and ask, how can I get that? You stop relaxing and you'll get it.

Naila: I can't get my hair to look like that. And that's the thing about Black people, because the way my hair takes a perm, to how my sister takes a perm, and my Mom is all different, and we're all in the same bloodline. My Mom can perm her hair all year long, but she will still when she wets it, have a wave. My hair is dead straight. So we all have our own, yes we're all women, but we all have a completely different hair texture. And I have like 8 hair textures in my hair.

Malene: We're willing to deal with our hair textures. Many people are just like, put it in extensions, put a weave on it.

Hirut: It's all about pride, and being creative. I do different things, I don't get bored. It's not somebody else who's doing my hair for me, I'm doing it myself. And I'm not burning myself, there's nothing destroying my brain.

Frank: There's a difference between perming your hair and doing styles with that hair. I used to think that women who went and permed their hair wanted the white hair, and then when they went and curled it, they wanted the curly version of the white hair. I thought it was crazy. But then I realized, if it's about style, press the hair, it can go back to its natural state. If it's about style and variety, then why not do that instead of permanently altering the chemical make-up of your hair.

Malene: There's that whole notion that you don't look beautiful with natural hair, and running your fingers through it. It's not happening, breaking nails. How many combs have I broken, how many teeth are missing from my comb.

Naila: There is no running hands through hair, that's just a crazy lie.

[Judy, with locks, comes and joins the group]

Hirut: My hair breaks my nails. If I attempt to put my hands in it (laughs).

Malene: I have no desire to have my hands running through my hair. I like it the way it is.

Naila: Now I enjoy taking care of my hair.

Malene: Giving yourself massages…

Naila: Yeah, now it's an enjoyable experience. Yeah, it's nice.

ANOTHER PERSONAL HAIR HISTORY:

Judy: My name's Judy and I've had my hair like this for the past six years. I had my hair in dreadlocks since I graduated from film school in Calgary. I decided I was going to go and do it because there weren't very many Black people in Calgary. I felt like I was kind of disappearing. So I felt like I had to go and do something about it, and I did. I walked into a Black hairdressing salon and I asked the woman how can I get dreadlocks. And she said, just don't comb your hair. That's it, yup, don't comb your hair. Another friend of mine told me that you can help your dreads along if you twist a bit after you wash your hair. And I really enjoy this hairstyle the most after I've had a lot of things. I've had the braids, the weave, Jherri Curls, remember those…

(Laughter and comments)

I've tried them all. I think I have sort of a sensitive scalp too. I don't like anything pulling on my scalp, so dreads have really been great for me. It's a really low maintenance hairstyle, so if I have to work really long hours I don't have to worry too much about anything. Definitely it's a look for a woman of the 90s. However, we're living in a White society, it's a bit difficult, sometimes I think the way people perceive you.

They see the image of a gangster when you have dreadlocks on. I've had a lot of different reactions. It's either people really like you, and they want to come up and talk to you because they assume you're counter-culture and they want to talk to you. Or, I've had like little ladies cringing, things like that. But it's been very good. A lot of Black people come up and talk to me now, they feel more comfortable talking to me.

LOCKS IDENTIFY:

Frank: Do you feel you know every dread in Montreal? I feel like I know every dread in Montreal. You walk up to them and you do a head nod.

Judy: Yeah, that's right.

Frank: I love that, I really love that. You get that kind of shock, with anybody?

SHE WORKS HARD FOR THE MONEY:

Judy: Usually, it depends on the age. I find that with young people, they're cool with it. Some people, some older people, not all people, have a harder time with it. It depends on what you do for a living. I could not have my hair like this if I worked at the Bank of Montreal, or something like that.

Frank: But you could, that's the funny thing.

Malene: I worked with about 6 Black women at the Bank of Montreal. And all of them looked at me funny because they were like you just don't look neat, you don't look finished, professional enough to be presenting presentations. They just have this mind set that if you relax your hair you have a more polished look, and no matter how polished I look, I still look a little bit rustic, not rusty.

Frank: It's true. I beg to differ somehow. I've seen dreads in a lot of places they should be. I go into big companies with big head honchos and I go in there with my hair waving around and you have to listen to me, you have to listen to my mouth. I know as soon as I turn my back they are thinking all kinds of things.

Hirut: Are you sure that it's not because you're a Black woman with dreads. I'm sure if you were a Black man, you probably wouldn't be able to come into the office.

Frank: But there's a big difference in the way of the confidence level. I don't want to be a natty dread, I'm not a Rasta, there's a big difference between me being a Rasta and a dread. I aspire to be a Rasta, but I'm not. Neatness does matter to me, I don't want nasty looking hair, so that comes into it. I've never had that problem, but if I had, I guess I didn't approach it that way, or see it.

Naila: I think that people always think about how White people the quote unquote corporate North America will view it. But I don't think White people know enough about Black hair to know the difference from locks, from braids. (Laughter) Sincerely, what I think is because I know that when I started locking my hair, my grandmother sat me down and spoke to me about it and told me her concerns. Because she was saying that in Jamaica if you're hair is locked, that means that you're a Rastafarian, they don't have dread and Rasta. When I went to Jamaica, that meant I was a Rasta. That week I was there, I was a Rasta. I was like no, I'm a dread. They were like no, if you're hair is locked, you're a Rasta. I'm like okay. But here there is a distinction. She sat me down and she said how people are going to view you from our country and our culture is that you are a Rastafarian and with that you have a lot of negative connotations. But I don't think that a lot of North American White people know about Rastafarians.

Frank: They know Bob Marley, and Peter Tosh, and all of those people.

Naila: I wouldn't even go as far as Peter Tosh, it might be Bob Marley (Laughter). But the thing is, they just see it as another style that we have.

Frank: But they've adopted that style too.

Naila: But they don't have the same connotations that Black people have of dreadlocks. So I don't know if it really matters that much if you're in a bank with dreads, or extensions, or a weave, or a perm. You know, because they don't have the distinctions. Whereas a Black person that walks into a bank, will notice the difference between a perm, braids or locks. And they'll probably treat you differently between a perm, braids and locks.

BLACK MEN AND HAIR:

Frank: You said something I think is quite poignant. Because if I were a man, that whole set up between a man and me, a Black man in White society is completely different. They're scared of Black men period, and a dreaded Black man…oh God, they're going to come and shoot the place up. So maybe I wouldn't be able to do that.

Hirut: Already a man with long hair is not acceptable, so like Black, dread, and long hair…it's just not kosher. (Laughter).

A HAIR WRAP:

Hirut: Hair wraps though, I started using them recently. The first time I started using them I felt odd, like everyone was staring at me. But it comes in much handy, when I don't comb my hair, when I have like a bad hair day, it's this miracle, I just wrap my hair…

Malene: It also shows your face more, and when people wrap their hair it's just beautiful because you get to see just them.

SHE IS STILL WORKING HARD FOR THE MONEY-MORE THAN 9 TO 5:

Judy: I have a question for the dreads? Have you guys noticed if you're treated differently before you had dreads and now you have dreads when you go out on the job hunt?

Frank: No, it's pretty much been the same thing. Talk to them on the phone, and then you show up and it's like...(her mouth drops). I tend to try to tie my hair back when I go, the first time, so it's not so noticeable. You don't want that to be the first image they see. There is a difference, I have to talk my way around it more.

Hirut: Are you sitting at the interview thinking are they looking at my hair, are they thinking about my hair?

Frank: I really try to make my hair as inconspicuous as possible, so it's not the first thing they see. I know that the minute I see a little thing sticking out, I have to do some fast talking, or they're not going to bite. Because the connotation is there, if you are a dread, you're smoking up, you know, that's what you're doing, you're not doing anything constructive. I think from the Whites that I know that have adopted a dreadlock hairstyle, they know a bit, but not as much as a West Indian, or an African would know, but they know more about it. The older ones, I don't think they have a clue.

Judy: Unfortunately it's not the hip ones who are working in human resources. (Laughter)

Malene: Have you had problems when you would go out on the job hunt?

Judy: I think being Black is enough of a shock usually. And the fact that I'm a woman as a camera operator in film and video, I'm already out on the edge, so. I don't really think that makes too much of a difference, but I think it would make more of a difference if I was looking for a job in an office, or working at Jean Coutu in a pharmacy. I think it would be something different. Frank: That's true, I haven't really seen a lot of dreads working in cosmetics and things like that.

Naila: I really haven't had any problems with it, because I don't have a problem with it. I just feel like it's not an issue for me. It's not an issue for me. But then the work I've been pursuing is on a part-time basis, I am still in school. But I plan to work in broadcast TV. But I will be on TV, and I will be reading the news, and people will be, but what is this, but that's how life go. And it comes from too many years of watching TV and not seeing anybody that looked like anybody I knew, like close in my family. So, for me it's not an issue, and that's a lot of reasons why my family counselled me against it.

Frank: You just put your best foot forward when you go. You don't have one sticking out like this (hand in the hair).

Naila: That's how I look in the morning. (Laughter)

WHITE PEOPLE AND LOCKS:

Hirut: White people that you come across with dreads, do they identify with you. Do they act like they can identify with the Black cause because they have dreads?

Frank: I know they try.

Judy: Out west it's different. When I was out west I was like what is with all these white people, blond people with dreadlocks. For them, it's like the hippie thing, the Sinead O'Connor look, it's like all that kind of gang that are in it. It's like they've distanced themselves from the Black experience.

Naila: You know that in 5 years, they are going to be like clean-shaven…

Malene: Not even 5 years.

Naila: I know for me what I've found with my hair that you're forever teaching. It's like you're forever teaching all the time. Can I touch it? It's not a petting zoo. I have to tell people you can't come behind and touch my hair.

Frank: You should charge them. (Laughter)

Naila: The most recent experience was when a man came up to me and he said, I don't know if I should say this but you look like Medusa with you hair, I said see, you and me have to talk. It is an issue, you know. It is an issue. But the more of us out there that are just going on with our lives…

Frank: I don't explain my hair to anybody, not even my mother.

NOTION OF PASSING AND HAIR:

Judy: My mother is really status quo. She said, if you ever want to change your hairstyle, I'll pay for the hairdresser. The question I think of trying to assimilate, you live in a White culture, you should try and assimilate.

Frank: To pass as much as possible. No, I don't explain my hair to anybody. If a Black person asks me, I say just leave it alone, don't play with it, that's different. But I'm not explaining my hair to…no, I'm not doing it. You don't explain your hair and your hair rituals to me in the morning, I don't want to know. So why should I explain mine to you.

HAIR EDUCATION:

Naila: I see it differently. Most Black people can't wash their hair everyday, no. It becomes tedious, but this is like an opportunity for them to know. Maybe it's not my job.

Frank: I can't explain for every Black woman, I can only explain for me. And I don't.

Judy: There was a dreadlock in Calgary and I went up and talked to him and he said, mother nature, that was his explanation. (Laughter)

Frank: I like that.

Naila: People would get into big discussions with me about why I locked my hair, and finally I just said, who feels it knows it, as Bob says in his songs. And that's it.

OTHER CULTURES AND HAIR:

Naila: The thing that's weird…do other people do this stuff. With Black people there is such a cultural and political culture that your hair is in. It's never just a style. I know some guys who will only check for those who have natural hair, and some guys will not check a woman who has her hair natural. I don't see other cultures or races having to do that.

Frank: Sure they do, it's just different.

Malene: It might be the actual colour of their hair.

Naila: But it's not a political statement.

Frank: Please, go to Japan. We have to deal with hair, we have to deal with body type, we have to deal with skin colour, and we have to deal with a whole lot of things that are not of the White people. But then you have Asian people, there are a whole set of different imperatives that they have to deal with. So you'll have Chinese women going in to put in a bone so they're eyes are not like that, and blonding, it's insanity, whatever you do to make you more White. There are Indians who will not marry anybody close to our colour. They're Indians, but no, no, no, you're too black.

Hirut: I watch a lot of Japanese animation, and even the hair colour is blond, they're very White looking.

Naila: I'm not worried about them. As Black people, we don't have a unifying language, we don't have a unifying religion, because the religion many of us have was put onto us, we don't have a unifying culture, so I'm just more concerned.

Frank: But I think it's all moving that way though, it's moving towards whitisizing everything. So Japanese people have Japan but not for always. There are Chinese in Trinidad that don't associate themselves with Chinese. You tell them they're Chinese and they go what, I'm Trini, don't talk to me, they don't speak no Chinese. They're Indian people in

Trinidad that go India, they tell you do I look Indian to you, you go yes, I'm a Trini. It's different, it's changing, we've been displaced a lot longer, but we can't go back, like you just said. We have to accept that you're different, and you're different, and we're all different, there's a diaspora, but it doesn't mean Blackland is here. We can still be unified. We can't go back, but we're here.

Hope you enjoyed the salon talk. You can lengthen the discussion in the Salon Utopia community.

SHEA BUTTER MARKET – BRINGING GIFTS TO THE MASSES

In [Beauty](), [Business](), [Culture](), [Health](), [Living](), [Media Writing](), [Pets](), [Writing (all kinds)]() on **June 22, 2009** at **06:58**

Shea Butter Market is the Brainchild of Gifty Serbeh-Dunn

I Called Gifty Serbeh-Dunn As She Was Feeding Her Cat. Her Boys Walked By The Cat Without Feeding Her. Her Big Boy Is Her Husband Wayne Dunn Who Has A Business Degree From Stanford. Her Small 7-Year-Old Boy Is Her Son Kaboré. Serbeh-Dunn Has Many Things To Do Such As Feeding Her Cat And Running A Successful Business Shea Butter Market.

"Shea Butter Market Was Inspired By The Women In My Community And Encouraged By My Husband," Says Serbeh-Dunn.

When She Would Travel To Her Homeland Ghana, She Would Get Some Shea Butter And Bring It Back To Canada. Another Time She Went Home She Asked People There What They Wanted Her To Bring Back From Canada And They Said – "Nothing, We Just Want To Work."

Her Husband Is Involved In Corporate Social Responsibility Work. She Ran The Idea By Her Husband To Start A Business With Shea Butter From The Women She Knew In Ghana To Help Them To Get Work.

Mainly Her Focus Was On Wholesale Accounts. She Connected With Greg Sullivan Who Lived With Her Family 30 Years Ago And Was In Support Of Her Business. Sullivan Lives In Colorado And Worked With The Peace Corps In Takpo As A Volunteer. He Introduced Her To The Widows' Collective Who Now Produces The Shea Butter For Her.

Takpo Village Is Where The Women Who Work For The Business In Ghana Are Based.

"We Went To The Village, We Met With The Chief. His Wife Monica Is The Secretary And Does The Books For The Widows' Group. The Chief Was Familiar With My Concerns With Quality Control And Timely Delivery Of The Product, Because He Lived In Canada He Understood. He Went To Laval University Years Back. Nothing Was Foreign To Him."

The Women Were Jumping Up And Down With Joy. The Women Just Wanted To Work And Needed A Market To Sell Their Shea Butter. She Was Giving Them That Opportunity.

The Takpo Women in Ghana Make the Shea Butter Market Products

"RIGHT THEN AND THERE I ORDERED. I TOLD THEM IN ONE MONTH…CAN YOU MAKE THIS AMOUNT OF SHEA BUTTER?"

SERBEH-DUNN WAS IN GHANA FOR ALMOST TWO MONTHS AND SHE TOOK HER SON, KABORÉ. IN THREE WEEKS, THE WOMEN HAD A TON OF SHEA BUTTER.

"WHEN I BOUGHT THAT SHEA BUTTER, EVERYONE IN THE FAMILY, EVERYONE IN THE COMMUNITY PITCHED IN SO I COULD PACK IT AND SHIP IT. THERE WAS SO MUCH EXCITEMENT AND ENCOURAGEMENT AND SO MUCH SUPPORT, THERE WAS NO TURNING BACK ON THIS THING."

A MICRO-LENDING FUND HELPED THE WOMEN TO PRODUCE THE SHEA BUTTER. SERBEH-DUNN USED HER OWN MONEY TO BUY THE SHEA BUTTER AT FAIR TRADE PRICES. A PERCENTAGE OF THE PROFITS ARE PUT BACK INTO THE FUND SO IT KEEPS IT GOING.

"YOU SEE HOW ENTREPRENEURIAL THESE WOMEN ARE," SERBEH-DUNN SAYS. "THEY REALLY ARE CREATIVE. IT'S THEIR WILL, IT'S THEIR INTEREST, IT'S THEIR BABY. I'M NOT A PHILANTHROPIST. I'M TRYING TO CREATE EMPLOYMENT FOR MYSELF AS WELL."

SHE WAS INTERESTED IN CREATING A JOB FOR HERSELF AND THE WOMEN IN HER COMMUNITY, BUT ALSO TO BRING…CLEAN SHEA BUTTER TO NORTH AMERICA.

"I WAS NAÏVE IN THE BEGINNING," SAYS SERBEH-DUNN. "[IT WAS HARD TO SELL]. PEOPLE GO INTO THE STORES AND BUY."

HER CHALLENGE WAS WHOLESALING THE PRODUCTS. SHE TOOK A COURSE WITH A WOMAN IN BRITISH COLUMBIA WHO TAUGHT HER HOW TO MAKE BEAUTY PRODUCTS. SHE MET HER THROUGH THE FIRST STORE THAT SOLD HER SHEA BUTTER.

The Shea Butter Market Products Products Come in Beautiful Packaging

"IT WAS JUST ALL COMING TOGETHER," SERBEH-DUNN SAYS. "I GOT EIGHT PEOPLE TOGETHER FOR THE COURSE AND WE TOOK THE COURSE AND EVERYTHING WAS COMING TOGETHER."

ANOTHER FRIEND WHO TOOK THE COURSE IS A HERBALIST BY TRAINING. SHE HAS A MASTER'S DEGREE IN NATURAL PERFUME MAKING. SHE CURRENTLY HELPS SERBEH-DUNN WITH PRODUCT DEVELOPMENT.

THEN CAME THE MARKETING. THE HEALTH FOOD SECTOR WAS THE PLACE TO GO. IF YOU GO THROUGH SERBEH-DUNN'S WEBSITE, YOU SEE AN IMPRESSIVE LIST OF PLACES WHERE YOU CAN BUY HER PRODUCT: HTTP://WWW.SHEABUTTERMARKET.COM/PURE_SHEA_BUTTER_MARKET_RETAIL.HTM

"OCTOBER 2004 WE LAUNCHED THE BUSINESS AT THE CANADIAN HEALTH FOOD SHOW IN TORONTO," SERBEH-DUNN SAYS.

THERE HAVE BEEN INCREDIBLE STRUGGLES ALONG THE WAY.

"OVER THE YEARS IT WAS DIFFICULT TO KEEP THAT PRETTY, PRETTY PACKAGING. NOW THE PACKAGING IS FAR MORE SIMPLE, STILL BEAUTIFUL, WITH THE SAME DESIGNER. THE MAN THAT DOES THE DESIGNS FOR THE PACKAGING IS PAUL FREISEN.

"SALES…WE STARTED OFF WELL," SAYS SERBEH-DUNN. "TWO SUMMERS AGO I HAD TO DECIDE TO DOWNSIZE. THE BUSINESS WOULD HAVE DIED TWO SUMMERS AGO IF I HAD NOT TAKEN CHARGE. I WAS GETTING THINGS TOGETHER, BUT I NEEDED AN ADMIN PERSON. I HIRED CINDY. IT'S BEEN GREAT WITH HER."

SHE HAS BEEN ABLE TO PAY AN EMPLOYEE FULL-TIME, BUT HAS NOT BEEN ABLE TO PAY HERSELF MUCH. SHE CAN ALSO PAY HER LOAN.

"SALES COULD BE BETTER. THE RECESSION THERE WAS A DROP. WE HAD STARTED TALKING ABOUT INCREASING SALES BY GOING INTO THE GIFT SECTOR."

SERBEH-DUNN WAS RELYING ON HER HUSBAND'S INCOME FOR HER SURVIVAL BUT THE BUSINESS PAID FOR HER EMPLOYEE. SHE NOW HAS AN AGENT IN THE

PHARMACY AND GIFT STORE SECTOR. THEY RECEIVE SOME OF THEIR ORDERS THAT WAY.

GIFTY SERBEH-DUNN HAS A MA IN CANADIAN STUDIES FROM CARLETON UNIVERSITY AND A MA IN CONFLICT MANAGEMENT AND ANALYSIS FROM ROYAL ROADS UNIVERSITY.

"I'M FROM NORTHERN GHANA, EVERY TIME I SAW HOW THE RESOURCES IN GHANA ARE NEGLECTED JUST BECAUSE OF POVERTY. THE SHEA TREE IS A TREE OF LIFE. IT WOULD BE SO PAINFUL FOR THEM [THE WOMEN] TO CUT DOWN ONE OF THOSE TREES. WOMEN TAKE GOOD CARE OF THE ENVIRONMENT WHEN THEY ARE WELL-POSITIONED."

THE WOMEN HAVE APPROACHED HER ABOUT A TREE-PLANTING PROJECT. YOU NEED $5,000 USD TO MAKE IT HAPPEN. SERBEH-DUNN IS WORKING ON RAISING IT.

SHE OFFERS MANY EXCELLENT PRODUCTS – ALL NATURAL. SPLAX IS A PRODUCT THAT CAN BE FOUND AT MOUNTAIN EQUIPMENT COOP. IT IS A NON-CHAFFING PRODUCT.

Shea Butter Market Offers Many Products, Including Splax Available at MEC

"THEY WERE LOOKING FOR A CLEAN NON-CHAFFING PRODUCT," SAYS SERBEH-DUNN, AND SHEA BUTTER MARKET DELIVERED.

"LATELY, I'VE STARTED TO HEAR FROM CUSTOMERS 'AH, YOU'RE STILL AROUND – GREAT I'LL TAKE ONE OF YOUR PRODUCTS.'"

JUST AS WE WERE GETTING OFF THE PHONE, FRIEDA, HER CAT IS BY THE CREEK AND THE BOYS ARE OUT PRAWNING. SHE LIVES ON VANCOUVER ISLAND.

SERBEH-DUNN TOLD ME A STORY THAT ONE TIME A GROUP OF GIRLS PHONED HER AND SAID, "WE LOVE YOUR LIP BALM. IT IS THE BEST LIP BALM IN THE WORLD! WE CALLED BECAUSE WE WANT MORE." THEY DID NOT LEAVE THEIR NAMES OR NUMBERS.

"I COULD NEVER REACH THOSE GIRLS BECAUSE IT DID NOT SHOW UP ON CALLER ID."

ALSO WHAT SHEA BUTTER MARKET HAS IN THE WORKS IS BEING PART OF A FUNDRAISING CATALOGUE. THE CATALOGUE SELLS PRODUCTS AND SOME OF THE FUNDS GO TO THE SCHOOL.

"THEY WANTED GOOD STUFF, SO THEY CAME TO US," SAYS SERBEH-DUNN.

FOR MORE INFORMATION ABOUT SHEA BUTTER MARKET: HTTP://WWW.SHEABUTTERMARKET.COM/INDEX.HTM#.

The Radio Call

In [Education](), [Health](), [Living](), [Media Writing](), [Opinion](), [Writing (all kinds)](), [travel]() on **July 18, 2009** at **01:46**

When It Comes To AIDS, It Is Better to Light A Candle - Photo Courtesy of StockExpert

It was a Saturday afternoon and the radio was on. I was living in Uganda in the fall of 1996 and the winter of 1997. The radio was calling out a list of names. I could not understand why.

I asked my aunt why the radio was calling out so many names. She said they are calling out names of people who have funerals; most of those people had died from AIDS she had told me.

I was shocked. Were there really those many people dying from AIDS in Uganda? The name calling went on for hours. One name repeated after another.

I guess it was true. The day after I had arrived in Uganda, I was over at my cousin's house. She showed me one of her wedding photos and there were about eight people in the picture. She said that five of the people had already died from AIDS. She cautioned me not to have intimate relations with anyone I would meet while in Uganda.

The statistics are shocking and growing. There are more than 30 million people living with HIV/AIDS around the world. About half of these are women. These statistics come from Worldwide AIDS and HIV statistics. More than 25 million have died from AIDS since 1981. Imagine…

Those people could have found a cure for cancer. Those people could have found a cure for AIDS. Those people could have come up with a work of art that would have stirred the souls of millions. Those people could have written a book that would stir the souls of millions. Those people could have been in the Book of World Records for being the best soccer player. They also could have simply lived, loved life and enjoyed raising a family, as well as working and contributing to the world's economy.

The travesty of AIDS is enormous. The spread of it mainly comes from a lack of education. While I was in Uganda, some people thought that you needed to be gay to get the disease. They did not believe that having unprotected heterosexual relations could result in transmitting HIV. These thoughts even came from people that were training others in understanding how HIV was spread.

Efforts were made though. While doing a story for YTV Canada while I was in Uganda, I followed an organization that would go to schools and use bananas to show students how to put on a condom. Condom use was low at that time, however has grown since.

Creating Things: Profile of Roger McTair (Originally Published on Impowerage.com)

In Creative Writing, Culture, Education, Entertainment, Health, Living, Media Writing, Writing (all kinds), book reviews on **July 19, 2009** at **04:34**

Roger McTair Creates Magic - Photo Courtesy of Seneca College's Website

Roger McTair is a director, poet, professor and writer who lives in Toronto, Canada. He has had short stories air on CBC Radio and BBC Radio.

He was born in Trinidad and Tobago on October 7, 1943. Not having much to do while growing up galvanized his love of creating things.

"I grew up in a film-loving country and there were few outlets, one of them were sports for boys, soccer, cricket, the movies, hanging out – the movies," says McTair. "There were very limited things to do. There was some theatre if you were middle class, but there wasn't a lot of theatre.

"Yeah, we would go to the movies," continues McTair. "Very specifically what happened when I was about 17 they would only show European movies and I found them so different. A lot of Italian movies, a lot of French movies, so I sort of realized at that point that you didn't have to make movies only about cowboys and Indians. I looked at a lot of Japanese movies too."

McTair came to Canada in 1969. He went back to Trinidad and Tobago for awhile, then returned to Canada in 1970.

"I had a lot of friends here," McTair says. "I had friends in Brooklyn too."

He went to what is now known as Ryerson University. He has also taken some courses at the University of Toronto and a lot of workshops. He studied film and a lot of philosophy at Ryerson.

"I did a lot of freelance writing for Caribbean newspapers and the black newspapers in Toronto." McTair says about what he did after he graduated from Ryerson.

He started making movies in 1979. Mainly his career has focused on documentaries. His first film was called, It's Not an Illness. It was about being able to run while pregnant to the very end. This film garnered McTair a finalist position at the Genies (Canada's version of the Oscars). It also won an award with a medical association in California.

"I made Home to Buxton [next]. Home to Buxton won a Genie and it showed in New York and California. I made a film with Jennifer Hodge called Home Feeling. It showed a lot. It was about the relationship between the police and the Jane-Finch community in Toronto."

McTair has done some work with Vision-TV. His almost complete filmography also includes Hymn to Freedom done in 1994 with Almeta Speak Productions. Children Are Not the Problem done with the Congress of Black Women of Canada in 1991. Jane-Finch Again done with Prieto-McTair Productions in 1997. Different Timbres that was a short at 14 minutes. His latest film was Journey to Justice done in 2000 for the National Film Board.

McTair has been teaching at Seneca College for about 16 years or more. He teaches media writing (basic writing), documentary, film, second semester media writing, advanced media writing, analyzing short stories and doing film and documentary.

McTair has done a lot of short story writing and written a couple plays, plus opinion piece writing. He used to write for the Star quite a bit. McTair has also done some poetry. He has been published with Caribbean newspapers and one of them broadcasted with the BBC, the fable book of Caribbean short stories is published with Faber. It's called the Faber Book of Caribbean Short Stories.

"I have stories published in an academic text in Boston," says McTair. "It's for students doing courses, such as English and writing with a huge press in the States."

He's done so many things and no longer keeps a resume, so he has stopped keeping track.

In terms of health, McTair describes his as "mediocre for 65." He has high blood pressure and could be in a lot better shape. McTair goes to his doctor on a regular basis and also walks.

"I'm quite casual about life, I don't always know when I'm stressed."

You can hear the pride and joy in McTair's voice when he speaks of his son Ian Kamau Prieto-McTair.

"He had an Ontario Arts Council grant to work with Schools Without Borders. Now he is working on some youth project."

Prieto-McTair is an artist-at-large.

"The apple did not fall too far from the tree," that's what McTair agreed his son says.

"I have always done the same thing that I have done. I have always worked in writing and creative fields. And when I leave Seneca I will continue to do that."

Study Finds New Technology For Fossil Fuels Can Cut CO2

In Business, Culture, Education, Environment, Health, Living, Media Writing, Writing (all kinds) on **July 20, 2009** at **07:11**

EPRI Did a Revealing Study on Electricity - Photo Courtesy of Stockexpert

A study by the Electric Power Research Institute (EPRI) has found the replacement of fossil fuels technology with electric ones would result in energy savings. The energy savings are as high as 71.7 quadrillion BTUs.

These savings would cut CO2 by 4,400 million tons between 2009 and 2030.

The new technology is meant for residential, commercial and industrial use. Sixty per cent of the fossil fuels that are currently in use are mainly come from cars and automobiles. Residential, commercial and industrial areas are also heavily used by fossil fuels. Electricity is becoming more de-carbonized and this will have a huge impact on the cars we drive, the houses we live in, its use in businesses and the industrial sectors.

"The Potential to Reduce CO2 Emissions by Expanding the End-Use Applications of Electricity" is the title of the EPRI study. The 2008's Energy Information Administration (EIA) was used as a case study for the report.

Federally mandated appliance standards and building codes, plus market-driven efficiency improvements and rule-making procedures were taken into account with the case study. In the report, projections are made that between 2008 and 2030 there will be a flat fee for electricity. As well, the report also predicts that before 2008 there will be government-sponsored and utility-sponsored end-use energy programs to reduce fees for electricity.

The report also goes on to say that the residential sector will prove to benefit the most from the reductions in CO2 emissions. The commercial and industrial sectors will benefit from a decrease in CO2 emissions at about the same rate.

Reductions in CO2 emissions of 320 million metric tons each year will result in a 4.7 per cent decrease in emissions in 2030 compared to the previous forecast of reduction of CO2 emissions.

The report found that there are two key ways to save energy and reduce CO2 emissions with the use of electric technologies. The first is to retrofit older equipment with new and more modern technologies. The second is to replace fossil fuel technologies with more efficient electric-based technologies.

"It is clear in order to meaningfully address the issues of climate change we will need to fully explore and develop existing, as well as new technologies that will address this important issue," said Mike Howard, a senior vice president at EPRI. "This study explores the greater potential for CO2 reductions through a review of demand-side opportunities, including furthering the advancement and utilization of energy-efficient end-use technologies."

Conducting research and development relating to the delivery and generation of electricity to the public is what the Electric Power Research Institute, Inc. (EPRI, www.epri.com) does. EPRI brings together scientists, academics, engineers to address how electricity can be improved based on reliability, efficiency, safety, health and the environment. The members of EPRI represent 90 per cent of the people who work in the electricity industry and its members span across 40 countries. Their main offices and laboratories are in Palo Alto, CA, Charlotte, NC, Knoxville, TN and Lennox, Mass.

Donna Kakonge is a professor, journalist and author living in Toronto. Her books can be bought at her online store at: http://stores.lulu.com/kakonged. She also has an online magazine called *Donna* at: http://kakonged.wordpress.com. Her official website is www.donnakakonge.com.

Source:
http://my.epri.com/portal/server.pt/gateway/PTARGS_0_95399_317_205_776_43/http;/uspalecp604;7087/publishedcontent/publish/epri_study_finds_greater_efficiency_in_electric_end_use_technologies_da_653269.html

The Fool (Excerpt from Stories in Red and Yellow)

In Creative Writing, Culture, Education, Entertainment, Living, Writing (all kinds), travel on **August 5, 2009** at **07:49**

Afro Almost Plays Dice With Her Life - Photo Courtesy of Stockexpert.com

I was embarrassed to tell my boyfriend's parents I was out of work again. It had been a year and I was on welfare, but at least I had love in my life. Richie, my boyfriend, just got a job as a public relations officer at the University of Toronto. He had been looking for a long time and was feeling lucky. When his parents came into town one mild January weekend for his birthday, we all decided to go down to Niagara Falls to the casinos. Gambling had never been my thing, but going was the only present I could afford for him.

The line into the casino was long, even for January. With my laugh lines no longer coming out just when I laughed, I figured I would have no problem getting in.

"You're ID, please," a man with arms as big as my legs asked me.

"I forgot it in the car."

"You have to be 18 to get in, miss."

"I'm more than 18. I'm 32."

"I need to see ID."

Richie and his parents whispered to me it was no problem for us to go back to the car, but I shook my head.

"Look, I don't even want to gamble. I don't even have any money on me," I showed him my empty wallet. "Plus, I am 32, turning 33 April 19th. My name is Afro and my parents called me that because Cornell University's Afro-American society seized the Student Union that day. Plus, I remember just turning 10 and watching the volcano Soufriere in St. Vincent erupting on CBC, the only channel we could get."

The other bouncer at the door, who happened to be a black woman, came up and looked at me closely.

"I remember both those things. Oh yeah, Steve, let her in."

"I've never even heard about that." He smiled at me and stepped aside.

We all went into a colourful and smoky wonderland, the casino.

"Af, I'm going to win big, I can feel it," Richie said as we stood in line to get our coins. His parents already got their coins and were off to gamble.

"Just calm down, Rich. These places are money pits. My mother has always said there's nothing like good, honest work to gain money, and you have that now."

"I know baby, but I want to win big. God, let me be lucky tonight," he said looking up at the chandeliered ceiling.

Richie was going to spend a $100 on those silly coins and I convinced him to only start with $20.

We walked around the casino trying to find an empty slot machine. Neither of us knew the card games well enough to play at those tables. I could not help but think how pathetic these people looked. Some people had two buckets of coins and their leg draped over the chair beside them so they could play two slot machines at once. At the same time, they would have a cigarette perched on their watering lips.

Richie and I finally found a slot machine and he plugged in three coins with no success, then he moved on to the next one. We kept doing this for about 10 minutes before I told him I was tired of flitting around this crowded place like a leaf in the wind.

We rested beside this old black woman who I noticed had American quarters in her bucket. As Richie played, I watched. I wondered where the black woman found the money to waste. I hoped she was not using her social security to pay for her gambling habit. I believed if I stripped down naked, this older woman or even Richie would notice at this moment. The focus people had while playing their games amazed me.

"Damn, baby. I lost everything."

I started to laugh. "I told you not to gamble.

Well, don't cry. At least it's only $20 and not a $100."

Richie and I met up with his parents at the exit, had dinner at a diner since no one had money for anything more than that, and we drove back home.

***

My first thought when I woke up in the morning was I could not wait to get out of the room I was renting in Little India, east of Toronto, so I could move in with Richie like we had planned. I would need a job first. Then the phone rang.

"Hello, Afro speaking." I was so used to working in offices I still answered the phone like that.

"Hi Afro, it's John."

"John?" I was trying to place the voice.

"John, from the temp agency."

"Oh, John, how are you?"

"Fine, Afro. Do you have a job, yet?" Just like John to get down to business.

"No."

"Well, I have good news. There's an assignment in Yorkville that starts tomorrow with a property management firm."

"Really?" I was grinning now.

"Yes. Can you start tomorrow?"

"Yes, what time?"

He hesitated and I could hear him shuffling papers. "Be there by nine o'clock sharp. They need you for a week, but the last time they took a girl from this agency a week turned into three years and she left because she found a better job."

John told me about the money and reminded me to fill out my timecards that were gathering dust in my desk. I hung up the phone excited. I would be making $500 a week, almost as much as I made on welfare in a month. I spent the day doing laundry for my good clothes, shining my shoes, dusting off my office purse, making my lunch for tomorrow and Richie treated me to dinner.

The next day I showed up at the office 15 minutes before nine. I could have been there earlier, but there was a 20 minute delay on the subway. I lived in the east end and it took almost an hour to get to Yorkville. I did not mind, I had a job now.

I walked into the office knowing I looked great. I had on a navy dress with a matching blazer. The outfit was a graduation gift from my mother years ago and still fit. My legs were itching from the pantyhose, but I still grinned at the receptionist.

"Hello, my name is Afro Kingston. I'm here to see Mr. Dirch. I'm from the temp agency."

The receptionist gave me a cold stare. "Afro? You were supposed to be here at eight."

"At eight?"

"Don't look so surprised. The agency must have told you. John is completely reliable."

"I was getting irritated with this bitch's attitude. "Look, John must have been smoking crack or something, because he told me to come at nine."

Before the bitch could pick up the phone that was ringing she said I could leave, now.

I walked around Yorkville looking at all the things I could not afford, and looking like I could afford them. Close to the shopping mall,

Hazelton Lanes, I passed by a sign for a fortuneteller. Satisfaction guaranteed it read.

I took a deep breath and let it out heavily. I needed to know where my life was going. It had been almost a year now I had been on welfare since I lost my job as a sales associate at The Bay. I left to follow my ex-boyfriend to Thailand and blew all my money on that trip. He lost the job promised to him there, and we broke up soon after that. I came back to Canada with my tail between my legs and a sexual disease that is not fatal but would rather not mention. The dog was playing around all along.

I walked into the psychic's place without even realizing what I was doing.

"Hello, welcome."

This beautiful tall blonde woman greeted me. "I'm Brenda."

"Are you the psychic?"

"Yes, my dear. What are you looking for? Crystal ball, tarot cards, palm reading, runes…I can help with anything you prefer."

"What's the cheapest thing?" I asked by reflex.

"We have a $40 special on our full tarot readings. You can ask any questions you want. It lasts about an hour."

Well, I had nowhere to rush off to, except a cramped room and roaches to feed.

"I'll take that."

"Fine, let's go back to this private room here."

We went behind a curtain and Brenda spent the next hour talking to me more than me asking questions. She knew about my ex-boyfriend, and my trip abroad. She knew I was having financial problems and was on social assistance. She also knew I had another love in my life and was struggling to get a job so we could get property together.

"I wanted to tell you stuff in your past and present so you know I'm for real," said Brenda. "But, you must understand, it's difficult to see your future because there is such a dark cloud around you. There is a lot of negativity around you and jealousy. God has guided me to you today to improve your life."

I got chills when she said the word God. "You can improve my life?"

"We can do it together. You try to do everything yourself. You need help, Afro. And I believe in karma. The good I do for you will come back to me three-fold. And the good you will be able to do for others in the future, which I do see, will come back to you three-fold."

"Is this going to cost me anything?"

"Well," said Brenda while punching on a calculator. "I need to buy the materials and give you a special bath and candle burning to do for three days to clear you're aura."

I sat silent thinking about how much I could afford. I only had $350 in my bank account. I needed that for rent. But I was getting another cheque coming soon.

"It would cost $350."

"I don't have that kind of money," I said in shock. "Well, I do, but I need it for rent."

"Well, how much do you think you can afford?"

"Well I have to have some money in the bank for emergencies. I am getting another welfare cheque in a week."

Brenda smiled. "Well, how about I make it $350 for the reading and for the psychic work and materials I will have to do for you. I guarantee you, you will get results. You're life will turn around. It will be like having money in the bank."

"Well, I don't have that kind of money on me. Do you have an Interac machine"

"No, but I'll wait for you, there are banks around here."

I left Brenda's place and walked to my bank on Bloor. The man in front of me was taking a long time and I was thinking about changing my mind before I was stunned when the man turned around.

"Mark?"

"Afro! You're back from Thailand?"

"Things didn't work out there."

"That's too bad, Afro."

Mark was my ex-boss at The Bay.

"How are things at The Bay?"

"Great. We're really expanding. We have a new home decorating section you would be perfect in, but it looks like you already have a job."

My eyes bugged. "No, Mark, I don't have a job."

"Really, Afro. We have an orientation for new workers in the decorating section tomorrow, and we're short one person who didn't show up for the interview. Are you interested?"

"I'll be there as long as you care."

Mark laughed. "I do care, Af." He patted me on the arm. "Good to have you back."

I went to the bank machine any ways and took out $20 so I could treat myself to lunch.

***

Later that day, I called my mother who had retired in St. Vincent. I told her about my experience with the psychic and how it made me blush to think I chastised Richie for gambling $20 after almost gambling with tarot for $350 myself.

"You know, Afro-sheen, there are no quick fixes, only ups and downs you can't avoid. Even the true fool knows that."

Channel Zero (Originally Published in the Queen's Alumni Review)

In [Business](), [Culture](), [Education](), [Entertainment](), [Living](), [Media Writing](), [Opinion](), [Video Work](), [Writing (all kinds)](), [travel]() on **August 6, 2009** at **04:53**

Stephen Marshall Traveled Around the World for a Video Magazine - Photo Courtesy of Stockexpert.com

By Mary Luz Mejia and Donna Kakonge

He's been dubbed "guerrilla film maker," "boy wonder" and "video artist" – titles he doesn't seem to mind and takes in stride as he charges toward the goal: "to establish and alternative universe to that of broadcast television."

Equipped with a super hi-8 palmcorder, Stephen Marshall did just that. From a crack house in Belize to the streets of Thailand people from all walks of life shared their stories with the inquisitive young man behind the camera.

Marshall, a Queen's arts '91 graduate who majored in philosophy has set out to live his belief that "life is about experiences." Traveling the world has provided him with an interactive education of sorts. Part of that education included probing the overtly racist minds of some neo-Nazis in Slovenia. As a Jew, Marshall admits he was afraid, but that he walked away thinking "at least they're honest."

Not everyone he met in his travels was scary. A beautiful little boy named Hope in South Africa shared his feelings of forgiveness about his country with Marshall.

Traveling around the world and meeting enlightening people was not just about becoming more culturally aware. It was and is about Channel Zero – that alternative universe to mainstream television. In more specific terms, Channel Zero is an advertisement free quarterly video magazine that you can't tune into – rather you have to buy it.

Channel Zero is meant to promote "participatory viewership."

Varda

In Beauty, Business, Culture, Entertainment, Living, Media Writing, Music, Video Work, Writing (all kinds) on **August 7, 2009** at **05:41**

Varda Etienne is now a Host of a Radio Show in Quebec

As she bops and moves looks real pretty and talks a fast game on Canada's French music station, Musique Plus, Varda Etienne, 27 and a VJ, works on two shows: Bouge (the highest rated show on Musique Plus) and Groove. She does not like music that lacks movement, but, she has other things on her mind.

"What bothers me is how corrupted the world is today," she says.

Musique Plus's age group target is 12 to 24. For the shows Varda works on, it's a bit older. Varda says what really makes the music station a different place to work in – it's the only TV environment where she doesn't feel trapped. The atmosphere is really cool and hip.

Etienne says it is hard in her business of glamour TV to find people you can trust.

"The hard thing of being in the business is to find the real ones, the real people who are not just using you and wanting free tickets (to a show)."

Etienne finds it hard to disassociate her from her sex symbol image. "I'm 27 now, but I'm going to be 30, and 40, and 50…this can't last forever. I'm sick of old men only after my ass," she says.

Etienne notes it is also hard for her to find a good black man that shares the same vision as she does. She feels blessed for all she has…but the glamour life can be lonely. In the area of relationships with men, she has been unsuccessful.

The one man in her life, who keeps her sane and helps her persevere, is her 7-year-old son Alexis.

Varda gets paid less than in other places on TV, but she makes more money than many dream of from working three hours a week live, with repeats that put her on-air for 20 hours.

With her more pay and less work attribute, she takes care of her son Alexis. She had him at the age of 20, unplanned, but no accident.

"It's crazy but I do manage to do everything. Being a Mom is a full-time job. I could never manage to work a 40-hour shift. My goal is to be a full-time Mom. Alexis is the one man who doesn't make me feel like a star. I don't have to wear make-up for him or dress-up," she notes.

Alexis has been her reason for keeping on in the tough competitive world of TV music. The love of her son is her philosophy of life. He balances everything.

"It's unconditional FREE love, and unconditional on top of that."

Her contractual love comes from her work environment at Musique Plus.

What has set her apart in success at work was finding someone she believed in, and who believed in her. A great person to always have in her corner – her boss, Moses Znaimer.

Next and foremost, she believed in herself, and maintained the obligation she had to follow her heart.

"I didn't become Varda. I was always Varda before TV." Varda also finds love through music and men.

"Barry White is the only man who brings palm trees and sunshine in your living room when it's raining outside," says Varda.

She listens to disco and Teddy Pendergrass too, as well as Creole music from her roots.

For her future, Varda hopes for wisdom.

"It's a hard thing to achieve but I want to be the best human being I can be, I want to be the best Mom, I want to be happy. I want to sit in my backyard, reading, just happy to be breathing."

Book review of Cane by Jean Toomer

In [Beauty](), [Creative Writing](), [Culture](), [Education](), [Entertainment](), [Living](), [Media Writing](), [Opinion](), [Writing (all kinds)](), [book reviews]() on **August 9, 2009** at **02:41**

Jean Toomer is the Author of Cane

I came across this book for three dollars at a Lebanese restaurant in the McGill ghetto of Montreal. It was worth every penny, and proves that you can find good books for affordable prices.

Jean Toomer was a genius. Cane is part of the Harlem Renaissance of the 1920's. This book has influenced such writers as Langston Hughes, Countee Cullen, Eric Walrond, Zora Neale Hurston, Wallace Thurman, Rudolph Fisher and his other contemporaries of the 20s. When reading the book, there is no wonder that it had a tremendous impact, and should be revisted for some reasons I will point out now.

The book is unique in style. A combination of short stories, with poetry which all have an undercurrent of the racism that existed during the 20s. Toomer himself was a mixed race man, living a borderline life between the black and white worlds, and his characters are sometimes white, sometimes black, probably reflecting his inner feelings.

There's Esther who lusts after a black man who had a religious experience in the street and she spends years pining for him. And then there's Becky who had two Negro sons who live in a house by the road and no one knows whether she's dead or alive.

He writes of sorrow such as this between blacks and whites, but also of beauty of women, and the ugliness of women. For a man, he writes women well.

His description of people and places is so lively, it is like the book is a TV screen where you can hear and see. Here's one example from his poetry, this one called « Face »:

Hair-
Silver-gray,
Like streams of stars,
Brows-
Recurved canoes
Quivered by the ripples blown by pain,
Her eyes-
Mist of tears
Condensing on the flesh below
And her channeled muscles
Are cluster grapes of sorrow
Purple in the evening sun
Nearly ripe for worms.

His imaginary is startling. I would recommend this book to anyone who wants to understand the desperation of living with the race relations of the 20s of the United States. Also just anyone who loves good writing. The sentences are short and clear. He wastes no words to strengthen his point. Just like chewing on sugar cane strengthens the teeth. Cane.

The Color Complex: The Politics of Skin Color Among African Americans

In Beauty, Culture, Education, Living, Media Writing, Movie Reviews, Opinion, Writing (all kinds), book reviews on **August 11, 2009** at **06:10**

The Color Complex is a Book that Discovers Some Blacks Obsession with Colour - Photo Courtesy of Stockexpert

Too many blackfolks are fools about color and hair. -Mabel Lincoln, interviewee in Drylongso: A Self-Portrait of Black America, by John Langston Gwaltney (1)

The Color Complex mentions the references made to skin colour in Spike Lee's movies such as School Daze and Jungle Fever. Is hair one of the factors that lures many Black men like Flipper (Wesley Snipes) in Jungle Fever to white women? Why is it that it seems like the more successful a black man is he will have a white woman as his wife or girlfriend? Do black men have more a complex about colour and hair than black women do? Is this evidenced in the fact that fewer black women marry outside of the race and MAY feel more comfortable marrying and dating men darker than they are?

Movies by Spike Lee and other African-Americans do lead to questions and insights about skin colour and hair – what about the films and videos found in Canada? There are a number of home-grown productions that can be looked at that directly or indirectly deal with hair, such as Clement Virgo's Rude.

The colour complex does manifest itself in a number of situations. This links to the ideas found in "Internalized Oppression" by Suzanne Lipsky. It is just another expression of black self-hatred. Black hair, being a marked difference from European ancestry can be a symbol or a target for expressing black self-hatred.

In The Color Complex an attractive medium-toned Black woman in her 20s was told by a man she was dating that she was too dark and that it was important for him to have light-skinned children. I can completely relate with this comment. A light-skinned (biracial) man I dated for almost three years was walking with me at a beach close to my house when he expressed a comment about my colour. This was months after we broke up and I knew that he had started seeing another biracial person. It was night when we were walking and he commented on how dark I was. It made me think that he never complained about such things when he was in bed with me for all those years, but I was too stunned to say anything. During our relationship I do not remember an instance when my colour ever seemed too dark for him. Actually in the summer when he would tan to a shade closer to mine he would seem to be almost in a rivalry with me to come close to my dark brown shade. It's interesting how colour can become a cruel reminder of why you may no longer be with someone.

A light-skinned woman with long straight hair comments about how her looks separated her from a relationship with her siblings. Although as a dark-skinned woman with African hair (who would not change a thing if I could turn back the hands of time, if push came to shove) does not have a lot of sympathy for the problems associated with those who have skin and hair privilege. It is only fair that in my quest to talk to women who are wearing their hair naturally that I also include those people who are by self-definition black and may have straight or wavy hair, such as light-skinned Blacks, biracial people who identify as black and Africans from Ethiopia and Somalia who on average seem to have a different texture to their hair.

*Reference is made to a manuscript The Bleaching Syndrome by Ronald Hall

As is stated in the introduction of The Color Syndrome the book is not trying to make anyone feel bad for having light skin or straight hair (naturally or chemically). The conviction is to inform. This is my aim as well with my thesis, to build understanding around the concept of black hair.

This book goes into a historical analysis that mentions among many things the "one drop rule" for blacks in the States. With this rule in effect in the States, not being sure of how much it holds true in Canada, what is black hair? How exactly do you define it? Is the hair of an Ethiopian just as black as mine is? The hairstyle books seem to define it as super curly hair and seem to have no problem with it, but I feel it is a bit problematic.

*Reference is made to Harriet Jacob's Incident in the Life of a Slave Girl

The thing about having a broad definition about black hair is that it does not factor in that those without super curly hair get treated differently. Such as during slavery, those with light skin and straighter hair would get preferential treatment, be the first to be educated, seen as more worthy by whites by garnering more money on the auction block. Later in history during the Black Renaissance exclusive black social clubs, elite neighbourhoods, churches, and schools would also be restricted to people who could pass a paper bag test in terms of colour and who most likely had "good hair." (25-28).

And in still other 'houses of worship' throughout Virginia and in such cities as Philadelphia and New Orleans, a fine-toothed comb was hung on a rope near the front entrance. If one's hair was too nappy and snagged in the comb, entry was denied (27).

Information like this establishes how far-reaching the politics of hair are:

Students on Black college campuses also claim that skin color affects their social opportunities, especially within the Greek system. Some maintain that membership in the more exclusive organizations still depends largely on having the right hair texture and skin color. However, many "Greeks" dispute this claim, arguing that skin color has never been a factor distinguishing Black fraternities and sororities, since most were founded at the turn of the century when the vast majority of students were mulatto. Others confess that when students from varied backgrounds started attending college, color did start to become a factor in the hierarchy of Greek organizations: the more elite the fraternity or sorority, the lighter-skinned its members. The highly regarded Alpha Kappa Alpha sorority and Kappa Alpha Psi fraternity must still contend with reputation for being partial toward Blacks with light skin and "good" hair (30).

Just as much as blacks may have created a world where light skin and straighter hair can provide privilege, there are also cases where it falls short in determining black radicalism or militancy.

In proclaiming "Black is Beautiful," some dark-skinned leaders even questioned the militancy of light-skinned Black radicals, believing that they had benefited too long from color privilege to understand oppression. Dedication to the Black cause was occasionally judge by how well someone's non-kinky hair could be styled in an Afro, or by how willing a light-skinned radical was to sleep with someone who was darker (36).

This book also notes that the money made between dark-skinned and light-skinned blacks is proportional to the earning difference between blacks and whites. Light-skinned blacks earn a dollar for every 72 cents a dark-skinned black makes. This also translates into hair since it is closely linked to skin colour. This also draws into question all the law suits that have been filed by black women about their hairstyles.

*Reference is made to Maya Angelou's I Know Why the Caged Bird Sings – I would like to take the reference made about hair directly from the book

Angelou's story is one example of many references made by black authors about hair and skin colour.

In the "Embracing Whiteness" chapter it is pointed out that businesspeople like George Johnson, founder and chief of Johnson Products who make skin bleaches and hair straighteners says he is only providing a service to black women, rather than "getting rich off black women's insecurities"(43). There are an increasing number of women who are turning away from these products and going more natural. Will these companies be changing with the times too? Perhaps they have already showed signs of doing so since there are a number of products that promote natural ingredients and are made for natural hair that are more mass produced.

These beauty practices have a long history. While still under the cruel and dehumanizing conditions of slavery, many Negro women tried to alter the texture and appearance of their hair. Most of the time, a slave woman kept her head wrapped in a "do-rag," or bandanna but on special occasion she might straighten her hair with some kind of grease, as her African ancestors may have done. House servants fared better in this regard because they had access to hog lard, margarine, or buttr. Sometimes they could even borrow "Miss Ann's" fine scissors to give themselves a stylish trim. But field hands had to use shears and axle grease, which was not only tough to remove but also caused the hair to stretch and break (43).

*Reference is made to a book Madam C.J. Walker: Entrepreneur by A'Lelia P. Bundles (more is written about Walker in Hairraising).
*Reference is made to a turn-of-the-century song called "Nappy Headed Blues"

My hair is cantcha, don'tcha.
You can't comb it.
Don'tcha try.
Nappy, that's the reason why.

Until the 1960s most Black women, and some Black men, regularly straightened their hair. It was rare for a Black woman to be seen in public with unprocessed hair, and those who dared risked the ridicule and even the chastisement of close friends and family members. When the Afro became fashionable during the sixties, it was radical in more ways than one. It not only associated the wearer with the politics of the Black power movement, but, for women, it also signalled the abandonment of the hair-straightening products they had been conditioned to use since childhood. The Afro eventually went the way of all trendy hairstyles, and by the mid-seventies most Blacks (although not as many as before) had returned to processing their hair (47).

Sociologist Bertice Berry found through an analysis of Ebony, Jet, Essence between 1985 and 1987, that a third of the ads were meant to fix the "bad hair" that is supposed to afflict many blacks. I have noticed in these magazines that they are filled with hair ads, as well as many community newspapers.

Perhaps there is a historical base for the desire for straight hair among Blacks:

One Black model and buisnesswoman, Naomi Sims, maintains that the use of hair straighteners and dyes should not be considered just a White assimilationist practice. Long before Parisian women of the 1920s made straight hair fashionable, the women of the Swahili and the Hova of Madacasar were straightening their hair with heavy oil and parting it down the center. And 'Beatle bangs,' named for the hairstyles of the Beatles of the sixties, can be traced back to the women of Chad, who twisted their hair into dreadlocks and then cropped it straight across the forehead. The same is true for hair coloring. Black women who dye their hair a lighter shade are often accused of trying to look White, but for a long time African women have been coloring their hair with henna, ocher, plant dyes, and other natural substances. In one tribe, women traditionally dye their hair blond, a cosmetic practice hardly related to wanting to be White (48).

*Reference is made to George Schuyler's Black No More, about a scientist who invented a machine that could magically transform Black people into Whites

The desire to lighten one's skin and alter one's features can be seen as a form of Black self-hatred. Yet Black women who straighten their hair or bleach their skin are in a sense behaving no differently than women of other cultures, who bind their feet or tighten corsets around their waists to achieve a culturally defined feminine appearance. Still, the reactions of Blacks to the grooming habits of other Blacks are deeply rooted and complex. When a White woman with brown eyes wears blue contact lenses, she might be thought vain for doing so, but most people would not assume that she was denying her heritage. When a White woman bakes under the hot sun all day to tan her pale skin, she might be admonished for risking skin cancer, but few would conclude that she hates being White. And when a White woman perms her straight hair, she is rarely accused of wanting to be something that she is not. But nearly everything the Black woman (or man) does to her (or his) appearance is interpreted politically (54).

When a thin-lipped White actress gets a collagen injection to give her a more sensual Negroid-looking mouth, or when a White rock musician wears dreadlocks for a more "street-wise" appearance, it is simply not the same as when a Black woman straightens her hair or goes great lengths to avoid prolonged sunlight. Whites can dabble in practices that amke them appear more Black, but for many African Americans enbracing Whiteness is a matter of economic, social, or political survival (54-55).

In the workplace, this books notes that there is a move for blacks to look less European. The authors mention that in professions like academia and journalism, blacks are wearing African garb and unprocessed hair. The reason is because these professions are supposed to promote freedom. Since both these areas are career goals of mine, this must be the reason for why my hair is not processed.

Alice Windom, coordinator of the James T. Bush, Sr., Center at the University of Missouri-St.Louis, thinks whites influence in Africa has created a colour complex. She mentions that in Zambia there is a phenomenon called "Fanta faces and Coca-Cola bodies," which is a result of women bleaching their skin. The same thing takes place in Uganda, I have seen it for myself and it is a terribly saddening sight for a Black North American wanting to find assurance of her Blackness in Africa. The same disease of self-hatred plagues Africa it seems as much as it plagues Canada or the States. And most likely all over the world. These would make for other interesting areas of investigation.

Psycho-sociological theories like these might adequately explain color prejudice were it not for one important fact: around the world, ancient stories and proverbs praising the value of pale skin, especially in women, long preceded the arrival of the White man. In Central America, thousands of years ago, bronze-brown Aztec women during courtship sed to smear themselves with an ointment made of yellow earth, since golden skin was considered more attractive than brown (57).

*Possible interview: Bertice Berry, a sociologist and stand-up comic (mentioned on pg. 62).

It has been found in the late thirties and early forties, self-hatred among Black children was expressed in the fact that many of them chose to play with white dolls instead of black ones. I had a few black dolls when I was younger, but many more were Barbie dolls with blonde hair and blue eyes. I loved these dolls and they always played major roles in the scenarios I would act out with them. It is sad to know that my upbringing in the seventies had not changed that much since 30 or 40 years prior. What I really liked about Barbie dolls was the hair. I loved combing it, braiding it, maybe cutting it. It's hard to even call the black dolls I had black because they never looked like me, they all had hair like Barbie's except darker. I could project a lot of my fantasies and desires into these dolls. These dolls inspired a many hours of play in me. I even created a magazine called Miss Sassy which featured many drawings of my White Barbie dolls on the cover, and some other fictional women, mainly White as well. Even in creating my own media I was not doing anything differently than what already existed in the media at that time.

And sometimes this is still true of many media moguls now, such as the man who owns Black Entertainment Television. (This part could be included in the analysis of the media).

It seems like many dolls of today have not changed much from ones I had in the seventies:

Dr. Powell-Hopson currently serves as a consultant to Mattel Toys and has helped that company develop a special line of dolls for Black children. One doll, called Shani, the Swahili word for "marvelous," has dark skin, ful lips, and a Negroid nose. Shani has two Black friends of different skin tones called Nichelle and Asha. Yet each of the new Black dolls has long hair flowing below the waist. More recently, Tyco Industries has introduced an African-American doll named Kenya. Her long, think, curly hair can be straightened with a moisturizing solution or it can be styled in cornrows. Kenya comes with colored beads and a manual describing various ways to style her hair. It will be interesting to see what effects, if an, playing with such dolls will have on the future choices of African-American children given the Clark doll test (64-65).

It is said that children rely on hair texture, facial features and eye colour to determine blackness, rather than skin colour. A part of this thesis that deals with children could be very interesting.

Charles H. Parrish was a pioneer in exploring skin-colour stereotyping in black teenagers. In the 1940s junior-high students used about 145 different terms for varying skin colour, many of which I heard at that age (to myself and others), such as "brownskin," "tar baby," "high yellow." Teenagers at this age also have very well developed ideas about hair as well which is talked about in the September issue of Essence.

Historically, the one-drop rule has both helped and harmed he Black community. While increasing its numbers, the rule has fractured the community's solidarity. In so broadly defining a genetically varied population with a wide range of features and skin colors, the rule has created a race grouping more social than biological. Nowhere else in the world does a single race encompass people whose skin color ranges from white to black, whose hair texture varies from tightly curled to straight, and whose facial features reflect the broadest possible diversity. Were it not for this artificial grouping, part of the legacy of racism, Blacks might not criticize each other so harshly for having skin or hair that does not meet some arbitrary standard (80).

How does this one-drop rule affect the definition of black in Canada? And what role does the definition of black in Canada have on hair?

As the twentieth century closes, I believe that black women have come to better appreciate the array of beauty we portray, despite subtle, and not so subtle, pressure from the media, the workplace and the larger society to conform to their standards of attractiveness.

Yet I am sometimes troubled that too many of us still make snide and cruel comments about the politically, professionally or socially acceptable way to wear our hair. We would be a lot stronger as a people if we used that energy to support each other economically, emotionally and spiritually.
-A'Lelia Perry Bundles, Great-great-granddaughter of Madam C.J. Walker, Black hair care industry pioneer

*Reference is made to Susan Brownmiller's Femininity about the triviality of hair. I would like to source this directly

Clearly, hair is less an issue for men than for women. Beginning in childhood, boys conventionally wear short hair while girls grow the their hair long. Adult Black males generally keep their hair cropped short, so its texture is usually not that important to them. But from an early age most Black girls, especially those with fuzzy edges and nappy 'kitchens'(the hairline at the back of the neck), are taught to 'fix' their hair – as if it were broken. Short hair is unfeminine but for many long hair is unmanageable. Still the hair of Black girls is braided and yanked, rubber-banded and barretted, into a presentable state. And when mothers grow weary of taming their daughters' hair, many opt to treat it with chemical relaxers. As one Black mother tired of fighting the comb declared, 'I didn't have time to mess with that child's nappy head any longer, so I went and got it permed. It's been a lot easier on both of us since' (83).

*Reference is made to Gerald Early's "Life with Daughters or The Cakewalk with Shirley Temple." Early is a professor of English and African-American studies at Washington University.

On a vacation trip to British Virgin Gorda, the Black poet, essayist, and writer Audre Lorde discovered just how easily her hairstyle could be interpreted politically. Wearing newly fashioned dreadlocks (a style in which the hair is either braided, twisted, or clumped together in separate strands all over the head), Lorde arrived at the Beef Island Airport and was told by the immigration officer – a Black woman with heavily processed hair – that her entry was being denied. Angry at the snag in her travel plans, Lorde demanded to speak to the woman's supervisor and was informed that her dreadlocks marked her as a dope-smoking Rastafarian revolutionary. Fortunately, the officer was eventually able to determine that Lorde was not a 'dangerous' Rastafarian, and her passport was stamped 'admit' (85).

BELOVED

In Creative Writing, Culture, Education, Environment, Health, Living, Media Writing, Opinion, Writing (all kinds), book reviews on **August 12, 2009** at **03:23**

Book Review of Toni Morrison's Award-Winning Book Beloved

Terry Otten suggests that while Sethe and the other slaves "might be considered simply victims in slavery, once they move towards freedom north of the Ohio River ... they assume responsibility for their own 'criminal' act and become 'victims' of their own flawed humanity as much as the viciousness of whites." In this essay, the validity of this statement will be tested against Beloved. References from the novel will show how Terry Otten is incorrect.

Otten compares "the visciousness of whites" with the actions of Sethe and the other slaves. Even a Canadian court of law punishes a crime differently based on the accused's explanation for committing the crime. Just as sure as there is a battered woman's syndrome that excuses the crimes of battered wives who kill their husbands, the same should be recognized by for slaves such as Sethe.

I will call them my people, which were not my people; and her beloved, which was not beloved. (Romans 9:25)

The question in this novel, Toni Morrison told PBS host Charlie Rose, was "Who is the beloved? Who is the person who lives inside us that is the one you can trust, who is the best thing you are. And in that instant, for that segment, because I had planned books around that theme, it was the effort of a woman to love her children, to raise her children, to be responsible for her children. And the fact that it was during slavery made all those things impossible for her."

Sethe is a woman who escaped from slavery but is haunted by its heritage. It shows how even when free, Sethe and the other slaves continually struggle to be free in their lives.

Same as Sethe's dead baby haunts their house in Ohio, slavery haunts their lives. Just as Denver, Paul D and Sethe sit in their home talking about the ghost in their house, they also talk about their former home in slavery.

'How come everybody run off from Sweet Home can't stop talking about it? Look like if it was so sweet you would have stayed.'

'Girl, who you talking to?' "Paul D laughed. 'True, true. She's right, Sethe. It wasn't sweet and it sure wasn't home.' He shook his head." 'But it's where we were,' said Sethe. 'All together. Comes back whether we want it to or not.'(Morrison 13-14).

This conversation between Sethe, Denver and Paul D shows the hold slavery still had over their lives. So much so that when Sethe had a chance to bring up at least one of her children without ever knowing slavery, she killed the child herself. Baby Suggs had eight children, all of them taken away from her because of slavery, no opportunity to know what beloved means.

"Anybody Baby Suggs knew, let alone loved, who hadn't run off or been hanged, got rented out, loaned out, bought up, brought back, sored up, mortgaged, won, stolen or seized. So Baby's eight children had six fathers. What she called the nastiness of life was the shock she received upon learning that nobody stopped playing checkers just because the pieces included her children." (Morrison 23).

The "viciousness of whites" seemed to be the playing of a game of checkers. Unmotivated by the actions of blacks to whites, but justified in their beliefs of superiority. Whites in America did not know the horrors of slavery by the hands of blacks. What was freedom after a lifetime of bondage? Sethe had known many tragedies under slavery, and she also knew that this baby's life was doomed to be hard, doomed to working in other people's kitchen, hopefully getting some sewing on the sly, and this would be her free life. Sethe killing her baby is a criminal act. But is she a flawed human being? Do her actions compare to "the visciousness of whites?"

'Men don't know nothing much,' said Paul D, tucking his pouch back into his vest pocket, 'but they do know a suckling can't be away from its mother for long.'
'Then they know what it's like to send you children off when your breasts are full.'
'We was talking 'bout a tree, Sethe.'
'After I left you, those boys came in there and took my milk. That's what they came in there for. Held me down and took it. I told Mrs. Garner on em. She had that lump and couldn't speak but her eyes rolled out tears. Them boys fould out I told on em. Schoolteacher made one open up my back, and when it closed it makde a tree. It grows there still.'
'They used cowhide on you?'
'And they took my milk.'

'They beat you and you was pregnant?' 'And they took my milk!' (Morrison 16-17).

The action of these young white boys who treated Sethe as though she were a cow, and were then responsible for her beating while pregnant did not have their experience with slavery to explain their actions. These were young boys who saw Sethe not as human, not as their mother or sister or friend. She was black, a slave, and therefore as useful to them as a cow. This judgement of another human being is indeed a flaw in their humanity. They showed no humanity to Sethe, and most likely not to any black.

Now despite all the horrible things Sethe went through during slavery, she did live to tell the story of what the white boys did, unlike what millions of other slaves went through. Sethe killed her baby, denying it life. The baby was born at the same time that her freedom was born. But even Sethe's baby did not promise beloved for her.

"Sethe couldn't think of anything to do, so grateful was she, so she peeled a potato, ate it, spit it up and ate more in quiet celebration." 'They be glad to see you,' said Ella. 'When was this one born?" 'Yesterday,' said Sethe, wiping swaeat from under her chin. 'I hope she makes it.' Ella looked at the tiny, dirty face poling out of the wool blanket and shook her head. 'Hard to say,' she said. 'If anybody was to ask me I'd say, 'Don't love nothing.' Then, as if to take the edge off her pronouncement, she smiled at Sethe. 'You had that baby by yourself?' 'No. White girl helped.' 'Then we better make tracks.'

Sethe's baby held much promise. Born with the help of the very race who had taken so much of her life away, so many of her children, a white girl helped her give birth to her baby. Sethe herself says that she hopes that the baby makes it. But was this child ever going to be free?

Eighteen seventy-four and whitefolks were still on the loose. Whole towns wiped clean of Negroes; eight-seven lynchings in one year alone in Kentucky; four colored schools burned to teh ground; grown men whipped like children; children wihpped like adults; black women raped by the crew; property taken, necks broken (Morrison 180). This was all going on while Sethe and the other slaves lived in 124. Sethe killed her baby because she believed it would have a better life dead than alive. Just as slavery haunted their lives, so did the baby. After Paul D scared the ghost out of the house, it came back in the form of Beloved.

"Beloved, she my daughter. She mine. See. She come back to me of her own free will and I don't have to explain a thing. I didn't have time

to explain before because it had to be done quick. Quick. She had to be safe and I put her where she would be. But my love was tough and she back now. I knoew she would be. Paul D ran her off so she had no choice but to come back to me in the flesh. I bet you Baby Suggs, on the other side, helped. I won't never let her go. I'll explain to her, even though I don't have to. Why I did it. How if I hadn't killed her she would have died and that is something I could not bear to happen to her. When I explain it she'll understand, because she understands everything already. I'll tend her as no mother ever tended a child, a daughter. Nobody will ever get my milk no more except my own children. I never had to give it to nobody else-and the one time I did it was took from me-they held me down and took it. Milk that belonged to my baby." (Morrison 200).
Sethe tries with Beloved to make up for everything she did to her baby, but Beloved leaves anyways. What Sethe is left with to understand, is what Paul tells her.

`She was my best thing.'

Paul D sits down in the rocking chair and examines the quilt patched in carnival colors. His hands are limp between his knees. There are too many things to feel about his woman. His head hurts. Suddenly he remembers Sixo trying to describe what he felt about the the Thirty-Mile Woman. `She is a friend of my mind. She gather me, man. The pieces I am, she gather them and give them back to me in all the right order. It's good, you know, when you got a woman who is a friend of your mind.' (Morrison 272-273).

`Sethe,' he says, `me and you, we got more yesterday than anybody. We need some kind of tomorrow.' He leans over and takes her hand. With thoe other he touches her face. `You your best thing, Sethe. You are.' His holding fingers are holding hers.

`Me? Me?' (Morrison 273).

This is the only point where Sethe comes close to freedom, when she realizes that the best thing is herself. She is bound by slavery, bound to the horrible memories, bound to the guilt of killing her child, then bound to Beloved. This is not a woman motivated by viciousness, acting as a flawed human being. She wants to understand what beloved is. She wants to be more than a slave. Paul D once again helps her to chase away the ghosts that keep her from truly being free.

The "`criminal'" acts of Sethe can not be compared to "the viciousness of whites." Sethe killed her baby because she did not believe it was going to live. This was a mother, a woman, looking to be beloved, to know what this word means. Everything was taken away from her in slavery, even the milk to nourish her beloved children. Slavery taught her not to love anything, but Sethe still tried. As much as she wanted her baby to live, she killed her child out of love. Without the haunting of slavery, without provacation, "the viciousness of whites" enslaved black people physically, mentally and emotionally. The end of Beloved shows a glimmer of hope, a sign that Sethe may find her beloved within herself, and ultimately finding the finest part of her humanity, rather than the flawed. Sethe remains a victim of slavery until the very moment she begins to realize her freedom. The ending of the novel shows a glimmer of hope. Sethe and the other slaves can not be considered outside the contexts of slavery until their own lives seem free.

Not to Be Boxed In Always Wanting to Try Something New

In Beauty, Business, Contact Information, Culture, Education, Entertainment, Living, Media Writing, Writing (all kinds) on **August 13, 2009** at **04:52**

Hyacinth Harewood Continues to Live a Full Life - Photo by Donna Kakonge

Hyacinth Harewood is a civil servant with the Canada Revenue Agency (CRA) working from home, former college professor, former businessperson, former volunteer and mother of five living in Toronto, Canada. She worked as a sessional lecturer with Carleton University in Ottawa, as a professor with Algonquin College in Ottawa for 16 years, has been working with CRA since the late 1980s, and once had her own sole-proprietorship business focusing on communications and written work. This consummate professional used to get up at 3:00 a.m. to work on her business, and then take care of five children to get them ready for school. She would continue working on her business while her children were at school and tend to their needs once they were home. She played the role of a superwoman well. This impressive woman who was educated at the University of Western Ontario where she studied French and Spanish, then received her master's degree at the University of Ottawa in applied linguistics managed to juggle a life of work, family and children. She has been a terrific role model for her five children.

Harewood was born in Antigua, West Indies on October 15, 1946. She is the eighth out of a family of 10. Her parents were active in politics in Antigua. She spent a lot of time listening to them and observing them.

She says she was an ambitious student that aimed to come out on the top of the heap.

"When I was young it was books, books, books and competing, competing and competing and leaving the competition in the dust," says Harewood. "In high school I was the only person in school who actually passed the [high school certificate the year I graduated] exam. I passed it the same time. I came out first class. I moved up with an attitude of being the best, leave the competition in the dust. We do say that a lot to our young people, it is a very elitist kind of position. For the people who do not come out on top, what happens to them?

"I do feel I have a responsibility to everybody," Harewood continues. "The idea of always being the best, the only one left sitting on the top of the heap, I do not believe in that approach anymore. I believe in a more balanced approach, not in mediocrity."

Harewood came to Canada at the age of 17 to attend the University of Western Ontario. Her children tease her that she was actually 18 because she turned that age shortly in October (a month after school started). She studied French and Spanish, including the literature of these languages. She also took German. This knowledge of languages has added to Harewood's international flair. After graduation, she got married and moved to Ottawa, Canada and attended the University of Ottawa to study applied linguistics in a master's program. She was still working on her master's thesis and she taught for a year at Carleton University as a sessional lecturer teaching a first-year general linguistics course. At that time, her oldest child, son Adrian Harewood, was attending the daycare at Carleton University. Adrian Harewood is the host of a Canadian Broadcasting Corporation's (CBC) afternoon show in Ottawa called "All in a Day." He is considered one of the best broadcasters in the Ottawa region and with a mother like Hyacinth Harewood it is easy to understand.

Needing to make more money, Harewood joined Algonquin College in 1972 as a "teaching master," however now the position is known as a professor. She worked at Algonquin for 16 years until 1988. Her experience in teaching has fortunately touched the lives of thousands of people who had the pleasure in knowing Harewood. She taught communications, technical writing, science fiction as elective courses and technology and social issues, as well as English as a Second Language courses. She left Algonquin to own her own business as a sole-proprietor for about two years. She recalls the contracts she would receive doing writing and communications work (writing, editing and developing brochures) for such places as the government and other businesses. She would be going out to lunches, "schmoozing," trying to drum up more work. In the end, she left that work because she needed to make more money.

That is when she joined the federal government in the late 1980s where she currently works now. She works in human resources and although she has mainly worked in Ottawa over the years, she now works in Toronto with CRA doing tele-commuting in both official languages of Canada, English and French. She has done a lot of training working with the federal government, as well she has taken business courses that did not lead towards a degree. She says if she knew then what she knows now about business, her sole-proprietorship would have been a greater success. It is a shame that Harewood did not continue with her own business efforts, to which she would be perfectly suited for.

While in Ottawa, Harewood did volunteer work with Centrepointe Theatre in communications. She would help to edit their newsletter. She also used to be a columnist with a community newspaper called *Contrast*. She writes poetry and has co-edited a collection of poetry. Harewood has been continually living a life of perfect balance – giving back to the community, as well as providing for those she loves.

Harewood says working from home is not for everyone. Some people really like being able to look over at the other cubicle and ask a colleague out to lunch. She says you really need to enjoy your own company – which she does. She will often make the best use of her lunch break by getting out of the house every day – rain, sleet or shine. She will visit the library, walk and run errands. She also does crafts and handiwork, not as a side business, however as gifts for friends and family.

Harewood dreams of the ideal retirement.

"My concept of retirement is not to start working in a different way," says Harewood. "These people who had retired and had not retired, that is not what I dream of as retirement. It is true you need to continue making a living. There are a lot of people I know who have retired who need additional income and need other kind of work. I'm dreaming of retirement, but the ideal kind of retirement."

Harewood has spent most of her life juggling the demands of work, as well as raising five children. The proof she has done both well are displayed in how her children have turned out. Adrian is a radio broadcaster for CBC and hosts "All in a Day." Pat is a lawyer with the Department of Justice and working with the Public Service Alliance of Canada. Anne is a criminologist. She teaches part-time hours at the State College in Antigua. She did a master's degree with a thesis at the University of Ottawa. Harewood also has twins: Joy who is several minutes older is doing optometry and is in her third-year at the University of California at Berkeley. June is doing dentistry at Columbia University in New York. This is a tremendous achievement when so many young people face problems in societies around the world. Her children appear to be extremely well-adjusted and most definitely accomplished.

"I was sort of thinking and saying to myself that the point is I try not to get boxed into one image. I look over the things I have done and I am not exactly a rolling stone that gathers no moss," says Harewood. "I do like to move onto different things and reinvent myself."

Donna Kakonge is a professor, author and journalist living in Toronto, Canada. Her books can bought through her online store at: http://stores.lulu.com/kakonged. She also has her own online multimedia magazine at: http://kakonged.wordpress.com. Her official website is: www.donnakakonge.com.

Continually Learning Aiming to Make a Better World

In Beauty, Culture, Education, Entertainment, Living, Media Writing, Opinion, Writing (all kinds), travel on **August 14, 2009** at **07:29**

Gini Dickie is a Teacher and Activist who is Making a Difference

Gini Dickie is a teacher-librarian, as well as a political activist in her own right living in Toronto, Canada. She worked as a teacher in northern Nigeria with CUSO-VSO, she worked at Expo ' 67 and she has been active working with Chilean refugees. She has worked in the inner-city Regent Park area of Toronto, as well as with York University. She also owned her own typesetting business for a brief period of time and everything she has done has taught her about the world around her, as well as about herself.

Dickie was born March 23, 1948 in Brantford, ON. She has two younger brothers and her father was still a student in optometry college in Toronto when she was born. Her father went to school on the GI bill after coming back from the war. After her father graduated, the family moved to Fergus, ON and her Dad was the one and only optometrist for 40 some odd years in their community.

"I was a good student and I guess I was always looking for challenges outside of the classroom too," says Dickie. "I have a high level of energy. I joined everything there was to join. I was involved with sports and brownies and guides and student government. I would go to conferences outside of the town to meet other people. The key thing that affected me was having a high school teacher from Africa who opened windows onto the world for me." Dickie went to Nigeria in 1969 to teach English. She arrived in northern Nigeria during the Biafran war. Dickie was there for two and half years. She also visited Tanzania and England (where she taught English for six months) before her return. She came back to Canada to get her education diploma from the University of Western Ontario.

Before she left for Nigeria, she attended McGill University after receiving acceptance to Queen's and the University of Toronto as well.

"I wanted to learn French. It was a very exciting time in Quebec and I got involved politically at the university. It was also the time of Canada's 100th birthday and Expo '67 and I was able to work as a hostess in the United Nations pavilion and that was very exciting and eye opening as well."

Dickie has taught on four continents. When she arrived back in Toronto after completing her education diploma, she wanted to teach, however it was a time of declining enrollment in the schools. She did other things for 17 years before she was able to officially teach again.

She worked at the Cross-Cultural Communication Centre, as well she was active with the NDP. She did solidarity work with Chilean refugees. She is actually still involved with the Chilean community and her children's fathers are refugees from Chile.

She worked for the school board as a school-community relations worker from 1977 to 1980. Then she and her Chilean partner went to Ecuador and lived in Quito for almost two years where she worked in community development and teaching. Her daughter, Aisha, was born in Quito.

She came back to Canada and ran a typesetting business for about two years. It taught her that running her own business is not for her. She worked at a legal clinic for Spanish-speaking people with a lawyer and one of the difficult things she had to do was transcribe the stories and testimonies of refugees who were torture victims. Dickie learned a lot.

Dickie later went on to be a senior project officer in the Association of Canadian Community Colleges (ACCC). The international bureau had just started and they were looking for people with international experience. Her Spanish-speaking skills came in handy, as she linked community colleges and CEGEPs in Canada with similar institutions in Latin America and the Caribbean. Her son, Nico, was born in Toronto in 1986.

Then she finally got her chance to teach in Toronto. She started working with the Toronto District School Board in 1991 with Jesse Ketchum Public School.

"I taught grade seven and eight special education, children with learning disabilities. I did that for five years and then I moved to a school in Regent Park called Lord Dufferin Public School, where I taught grade six for nine years."

Continually learning has been a theme throughout Dickie's life.

"In Nigeria that was obviously true because it was such a different culture, I learned so much about Nigerian culture and the language. We all grow up with stereotypes and prejudices that we need to be aware of and one of the things you learn from students is to challenge your thinking. I have taught kids with learning disabilities and now I can see the complexities of their lives. When I went to teach in Regent Park, I could see the richness of their lives and how they were proud of their community and their desire to learn and improve their lives and this challenged my own previously held ideas."

After working in Regent Park, Dickie was seconded to York University where she taught in a Faculty of Education program with an equity and social justice focus. She had the privilege of working with the professor who started the program, Dr. Patrick Solomon. She was there for three years.

Now she is a teacher-librarian at Clinton Street Public School.

"I plan to be teaching for several more years," says Dickie. "When I retire, I think I would like to become a full-time political activist. It would be carrying on the same thing. I see teaching as a 'subversive activity'. It is political activism in that sense. I'm involved in starting a solidarity museum, I'm involved in all kinds of things and I'll just have more time to do them [in retirement]. It's really about challenging the status quo and continually trying to make this a better world."

Power of the Third Eye Geomancer and Feng Shui Expert

In Business, Culture, Education, Entertainment, Health, Home Decor, Living, Media Writing, Opinion, Religion, Writing (all kinds), travel on **August 15, 2009** at **07:14**

Paul Ng Addresses a Crowd with his Feng Shui and Geomancer Expertise

Paul Ng is a geomancer and feng shui expert that helps to improve the lives of others, as well as former corporate manager. He has worked with Ernst & Young that was the largest accounting firm in all of Canada at the time as a data processing manager. He has been vice-president manager of a subsidiary of Canadian Pacific called Marathon Realty.

This was the largest company in Canada. He became a director at CIBC and then gradually owned his own company.

Ng was born on May 8, 1947 in Hong Kong. His sister died when he was in his teens from suicide. He predicted her death. He also predicted the death of his father. Being able to predict the death of others is a gift of sorts that he has had since very young. He would spend a lot of time at the seminary when he was young and read the tombstones by the gravesite nearby. From as early as possibly grade four up until university, Ng only had 20 to 30 per cent of his hearing. This taught him to read other people's body language well. He went through three surgeries in Kitchener, Waterloo to restore his hearing. He also had a phobia of heights. He would climb to the highest peaks to combat this fear. He truly believes that everything has a reason.

"I always had some kind of a bond with an unexplainable skill," says Ng. "Since I was very, very young I was very capable of observing people, especially in terms of death. My sister died when I was in my early teens, if not more.

"I took the bite of one bun. I told my father I would be surprised if he would live beyond the weekend. He died that Sunday night. I'm really connected with that psychic power. I studied in a boarding school. And I made a habit of going to the seminary school after school. When I would go and see the tombstones. Why are we here? I have been searching for years what is the meaning of life. Religion is really an escape from reality. So I read up a lot about Chinese culture. I read a lot of books and kept getting quite confused."

He came to Canada to study electrical engineering at the University of Ottawa in 1968. He transferred in his second year to the University of Waterloo in computer science. In 1972, he did a master's of business administration degree at the University of Toronto. Now it costs tens of thousands of dollars to study such a degree. In Ng's day, he spent $600 CDN.

He did his business degree part-time while working for Ernst & Young. In 1982 he became vice-president manager for a subsidiary for Canadian Pacific. The subsidiary is called Marathon Realty. This was the largest company in Canada. He was there for five years in the management department. After that he became director of information technology at Wood Gundy. Gradually over several years he had his own company. He became director of CIBC only for a short period in 1992. Then in 1993 he left the corporate life to be a geomancer and feng shui expert full-time.

What started Ng's career in geomancy and feng shui was when he contracted bone cancer in 1974 (the first turning point in his life), plus his gifts displayed as a young child. He went to Hong Kong in 1976 and became a disciple of a guru.

"Then I was at the point of life and death. They removed a bone from my leg. They said the cancer was to the right bone. I was lucky. The surgery left me weak. Then I refused to do anything with chemo or radiation. When I became a disciple of a monk I learned Qi Gong. It completely transformed my body to a different person. That is why I do not show my age even at age 63. They taught me the basics to bring me into the door. The house of feng shui and master arts basics. He [guru] said that one day I would way surpass him. So I understand my passion."

Ng began doing the feng shui in 1985. He was invited to a housewarming party and he told his friend the way to lay out the apartment. The way she laid out her apartment was very detrimental for marriage. It had already happened one week earlier that her husband had left her and he did not know that. He began doing what he does on a part-time basis from 1985 on. That became the second turning point in his life.

The third turning point in Ng's life was in 1990. He ran for MP in the Scarborough-Rouge Region of Toronto in 1993 knowing he would not win. When he got back to work, he could not even sit at his desk for half a day. So he quit his job and then he began his business full-time.

In 1994, the World General Newspapers organized four master debates and in his work they regarded him as one of the four top feng shui masters in Canada and that got his name out. In 2000, he was further renowned as the top master in Canada. January 2008 the media came and announced him as the top feng shui master in Canada. And that happened in November. Also in October, 2009 he will be showcased across the country with OMNI-TV, as well as judging a Miss Asia contest at the end of August, 2009.

He was invited by the United Nations to discuss feng shui to improve functionality and reduce crime in Jamaica.

"That was really something."

Ng finds his current occupation far more interesting and the money is better too. However he says he does not find the money important.

"People would have had a lousy life," Ng says of how his skills help to improve the lives of others. "It really can change your life. I can say that decent people live today because of that. I find that life works in karma energy and cycles. If we need to do something fantastic in our lives, then we need to go through fantastic challenges. If we want to achieve nothing then there are no challenges. Then there was the bone cancer and every single thing had a meaning. Most people would be depressed and be miserable and give up. I treat them as an opportunity to bring me to bigger and better things."

Ng has a wife who is a Chinese medicine doctor. He has two sons, one of them 30, the other 31. The older one is doing manual work and the younger one works at Nestle.

Forging a Career in Journalism A Pioneer Voice in Radio (Originally Published with Impowerage.com)

In Culture, Education, Entertainment, Living, Media Writing, Movie Reviews, Radio Podcasts, Writing (all kinds) on **August 16, 2009** at **04:25**

Robert Payne has Enjoyed a Life in the Limelight - Photo Courtesy of Robert Payne

Robert Payne has been a journalist for 40 years. He has worked in Quebec City, Montreal, Ottawa, Niagara Falls, London, ON and gained notoriety in Toronto, Canada where he now lives. In the early days of his career, he coupled his work at radio stations with being employed at Dominion stores while in the province of Quebec.

From a tentative start in Quebec City, his goal was to rise to where skies were blue and the compensation green. When the full-time radio career ended (after 18 successful years at CKEY Toronto), he moved seamlessly to chairing the Ontario Film Review Board, the provincial government body that classifies all films and videos released to the Ontario marketplace.

He also produced award-winning columns with various newspapers.

The flexibility he has shown to last in the competitive field of journalism is an example of his adaptability and willingness to "bounce back" from any setbacks that have come his way.

Payne was born June 12, 1941 in Montreal. Both of his parents are from Fredericton. The railroad brought his family to Montreal and at the age of two, Payne's family was transferred to Quebec City. He lived in Quebec City until he was 22. He calls it his hometown. His family rented a flat on the top floor of a house when they arrived in Quebec City and there was a French family living below. The teenage children who lived below found great interest in the young Payne and he learned to speak French. Mainly he only spoke English to his parents, although he went to English schools. He would speak French with his friends.

"We were 'the ghetto' in Quebec City back in the 40's and 50's," Payne explains with a chuckle, "the only blacks in a city of about 300-thousand. But rather than being victims, we seemed to generate warmth and curiosity among the locals. As a child, it was common for ladies to stop me and my mother on the street and pat me on the head adoringly"

Gosh, it's a wonder the English-speaking, Anglican, African Canadian son of a railroad porter and homemaker mother could not only survive a childhood among a sea of White, French-speaking, Roman Catholic denizens of Quebec City, but indeed thrive and live to tell about it.

Later on in life he got a part-time job at a Dominion store and also attended Laval University in Quebec City. He studied teaching and had planned to become a physical education teacher. He met someone at the school who invited him to apply to work for an English-language CBC-affiliate in Quebec. He auditioned and received the job.

Part of his job duties were making sure that everything was running smoothly. The other part of his job was being a DJ on the late night shift. He "fell in love with radio."

"Once I got into radio I knew this is what I wanted do for much of my adult life," says Payne.

His parents were eager to have him live on his own, so when he was offered a management job with a Dominion store in Montreal, his Dad left for the railroad over the weekend and Payne had left for Montreal before his Dad got back that Sunday evening. He also got a part-time job in Montreal working for a radio station CKJM (note: the Montreal station I worked at was CFMB. The one I subsequently applied to was CKGM, across the street at the time. They asked whether I wanted to go to Ottawa). He was making about $60.00/week and even owned a sports car. The station in Montreal was a multilingual station that was the equivalent to CHIN Radio in Toronto.

Part of Payne's tasks was editing audio in many different languages, as well as being a newscaster.

There was a radio station across the street from the one he worked at that was a rock station and the place where he really wanted to work. He went there asking for a job and they said we do not have one here, however we are opening a new station in Ottawa CKPM and would Payne want the job. He decided to do it and moved to Ottawa. He found the only action in Ottawa was drinking in Hull, Quebec.

He met many friends in Ottawa, as well as met the mother of his two children. Being ambitious, he knew that going to Toronto was the way to reach his goals of great success – since the major media markets are there.

Before he got to Toronto, he worked in London, ON, as well as Niagara Falls.

He got a call from CHUM to work in Toronto. He did not last long at CHUM, mainly because he was intimidated by the reputation of his colleagues – many of whom were known far and wide as the cream of the crop and did not perform as well as he could have.

After leaving CHUM, he enhanced his skills and credibility by going to meetings and taping them. He would freelance these stories out to different radio stations. One of the stations he would do this for was CKEY – eventually they offered him a job.

He ended up getting a job with CKEY in Toronto and learned his lesson from the experience with CHUM Radio by staying with CKEY for 20 years. He became quite a celebrity with billboards and caricatures made of him.

When management changed at the station and he was let go, it made the front page of the *Toronto Star*.

Close to the end of Payne's term at CKEY, he was appointed to the Ontario Film Review Board and subsequently became its chair. The offer for this job came from the premier at the time. Payne takes pride in instigating a process of standardized assessment of film and video content, such as pornography. When this story hit the papers, such as the Toronto Star – it caused quite a controversy.

"I learned a lot from that," says Payne.

Payne is also a notable columnist. He worked as a columnist with *Contrast Newspaper* until it folded in the early 1980s. He then wrote columns for *Share* until the mid 1990s. He also became a columnist with the *Toronto Sunday Sun*. He has received an award for his columns.

Once his tenure with CKEY Radio ended, he got a call from Rogers TV to host a show called "Lemon-Aid" about cars. He did that for three years, as well as continued to write columns, be a speech writer (for Ontario government ministers), plus a film reviewer.

He has also done casual work for the CBC, as well as worked on hiring committees with Centennial College (Ontario's oldest community college), as well as taught at Centennial College.

He was the ghost writer for Herb Carnegie's book Fly in a Pail of Milk which deals with Carnegie's 1940s hockey career, his unsuccessful attempts at persuading the NHL to accept a black player and his post-hockey successes.

Payne has served on a number of boards, including Arts Foundation of Greater Toronto, the Onyx Lion's Club that served mostly the African-Canadian community. In the early part of this decade, he served as vice president of the Canadian Association of Black Journalists (CABJ). He recently stepped down as Audit & Finance chair of Toronto Grace Hospital, a Salvation Army owned hospital and continues to write part-time as well as fulfill the duties to his partner, such as cooking, cleaning and doing the laundry. Payne also hosted the first five years of the Harry Jerome awards.

What does he have to say about being a pioneer in the journalism world as a black man?

"While I enjoyed meeting and serving with a broad range of men and women, I also think it served the purpose of some organizations to demonstrate a willingness to be inclusive," says Payne. "Not so much the radio, where most listeners don't have a clue as to what color you are. I confess to a touch of arrogance and ignorance at the time. Given my own upbringing in Canada, and because everyone in radio in the 60s and 70s spoke "like Canadians," I remember (painfully/Paynefully) telling newly-arrived Canadians they needed to speak like "the rest of us." I realize how negative and verging on racist my comments were. One of the great things about experience is that it shows you how stupid you were as your former self."

Payne has learned a lot from his early years in radio and journalism and the success he has achieved. For all those people he may have "pissed off" at one point, they can be safely assured that now in his golden years he is giving back to the community, plus giving back to his friends and family. He plays hockey three times a week and shows no signs of slowing down. Whatever arrogance he may have shown in his youth is not apparent in the humble older man who can still get up on a ladder at his age to make renovations to his home.

"I guess I come from good genes. My dad died last year at age 96, and my 94 year old mom is keeping up the good fight."

The resultant sense of acceptance and self-worth seems to have propelled Payne far beyond what the surface surroundings seemed to promise. Indeed it helped drive him to the upper echelons of his chosen profession.

The Politics of Hair (Proposal to Ryerson University)

In Beauty, Culture, Education, Entertainment, Health, Living, Media Writing, Movie Reviews, Music, Opinion, Writing (all kinds), book reviews on **August 21, 2009** at **07:35**

Everybody Does Something to Change Their Appearance for Advancement - Photo Courtesy of Stockexpert.com

The politics of black hair shows in books like Tenderheaded to the Princess of Wales plays 'Da Kink in My Hair and Hairspray to movies like Beauty Shop to songs played on Flow 93.5.

Everyone alters their hair to gain more power in society. Dr. Mariame Kaba, who received her PhD from Northwestern University, is also a contributor to the book Tenderheaded. In her work, Kaba discusses the straightening of black women's hair as an agent for political power. Keeping one's hair natural is also a source of political gain by using one's ethnicity to move forward in society. At the time I did my master's thesis with the title Afro Forever: Research Paper on Salon Utopia, I did not see I was using my natural hair to obtain personal and professional power in the employment I chose after graduation from Concordia University's Media Studies program.

I was an Announcer/Producer with Radio Canada International with an estimated audience of 600,000 listeners worldwide. I worked on a news and current affairs program called African Eyes which was broadcast to sub Saharan Africa. Educating Africans about Canada with my natural hair at the time made me belong with my fellow co-workers. The same is true for other cultural groups.

Francis B. Nyamnjoh, Deborah Durham and Jude D. Fokwang write in Identity, Culture and Politics, about "The Domestication of Hair and Modernised Consciousness in Cameroon: A Critique in the Context of Globalisation" that Africans women consume Western ideals in their choice of hair design and do not control the flow of hair aesthetics in the global marketplace. This is true, not just in Cameroon. However, even non-African cultures are strongly affected by Western ideals.

In Grant McCracken's Big Hair: A Journey into Transformation of Self, he focuses on the effect big hair had on a mainly Caucasian group of celebrities in the 1980s. These women used their hair, a big part of one's image, to advance themselves in their chosen profession of glamour. The same can be said of the South Asian man who gets a haircut to work in arts journalism, the Jewish and Hispanic women who straighten their hair for the job interview and the older men who colour their hair to look more hip or use their grey power. In all these cases, some form of alteration has been made with the aim for advancing economically. Our cues for the choices we make often come from media and culture.

My dissertation will analyze the media and cultures of people of colour; red, brown, gold, black and white to show how the majority of us succumb to the media and our culture for political gain through our hair. I am especially interested in taking the film courses offered at Ryerson and York.

I did my 90 page master's thesis entitled Afro Forever. I also did a master's project, a 26 page website called Salon Utopia. I've written articles on black hair politics for a Panache Magazine, an International black woman's magazine and written about beauty in general for Canoe.ca's Lifewise section. I have done commentaries for the CBC on black hair politics in Montreal which has been syndicated and replayed.

Also By Donna Kakonge:

What Happened to the Afro?

This graduate research paper is a case study that sheds light on the politics of black hair.

How to Write Creative Non-fiction

Writing is one of the hardest jobs in the world, and this book will give you the help you need to crack the market. Everything you wanted to know about the writing business and how to write, with exercises included.

Spiderwoman

This book of short stories crafted over many years and originally developed in a writing workshop at Carleton University includes the experiences of a young black woman in Canada, experiencing everything from travel to family tragedy and love.

My Roxanne

Written at the age of 17 and revised later in life, this novel is the story of Roxanne and Lance – an interracial couple who go through their ups and downs.

Being Healthy: Selected Works from the Internet

This book is a compilation of works from the Internet related to health that have been edited by Donna Kakonge.

Do Not Know

This book is a collection of literary explorations of madness. A young black woman experiences the challenges and adventures of mental illness.

My Story of Transportation

This book is a memoir of Donna Kakonge's transportation experiences. Everything from roller skates to Jaguars; this is a story of how she has managed to get around.

Draft: Spirituality Chats

On a desperate search for a PhD, Donna Kakonge actually produces doctorate-level work by discovering there is more knowledge in one's common sense than meets the third eye of psychics.

Journalism Stories Collection

From newspapers and magazines such as NuBeing International, Panache, Pride, Share and the Toronto Star – Donna Kakonge creates a collection of her journalistic stories that span five years of her writing career.

The Education Generation

Perfect for professors, students and anyone in the college or university system in North America, this book has articles and columns that explore the notion of the education generation.

Digital Journals and Numerology

This book is meant to emphasize how powerful keeping a journal can be with the aid of numerology. I started writing one at the age of seven and keeping a journal has been a constant for me – more than some friends, some jobs and some family members. I used to get a thrill selecting my journals to write in. Now I have decided to try something new by using the computer that I already spend so much time on and money on to show how powerful keeping any journal...even a digital journal can be. Using the principles of numerology can also help in chronicling your life.

Other Work:
"Nine"
This is a selection of some of Donna Kakonge's radio documentaries done with the Canadian Broadcasting Corporation, as well as Radio Canada International.
"Matoke"
This audio book brings the story of Matoke from the book Spiderwoman to your ears.
"Church Sunday"
From the book Spiderwoman comes an audio story of the story "Church Sunday," first published in Concordia University's *Headlight Anthology* and reviewed by the *Montreal Gazette*.

This book was written to help you during the perilous times we live in.

Morning English Lessons

This is a book that is ideal for helping you hone your English skills.

Where I Was

This is a memoir of Donna Kakonge's sometimes-difficult life spent in Montreal and her move to the place she grew up in, Toronto.

Draft: Part Two

What happens when you turn to psychics for answers? You discover God.

Radio and Television Announcing

This book gives some fundamental knowledge to radio and television announcing.

Donna Kakonge goes back to one of her homelands to discover where home really is.

School Works

A collection of essays Donna Kakonge has done about the black press, black journalists and ethics in filmmaking through undergraduate work at Carleton University in Ottawa, Canada and graduate work at Concordia University in Montreal, Quebec.

Yes, School Works

A collection of communication essays done at the graduate level at Concordia University in Montreal, Canada.

School Works – Other Essays

This is a collection of undergraduate arts essays done at Carleton University in Ottawa, Canada.

Honest Psychic Chats

This conversation with psychics is the last book in the series of psychic chat sessions online.

The Write Heart

This is the last in a series of books about journalism that started with How to Write Creative Non-fiction and followed with Radio and Television Announcing. This book deals with journalistic and non-fiction writing.

Story Ideas: Help For Writer's Block

This is a collection of unfinished stories that writers could pick up on to develop full-length stories.

Listening to Music

The experience of listening to Erykah Badu, Sting and India.Arie.

This is How the Egyptians Fell

Further conversations with psychics lead to a deeper understanding of how bogus this business really is. This is why the Egyptians fell.

Natural Beauty

Tips, information and advice on all forms of being a natural beauty.

Random Bibliography of Media Books and Internet Resources

This is a resource guide for media professionals, as well as students. It is also available as a free download.

My Mind Book

This is a guide of how to manifest the law of attraction.
Stories in Red and Yellow
This is a collection of fiction and non-fiction work.

www.ingramcontent.com/pod-product-compliance
Lightning Source LLC
Chambersburg PA
CBHW031626160426
43196CB00006B/300